Democracy and America's War on Terror

Democracy and America's War on Terror

Robert L. Ivie

THE UNIVERSITY OF ALABAMA PRESS
Tuscaloosa

Copyright © 2005
The University of Alabama Press
Tuscaloosa, Alabama 35487-0380
All rights reserved
Manufactured in the United States of America

Typeface is Goudy and Goudy Sans

∞

The paper on which this book is printed meets the minimum requirements of American National
Standard for Information Science-Permanence of Paper for Printed Library Materials, ANSI
Z39.48–1984.

Library of Congress Cataloging-in-Publication Data

Ivie, Robert L.
    Democracy and America's war on terror / Robert L. Ivie.
        p. cm. — (Rhetoric, culture, and social critique)
    Includes bibliographical references and index.
    ISBN 0-8173-1443-1 (cloth : alk. paper)
        1. War on terrorism, 2001—Language. 2. Rhetoric—Political aspects—United States—History—
21st century. 3. English language—United States—Rhetoric. 4. Democracy—United States. 5.
Democracy—Philosophy. I. Title. II. Series.
    HV6432.I94 2005
    973.931—dc22
                                2004013520

For my dear wife, Nancy, without whom there would be no such book, and in memory of my father, First Lieutenant Robert G. Ivie, United States Army Air Corps (World War II) and United States Air Force (Korean conflict).

Contents

Preface and Acknowledgments

I have been writing for more than three decades about American war rhetoric, a project that has evolved over time to the present critique of the war on terror. My early investigations of war as a genre of political discourse brought me quickly to a focus on the image of the enemy, which is central to any call to arms, to Kenneth Burke's theory of vilification and victimization, and now to George W. Bush's rhetoric of evil. Over the last number of years I have become increasingly alert to the centrality of democracy in all of this, how critical its various constructions have been to the national identity and motives for war and how its potential for building a positive peace in our time has yet to be realized. In the aftermath of 9/11, I felt a renewed urgency to address the problem and potential of democracy in a troubled and deeply conflicted world. Not since the traumatic experience of the Vietnam War, which launched my ongoing quest to understand how the United States talks itself into such wars, had I felt so strongly compelled to seek answers to the question of how we might talk ourselves out of an unnecessarily belligerent attitude. The answer I advance here is to reassess America's traditional distrust of democracy and to redeploy democracy robustly as a rhetorical idiom of engaging even nondemocratic Others through strategies of identification that partially bridge the human divide in order to articulate relationships of consubstantial rivalry. This is but a partial answer to the complexities of war and peace, but it drives toward the heart of the matter and, I hope, will stimulate further inquiries of its kind.

I have been working on the ideas specifically related to this book during the last decade, and some of these ideas have appeared in earlier versions elsewhere. Some of chapter 1 draws on my essay "Democratic Deliberation in a Rhetorical Republic," *Quarterly Journal of Speech* 84 (1998): 491–505. Portions of chapters 1 and 3 are drawn from parts of my chapter titled "A New Democratic World Order?" in *Critical Reflections on the Cold War: Linking Rhetoric and History*, ed. Martin J. Medhurst and H. W. Brands (College Station: Texas A&M University Press, 2000), 247–65. Some of chapter 2 is condensed in my chapter titled "Distempered Demos: Myth, Metaphor, and U.S. Political Culture," in *Myth: A New Symposium*, ed. Gregory Schrempp and William Hansen (Bloomington: Indiana University Press, 2002), 165–79. Chapter 3 draws from my essay "Democratizing for Peace," *Rhetoric and Public Affairs* 4 (2001): 309–22. A segment of chapter 5 comes from my essay "Evil Enemy v. Agonistic Other: Rhetorical Constructions of Terrorism," *Review of Education, Pedagogy, and Cultural Studies* 25 (2003): 181–200. Bits and pieces of other themes dispersed throughout this book can be found in other recent essays I have published, including "Democracy, War, and Decivilizing Metaphors of American Insecurity," in *Metaphorical World Politics: Rhetorics of Democracy, War, and Globalization*, ed. Francis A. Beer and Christ'l de Landtsheer (East Lansing: Michigan State University Press, 2004) and "Rhetorical Deliberation and Democratic Politics in the Here and Now," *Rhetoric and Public Affairs* 5 (Spring 2002): 277–85. This previously published material has been reworked and integrated with the bulk of the new writing that constitutes the present book and its original argument.

I am grateful for the opportunities provided to me to develop and test in various lectures and venues my thinking on the problem of the terror war. These presentations included a talk titled "Profiling Terrorism" as the Wayne N. Thompson Annual Lecture at Western Illinois University, March 25, 2002. It was also delivered as the keynote speech during "Communication Week" at Indiana University, Northwest, in Gary on March 26, 2002. Another talk, "Terrorism at Democracy's Frontier," was presented at Manchester College in Manchester, Indiana, during "Peace Week," April 17, 2002. I presented "Terrorism on Democracy's Rhetorical Frontier" in a plenary session of the Eighth Biennial Public Address Conference, October 4, 2002, held at the University of Georgia in Athens, Georgia. On a keynote panel at the Eighty-eighth Annual Convention of the National Communication Association, held on November 22, 2002, in New Orleans, I presented a paper on the theme "Profiling Terrorism: From Freedom's Evil Enemy to Democracy's Agonistic Other." My keynote presentation for an interdisciplinary and international conference on war, law, and rhetoric, sponsored by the Center for the Study of European Civilization, was presented at the University of Bergen in Norway on March 12, 2003, and was titled "Evil Enemy v. Agonistic Other: Rhetorical Constructions of Terrorism." A version of that talk was also given on a spotlight program, dedicated to critiquing the rhetoric of war, at the Eighty-fourth Annual Meeting of the Eastern Communication Association, April 25, 2003, in Washington, D.C. Finally, I spoke to the faculty and students of Alma College in Alma, Michigan, on May 13, 2003, on the subject "The Rhetoric of Evil and the Idiom of Democracy in the War on Terrorism."

My debt of gratitude extends to three of my closest friends and most engaging colleagues who, over the years, encouraged me in this work both by reassuring me it was worth the effort and by challenging me to explore new avenues of thought. Oscar Giner opened my eyes to the performative power of myth in human relations generally and in political affairs specifically, which led me to a compelling appreciation for the life-sustaining dirt work performed by Coyote and other trickster figures. John Lucaites affirmed my inclinations toward a productive mode of rhetorical critique, engaging me conceptually throughout the extended process of developing the argument of this book despite the daily distraction of departmental administration that kept us both otherwise occupied for ten years. Jeffrey Isaac engaged my developing notions of democracy agonistically, providing not only an enrichment of those notions but also a living example of productive agonistics. Each of these brilliant colleagues has enriched my work and my life. I have benefited immensely from their friendship and from their reactions to the manuscript. Its remaining limitations reveal my own shortcomings, not theirs.

The continuing inspiration for this work comes from the love and support I have received from my wife, Nancy Lee Ivie, these past thirty-seven years. She has been my compass through the maze of adulthood and my co-conspirator in selectively subverting outworn habits of the life world. She has taught me to learn from our grown children, each of whom has set out in directions both recognizable and unique. And she has inspired me by her own example to cherish the gifts of our parents. In particular, I wish to honor the memory of my father, Robert G. Ivie, who served his country faithfully and courageously as a commissioned officer in two of America's wars. He fought to preserve the principles we are now challenged to put into practice with renewed commitment and vigor.

Introduction

September 11, 2001, was a second day of infamy for Americans, or so it seemed, in which terror was visited upon a peaceful and unsuspecting people by the dastardly forces of tyranny. The United States was at war once again, more or less, with an axis of evil in defense of freedom and democracy. Sixty years earlier, Franklin Roosevelt's heroic oratory following Japan's sneak attack on Pearl Harbor had rallied the nation not only to defeat the agents of treachery and their wicked coconspirators but also to crusade for an end to the history of war by establishing an empire of democracy. From that moment of moral outrage to the present day of righteous fervor, America's quest for invulnerability and a democratic peace has placed the nation under "the shadow of war," to borrow Michael Sherry's felicitous phrase, its culture and institutions militarized, its foreign affairs intensified, and its passion for absolute security thwarted.[1] Thus, a cyclical drama of transgression, travail, and triumph has traumatized the nation from the beginning of the American century. Under the sign of great tragedy and in the image of heroic struggle, a beleaguered nation once again has been called upon by its president to defeat the horror of chaos and to secure the future of civilization, this time against the specter of global terrorism.[2]

The intersection of terror, democracy, and war is both strange and familiar territory for Americans to tread and conquer. They have defeated the threat of tyranny before, only to encounter it again in yet another virulent form. Danger is seemingly endemic to a demos—a democratic people and their leaders—forever besieged by demons from within as well as outside their polity. Thus, *democracy* is a troublesome term in the lexicon of American political culture. As a mark of national identity, it inspires greatness and suggests destiny but also stirs dread and loathing, fear and distrust, terror and counterterror. It is at once a powerful incentive for peace and a compelling motive for war, a reservoir of strength and a point of vulnerability, a dimension of the nation's awesome might and a source of its chronic insecurities. Democracy, in short, is a decidedly conflicted measure of American power or the failure thereof.

Joseph Nye makes an important observation about the role of America's democratic "soft power" in meeting the challenges of our time at home and abroad. As a mode of enticement and attraction, unlike military force and economic coercion, soft power shapes preferences to inspire imitation and sets political agendas to achieve consent. This kind of influence is derived from the way the nation expresses its cultural values and handles its domestic and foreign affairs by championing democracy, promoting peace, and cooperating with international institutions. In the global information age, the United States cannot afford to undermine its soft power without eroding its standing and security in the world. International cooperation is required to assure continuing economic vitality, for example, and to address global problems such as terrorism effectively.

Nevertheless, a parochial spirit of arrogant and heavy-handed unilateralism has emerged at this critical moment, especially after the events of 9/11, to define U.S. interests narrowly with indifference to the opinions of others and renewed devotion to the exercise of hard power. The hubris of this new unilateralism has motivated the United States to violate civil liberties, reduce foreign aid, eschew international treaties and conventions, and snub the United Nations just when "world politics is changing in a way that means Americans cannot achieve all their international goals acting alone" and will likely get themselves deeply into trouble if they alienate other nations by "investing in military power alone" while squandering the soft power of democratic values.[3]

The paradox of American military and economic power, as Nye observes, is that the United States is too strong to be challenged by any other single state but not strong enough to solve global problems, such as terrorism, by itself. America's security requires the help and respect of others. Accordingly, the exercise of soft power to enhance U.S. security necessitates a willingness to cooperate with other states and international organizations and thus to accept a reduced measure of direct control over world affairs. In Nye's words, "We may have less control in the future, but we may find ourselves living in a world somewhat more congenial to our basic values of democracy, free markets, and human rights." Hard power as the measure of American preeminence will prove increasingly illusionary in an information age of intense diversity and thick globalization that is changing the very meaning of control. "Fewer issues that we care about," Nye continues, "will prove susceptible to solution through our dominant military power."[4]

The irony of this paradox of power is that the United States must relinquish a degree of control in order to enhance its security. Yet, the irony itself is premised on an illusion of control, as if the United States can will its security unilaterally through military preeminence and economic hegemony. Americans cannot surrender a commanding global influence that is beyond their reach even as the world's sole superpower. They can only forfeit the illusion of control and place greater faith in the soft power of their democratic culture. That is the challenge facing an insecure nation at the peak of its power: will it entrust its future to strengthening democratic practices in the present or bet against the odds by trying to dominate the world?

Affirming the soft power of democracy does not imply abandoning the hard power of military and economic strength, nor does it mean treating democracy as an excuse for world domination or as a pretext for perpetual war in a quixotic (or even cynical) quest for universal peace. The point is that the United States cannot rely solely on hard power to ensure its welfare, nor can it sustain an arrogant and alienating unilateralism that undermines its democratic credentials by attempting to force its will on a world in which power is increasingly complex and widely distributed, a world requiring better cooperation and greater capacity to cope with diversity. Enriching the nation's democratic culture is key to enhancing its well-being and security.

Yet, democracy itself, as a troubled term in the lexicon of American political culture, is a source of chronic fear and national insecurity no less than a resource of domestic health and global influence. Tapping its full potential for adapting to the shifting challenges of a divisive and decentralized global order will require adjusting a severely conflicted attitude, which consists of a strong positive regard for the promise of democratic rule that, in turn, is diminished by a deep and abiding apprehension over the threat of democratic distemper. The purpose of this book is to confront that very tension between democracy's perceived promise and peril. My argument is that contemporary threats and challenges facing the United States can be addressed more constructively in a robustly democratic idiom than by perpetuating the debilitating image of distempered democracy, that the nation's well-being, standing, and security can be enhanced by giving primacy to democratic practices and values instead of degraded by surrendering to the antagonistic impulses and aggressive policies emanating from a republic of fear, and that enriching democratic practice promotes a positive peace over giving the presumption to war.

In order to develop a constructive critique of America's democratic deficit, I have adopted an overtly rhetorical perspective both for identifying the distinctly discursive dimension of the problem at hand and for advancing a corresponding corrective of enriching democratic culture and practice. From that perspective, I presume polities cannot choose between rhetoric and reality but instead must opt for more or less adequate interpretations of their multifaceted worlds, interpretations which necessarily are constructed rhetorically. Our choices are always between one kind of rhetoric and another.

Symbolic action is inherent to the human condition. As symbol-using and symbol-misusing beings, we make sense of things and develop strategies of adaptation, both individually and collectively, through language. Discourse constructs and reconstructs political realities as we know them within frameworks of interpretation. In Kenneth Burke's view, "Much that we take as observations about 'reality' may be but the spinning out of possibilities implicit in our particular choice of terms."[5] Such is the rhetorical fabric of political motivation understood as collective attitudes or predispositions toward action of one sort or another.

The more flexible these discursive constructions, or what Burke has called "terministic screens," the better they serve as "equipment for living," that is, as interpretive instruments for coping with the stresses and strains of a dynamic and complex world—a shrinking world in which social divisions, cultural diversity, and other sources of difference are increasingly compressed in the global information age to the point of intensifying friction and igniting conflict. The more rigidly these "terministic incentives" are constructed, the more likely they are to exacerbate tension, foster alienation and hatred, and provoke violence. Thus, the central function of language, considered as symbolic action, is "attitudinal and hortatory," an instrument of political "cooperation and competition." Pushed to the extreme, it yields untoward consequences, including guilt, hatred, fear, and "catharsis by scapegoat."[6]

Accordingly, a considerable source of America's chronically exaggerated fear of foreign and even domestic Others, its disinclination toward international cooperation, its propensity for unilateralism, and its motivation for war can be attributed to the rhetorically rigid construction of a term central to the national identity. As that term, democracy is all too readily degraded into an object of anxiety and containment, especially when it is closely articulated with the language of disease and with other reified tropes of endangerment. Under this condition of rhetorical degradation, the thoroughly literalized and elaborated metaphor of distempered democracy manifests and reproduces a troublesome state of mind that, at its worst, reduces a powerful nation to an aggressive republic of fear. As such, the United States is strongly predisposed toward violence and deeply motivated to rationalize war as the work of peace.

Managing this fear-induced tension within the nation's democratic identity, where an otherwise abiding aspiration for peace conflicts with an immediate incitement to war, requires constant rhetorical work to keep from destabilizing the prevailing but problematic rationale for relying so heavily on America's righteous force to pursue an illusive state of security. Absent a strong accent on a flexible and robust conception of democratic practice, a rigid rhetoric of evil, such as that practiced by George W. Bush, stirs the nation into patriotic fits of belligerence. This is a rhetoric that promotes the mistaken promise of a universal peace in a mythical world made safe for democracy and that inhibits any serious reconfiguration of democracy itself into a figure of strength rather than a sign of danger. It is a rhetoric too little contested at the present moment of growing national hubris and diminishing tolerance in a decidedly conflicted and complex world. Thus, it is a rhetoric that requires critique in order to redirect its force toward an attitude more conducive to coping with the challenges of the global information age.

The critique advanced throughout the pages of this book probes four interconnected points of tension in the problematic composition of democracy as a terministic incentive for war. One of those points is a restrictive conception of democratic deliberation that reflects and reinforces what might be called the nation's inclination toward demophobia. This idealization of deliberative democracy as a rational process best reserved for experts and privileged political leaders, a process easily degraded by the common people under the irrational influence of a demagogue, is elitist, culturally biased, and generally tone deaf to the challenges of pluralism and diversity. It is a discourse of rationality that masks its own rhetorical form and function and thereby impoverishes democratic culture, whereas a more rhetorically robust mode of political reasoning enriches public deliberation and democratic identity in a way that is responsive to a pluralistic polity and reduces exaggerated fears of foreign and domestic Others.

A second and related point of tension constituting a republic of fear resides in the irony of distrusting the very symbol of the nation's identity and purpose. This tension between democracy's legitimizing ethos and its unruly impulses is managed by invoking the myth of disease to fabricate the image of a distempered demos. The vehicles of the myth convey a caricature of the public as prone to popular rage and fits of passion, convulsions of factionalism that poison public deliberations, and a contagion of jealousy and avarice that reduces the people to a collection of mere dupes subject to the manipulation of unsavory politicians. Thus the founders fashioned a republic, grounded on the fiction of representation, that contained rather than entrusted itself to the rule of the people. Representation was the healing principle that removed the disease of the people from the body politic. It privileged supposedly rational elites over a presumably distempered mass on the premise that the public is vulnerable to unenlightened and debilitating influences, thereby predisposing the republic to discipline domestic differences and prevent foreign contamination.

A third affiliated point of tension locates democracy at the intersection of war and peace. Consistent with the fear of foreign contamination and a determination to control domestic distemper, the quest to achieve a universal peace is motivated by a desire to expand the domain of liberal democracy in order to contain the forces of disorder and curtail chaos within an ever-diminishing perimeter. The truism that democracies do not fight one another has become a commonplace of scholarship and public discourse alike and the centerpiece of a national security policy driven by the attitude that democracy is too frail to survive alien influences. The very pursuit of a perfect peace through global democratization belies an abiding uncertainty and deep suspicion of democracy that, in turn, provides an enduring and powerful incentive for war, so much so that Americans typically do not even notice the oxymoronic conceit of fighting for a democratic peace.

This festering conundrum of pacific belligerence extends to a fourth point of tension in the republic of fear. America's democratic appetite for war and corresponding inclination toward a politics of quiescence and coercion were intensified by the tragic events of 9/11, which spurred the nation to declare an open-ended war on international terrorism. As that vague but invasive state of hostilities expanded to various foreign and domestic fronts, it brought with it an evolving presumption of preemptive and perpetual war. A nation of reluctant belligerents who historically proclaimed themselves predisposed to peace no longer placed the principal burden of proof on those who advocated for war. The United States, it was now broadly presumed, was merely engaging in one battle after another in a seamless war on terrorism when it invaded Iraq, for example, not committing acts of aggression. Preemptive wars and curtailments of civil liberties were merely tactical requirements in an overall strategy to defeat terrorists who had initiated hostilities with their unprovoked attack on the twin towers of Manhattan and the Pentagon.

The administration's rigid and simplistic rhetoric of evil profiled the enemy crudely but powerfully in a manner that entangled the United States even more dreadfully in a theater of reciprocal and escalating violence perpetrated against civilians for political purposes and proving once again the gruesome validity of Nietzsche's observation that "every society has the tendency to reduce its opponents to caricatures": "'The good man' sees himself as if surrounded by evil, and under the continual onslaught of evil his eye grows keener, he discovers evil in all his dreams and desires; and so he ends, quite reasonably, by considering nature evil, mankind corrupt, goodness an act of grace (that is, as impossible for man). *In summa:* he denies life, he grasps that when good is the supreme value it condemns life."[7] Reciprocal demonizing spurred each side to participate in an escalating dance of death. By this logic, Americans were expected to fight for the hollowed-out symbols of freedom and democracy while succumbing to the righteous, even crusading, will of the administration and disregarding the underlying causes of terrorism.

Democracy was contained, diminished, deferred, and sacrificed on the altar of righteous force and in the quest to achieve national security by eradicating an ubiquitous evil Other. Democracy itself was thought to be too dangerous to practice safely and robustly during this open-ended war on terrorism if the nation was to stay the course and eventually prevail. Patriotic fervor and political quiescence were the preferred alternatives to debate and dissent. The perceived risk of, and threat to, exercising freedom and practicing democracy contributed doubly to the nation's sense of extreme peril.

Yet the rhetorical work required to suppress the twin impulses of freedom and democracy under the sign of danger generated tensions of its own inside a political culture that possesses a residual respect for and enduring devotion to democratic practices and principles. Herein lay an untapped rhetorical resource for displacing the language of evil and recovering the presumption of peace by giving primacy to a balance of liberal-democratic values and speaking in a robust democratic idiom rather than in a weak and demophobic voice. Addressing agonistic Others strategically as consubstantial rivals rather than as evil enemies reduces the impulse to exaggerate danger, invent scapegoats, and rely too singularly or heavily on the hard power of military coercion. It requires exercising rhetorical flexibility over ideological rigidity, keeping linguistic boundaries appropriately fluid and fuzzy within a prevailing framework of interpretation and motivation, finding points of identification that make adversaries concurrently adverse and consubstantial, identifying similarities where otherwise only differences prevail and underscoring differences where similarities have been reduced to simplistic identities. Speaking in the idiom of robust democracy is not a luxury to be reserved for addressing friends and allies but instead a necessity for keeping rivals from becoming sheer enemies. To the degree that war in a republic of fear is the bitter fruit of rhetorical rigidity, peace may regain some standing by bolstering democratic culture and speaking across rhetorically blurred boundaries out of respect for the complexities of an increasingly interconnected and deeply divided world. Such is the constructive role of rhetoric in advancing a positive conception of peace for a healthy democratic society, a rhetoric that resists the kind of extreme Othering that perpetuates the cycle of terror and counterterror.

This is the basic outline of the argument that the rest of the book develops into a more detailed critique. The four interrelated points of tension associated with an elitist conception of democratic deliberation, a debilitating identification of democracy with disease, an oxymoronic conceit of fighting for a democratic peace, and a counterproductive rhetoric of evil for protecting freedom and democracy from terrorism converge not only on a diagnosis of discursive sources of national insecurity and associated rationalizations of state violence but also a prescription for enriching democratic culture and decreasing aggressive unilateralism. The diagnosis points to how America's fear of its own demos is transformed into exaggerated articulations of vulnerability and extreme danger from exposure to alien influence. The prescription, like the problem itself, is a rhetorical derivative, but instead of projecting reified metaphors of disease onto foreign Others and treating them as sheer enemies and convenient scapegoats, it calls for articulating points of intersection between rivals to make them partially consubstantial with one another and to give primacy to liberal-democratic values in the management of serious differences. Democracy, like rhetoric, participates in the drama of life that pits protagonists against antagonists who may or may not choose to reduce one another to tragic enemies and, in the first case, learn the lesson of hubris the hard way by fighting one another to the bitter death or, alternatively, discover they are better off competing cooperatively across appropriately fluid and fuzzy lines of division.

I do not mean to suggest that I have identified the whole problem of American insecurity and belligerence or provided a complete solution. Instead, my aim is to call attention to an overlooked but important rhetorical dimension of public culture that can either hinder or help our efforts to live as peacefully and productively as possible in a deeply conflicted, richly diverse, and increasingly compressed global village. We are not yet accustomed to thinking of rhetoric as a potentially positive force for achieving a healthy democratic culture, but we live in a divisive world that requires us to look constantly for strategic ways of symbolically bridging the human divide enough to coexist without eradicating differences or ritualistically sacrificing convenient scapegoats. War is a perversion of rhetorical expression, as Kenneth Burke has written, whereas peace can be privileged rhetorically through the principle of identification.[8] I can only hope the present probe of democracy's rhetorical configuration will prove sufficiently revealing to motivate further consideration of how the democratic idiom might be rehabilitated and accentuated for the added enhancement of human relations.

1

Republic of Fear

The American republic, so powerful its leaders have proclaimed it the world's indispensable nation, is prone to war because, paradoxically, it remains forever insecure no matter how many weapons it adds to its arsenal or how strong its economy or widespread its influence. The United States is a violent nation motivated by a tragic sense of fear, a country tyrannized by an exaggerated image of the danger endemic to domestic politics and international affairs. Yet, no people identify more closely than Americans with the quest for peace or profess themselves so devoutly the champion of global democracy. How is it, then, that such a powerful force for freedom should feel so vulnerable and compelled so often to break the peace it seeks?

Perhaps this question about the source of U.S. insecurity seems inappropriate. After all, is it accurate or fair to presume America is a violent nation? Whenever the United States has been forced to fight, has it not been a reluctant belligerent—a victim of aggression defending itself and others in a just cause? Is not peace the national norm and aspiration, not war?

Any responsible answer to such questions must acknowledge that the United States is both violent and peaceful in its conduct toward others and its aims for international order. The problem is not whether the country and its citizens want war or peace but how to minimize the inducement to violence. Regardless of their aspirations for peace, Americans have found themselves engaged in an endless quest for security punctuated by small and large wars throughout their history as a nation-state. Yearning for "perfect safety from foreign threats," they have remained for more than two centuries chronically alarmed "by even potential dangers," observe James Chace and Caleb Carr, and thus have responded with military force to "real and imagined" threats to their own borders as well as the borders of other nations with whom they feel their security is "strategically or politically linked." Nevertheless, the "goal of absolute security" has always eluded the United States.[1] Oft-repeated warfare has failed to secure the peace or safety of the republic while Americans have continued to insist they are a "target nation."[2]

Why does security elude the nation and peace remain its unfulfilled quest? Because, as David Campbell explains, danger is "an effect of interpretation," not "an objective condition." Although danger most certainly exists, risk is such a common, unavoidable, and pervasive experience that Americans have to decide which risks are dangerous and which can be tolerated, decisions that necessarily operate beyond the limits of objectivity. Accordingly, the country is prone to represent some events, conditions, incidents, rivals, or acts, especially those characterized as "alien, subversive, dirty, or sick," as more threatening than others. Americans must always choose, not between reality and falsehood, but instead by "adopting one mode of representation over another."[3]

Although there is a material, nonsymbolic world beyond language and interpretation, it can be experienced and understood only within the framework of symbolically constructed meaning that, in Kenneth Burke's account, is a "terministic screen" that forms attitudes and a "terministic incentive" that comprises the motives or predispositions of a political community.[4] Objects exist external to thought but, as Ernesto Laclau and Chantal Mouffe state, they cannot "constitute themselves as objects" in our collective consciousness outside of discourse or without a "discursive field."[5] Discursive modes of interpretation, including the dangers they construe, endure over time in the identity of a people, especially as that identity is defined in opposition to threatening Others. As Campbell concludes, the "constant articulation of danger" is a condition of the possibility of a state's identity, not a threat to its existence.[6] Thus, the discourse of foreign threat demarcates American identity and constitutes national purpose. That is why peace and security elude the republic no matter how strong or prosperous it becomes or how often its armies are victorious. Without an image of the threatening Other the possibility of national identity is diminished. Americans must feel endangered in order to exist purposefully and meaningfully as a people.

But must they exaggerate routine risks so often and so greatly to remain a people? Or, more to the point, what inclines American identity toward overstating danger? Certainly, more than one good answer to this question can be found but none that cuts more quickly to the heart of the matter than the perceived vulnerabilities of democracies, for democracy defines the national identity and establishes a measure of political legitimacy more than any other single factor affecting the well-being of the republic. Yet, the republic is, and always has been, conflicted between democracy as a professed ideal and an actual practice. By choosing to contain democratic practice within liberalism's protective sheath, Americans have constituted democracy as something both dangerous and endangered. They have created a rhetorical dynamic that promotes excessive fear of the domestic as well as the foreign Other. They have grounded their national identity in a symbol of political legitimacy fundamentally feared and distrusted no less than revered and deified—a god-term or, more accurately, a term of awe that simultaneously attracts and repels, that connotes instability, vulnerability, and disorder more than trust in the rule of the people. The United States fears itself as a democracy subject to self-destruction no less than foreign attack or domination. It seeks security by containing democratic practices domestically and globally, by making the world safe for democracy and thus rendering itself safe from democracy's infectious influence. This is the special burden of the American republic, the burden of a republic of fear.

The cycle of fear and violence linked to national identity need not continue unabated in the post–cold war era, however, if Americans revise their ancestral attitudes toward democracy. The liberal tradition of containing democratic distemper is strong but not monolithic or impervious to change, nor does a constructive critique require Americans to abandon their liberal principles of freedom, individual rights, and economic opportunity. They need instead to correct an imbalance between liberalism and democracy that is inadequate for present times and purposes because it inflates and perpetuates national insecurities. The cumulative effect of previous historical reinterpretations, as Russell Hanson has demonstrated, "was to liberalize democracy so thoroughly that any tension between liberalism and democracy was almost completely sublimated" to the detriment of America's democratic imagination. This "taming of democracy" undermined the nation's "capacity for reinterpreting liberal democracy in appropriate ways," in ways, that is, that would democratize liberalism.[7] As Kenneth Burke once observed about the problem of ideological efficiency endangering a "proper preservation of proportions," the "apologetics of liberalism" has been too efficient in that it has "overstressed the element of liberty and strategically ignored the element of obligation."[8]

Reconstituting democracy as a more robust concept and increasingly vital practice in American political culture requires an appreciation of its currently unreconstructed role in perpetuating republican insecurities along with a clear recognition of its profoundly rhetorical properties. The tropes of democratic discourse, sometimes metaphorical and explicitly figurative but more commonly conveyed in the mode of literalized imagery, are a primary medium for embellishing routine hazards and ordinary risks. Particularly, the language of disease has been closely and intricately identified with democracy enough to exclude the possibility of an open rapport or even healthy competition with foreign and even domestic Others, so much so that the public itself has been routinely diagnosed by political elites as a distempered Other. Within such a distorted framework of interpretation, war and domination (represented as national defense and global leadership) are deemed the only realistic options for protecting freedom and preserving civilization against ubiquitous forces of death, destruction, and chaos.

A revised framework of interpretation would aim to avoid what Roger Burbach has termed "the tragedy of American democracy," a condition in which the United States manipulates the world's democratic aspirations to advance capitalism and special economic interests. Promoting neoliberal economics in this way systematically undermines democracy abroad, increases political cynicism, and shreds the internal fabric of democracy in the United States itself. The vitality of the democratic system is diminished, Burbach insists, when foreign policy becomes authoritarian and domestic problems are allowed to fester. With such a shallow notion of freedom and equality, "the institutions of representation tend to alienate and marginalise people."[9] Thus, any hope of democratic advance or legitimacy is severely constrained by the prevailing practice of what Benjamin Barber calls "thin democracy," itself a legacy of America's republican origins and a continuing source of national insecurity.[10]

Republican insecurity over democracy, even after the defeat of fascism in World War II and victory over Soviet communism in the cold war, is tragically ironic for a country now aspiring to a democratic peace that supposedly would end ideological struggle and warfare for all time. In the American tradition of liberal democracy—a tradition of thin or weak democracy wherein the voice of the people is muted by the principles of liberalism and contained within a constitutional regime of representative, republican government—a culture of fear has developed to the near breaking point. The origins of this culture of fear can be traced to the nation's founding years and even earlier to the political philosophies that so heavily influenced the rhetoric of the founders and informed their enduring critique of democracy. On the one hand, democracy is represented as especially vulnerable to alien influence and corruption. Accordingly, generations of leaders have shared Thomas Jefferson's "anxieties about the threatening, infectious nature of alien ideologies and political systems," as James Chace observes, in a futile search for "complete immunity to foreign threat" that has exaggerated the nation's sense of vulnerability and reinforced its distrust of democracy's staying power.[11] On the other hand, democracy is perceived as inherently corrupt. Certainly, James Madison harbored little faith in the demos or the democratic process, believing that even an Athenian assembly of individuals as wise as Socrates would soon deteriorate into a mob.[12] His distrust of democracy was widespread in eighteenth-century America, when the prevailing political ideal was for a republican form of mixed government designed to prevent the inordinate power of the commons over a virtuous elite. Violence and destruction were associated with the demos, just as factionalism and foreign invasion were deemed the two greatest threats to the republic and fearful images of a rebellious contagion of democratic distemper spreading to America were evoked by the French Revolution.[13]

Thus, a peculiar form of demophobia has marked the national identity since the advent of a republican polity more than two hundred years ago.[14] Two world wars in the first half of the twentieth century—one fought ostensibly to make the world safe for democracy, the other to defeat fascism—and a cold war against communism extending throughout most of the rest of the century raised the problem of America's democratic ethos to a crisis level. The nation's culture of fear reached a particularly ominous point during the cold war when it became entangled with nuclear politics. Dwight Eisenhower, consummate cold warrior that he was, dedicated his presidency to a campaign of psychological warfare aimed at totalizing a communist threat that could be met only by risking nuclear suicide. Rhetorically transforming the nation's perennial quest for absolute security into a nuclear pathology of perpetual insecurity, Eisenhower's crusade for freedom appealed to the spirit of democratic righteousness even as it reinforced traditional misgivings over the public's inability to resist foreign, in this case Soviet, propaganda.[15]

Through such manipulations American national security became inextricably linked, for good or ill, to the hegemony of one form of government. Global democratization, in the image of liberal democratic internationalism, emerged from the era of containing communism to become the linchpin of

U.S. foreign policy. "The dominant logic of American foreign policy," Tony Smith observes, "was dictated by concerns for national security; and the dominant way Washington saw to assure this security in terms of the construction of a stable world order congenial to America's way of life was that democratic governments be promoted worldwide."[16] Thus, Ronald Reagan initiated his administration's "crusade for democracy" in 1982 on the questionable premise that the best hope for peace and national security was a world of democratic nations. Beyond containment lies democracy, proclaimed George H. W. Bush's secretary of state, James Baker, and Bill Clinton campaigned for the presidency in 1992 on the theme of achieving national security by promoting "democracy's triumph around the world."[17]

Still, thoughtful voices caution against the viability or even desirability of seeking a democratic peace. Political scientist Amos Perlmutter, for instance, warns of this pervasive sense of mission "in the name of a hegemonial ideology that is intended to dominate the world system." The "world is not ready for democracy," he argues, nor is democracy necessary for international order and national tranquility.[18]

The "curious myopia," as John Lewis Gaddis calls it, that nations possessing different forms of government are hostile to the United States, has become an ideological litmus test that repeatedly exacerbates misunderstandings and grossly exaggerates the dangers facing Americans in a post–cold war world challenged by the centrifugal forces of nationalism, ethnicity, religion, and economic disparity. Caught between newly unleashed forces of fragmentation and its own rejuvenated quest for ideological integration, the United States risks chronic paranoia by asserting hegemony under the sign of democracy while much of the rest of the world devolves into regional and local struggles over divisive issues of protectionism; aggression; civil war; terrorism; and racial, ethnic, and religious self-determination.[19] As the immediate legacy of a cold war rhetorical presidency, global democratization has become, to borrow the language of Frederick Dolan and Thomas Dumm, a problematic governing representation of national security and salvation in a fearful "republic of words." It is both a vehicle of national hubris and source of tragic fear in a republic of rhetorical "fantasies and images," including the fantasy of transforming a barbaric world into a civilized haven of lasting peace and universal freedom.[20] Failure to recognize the futility of such a heroic dream and its incompatibility with the idea of democracy is to risk the demoralization of the nation—its already thin and fragile democratic ethos the near-certain casualty of cynicism.[21]

Rhetoric and Democratic Culture

How, then, might the United States come to terms with democracy as a source of national insecurity and thus diminish unwarranted or exaggerated fears of the Other that too easily become incentives for war? Not, I will argue, by abandoning the symbol of democracy or by further diminishing an already attenuated commitment to democratic practice, but instead by enriching the nation's democratic culture. A robust democratic culture is far more congruous to the present challenge than a strategically contained simulacrum of democracy. In the contest between the forces of global integration and unbridled fragmentation that defines the post–cold war world, strengthening the nation's commitment to the practice of democracy is key to securing the judicious "middle ground" of "healthy skepticism" that Gaddis prescribes as a hedge against the extremes of centripetal domination and centrifugal disintegration.[22]

Enriching the nation's democratic culture requires, in turn, a revised understanding and new appreciation of its relationship to rhetoric. Rather than reducing the intersection of rhetoric and democracy to demagoguery, which undermines confidence in the judgment of the people and transforms the demos into a threatening Other, chronic republican insecurities might be considerably alleviated by realizing democracy's rich rhetorical potential and rhetoric's aptitude for securing a democratic polity. Democracy necessarily exists within a rhetorical culture. As Hanson has explained in some detail, liberal democracy should be understood as a particular rhetorical tradition, especially when we are attempting to assess the vitality of such a tradition in which ideas depend upon their persuasive construction for "their standing within particular political communities." Thus, Hanson observes, "rhetorical traditions such as liberal democracy are always being constituted and reconstituted in the process of political argumentation." Although the prevailing sense of liberal democracy overemphasizes the role of power in opposition to collective deliberation and obligations, as a rhetorical tradition its efficiencies are subject to critique and modification.[23]

The possibility of constructively engaging the tradition of liberal democracy becomes increasingly evident when viewed from the perspective of culture, specifically the norms of rhetorical culture. The term *rhetorical culture*, as Thomas Farrell explains, refers to commonplaces or sources of invention, perpetuation, revision, and adaptation of meaning for situated audiences, the "symbols and families of practices that permit ongoing performance of meaning and value" by a community. It represents the practices that form and maintain community, for "no culture or public life project can survive for long without some form of rhetorical practice, some coherent, symbolic manner of securing collaborative public action." The norms of an institutional formation must be invoked rhetorically, articulated in rhetorical procedures and conventions, and cultivated in rhetorical practices that constitute and momentarily resolve in particular circumstances, and for specific audiences, the competing identities, motives, needs, and logic of civic life. Because it elicits an audience through public discourse, rhetoric serves as a culture's "collaborative art of addressing and guiding decision and judgment."[24] Thus culture, including the fearful republican tradition of thin, liberal democracy, is subject to rhetorical transformation in the normal course of public deliberation.

A productive critique and transformation of democratic culture, however, requires a more thoroughly rhetorical understanding of political discourse than either Hanson or even Farrell provides, for each in varying degrees defaults to the ideal of argumentation or rational deliberation in the service of consensus. In Hanson's words, following Habermas, "Only rational persuasion determines the outcome" in "an ideal of democratic discourse." Stratagems are corrupt with power where otherwise the force of the better argument should prevail in democratic transactions among equals.[25] Farrell, too, influenced by Habermas's ideal of emancipation through communicative rationality, appropriates critical theory to traditional rhetoric, even though from the vantage point of universal pragmatics rhetoric "constitutes a crude subset of perlocutionary [or strategic, success-oriented] speech" as opposed to the ideal of illocutionary acts aimed at achieving understanding. Farrell's revision of Habermas aims to make rhetoric the practical instrument of public debate that sustains critical publicity essential to realizing an ideal public sphere.[26] Nevertheless, the goal of rational deliberation, constrained by the vision of an ideal speech situation that brackets power, masks its own rhetoric even as it diminishes the rhetorical promise of democratic politics. This restricted sense of rhetoric not only is impractical but also ultimately inhibits democracy.

A singular emphasis on rational deliberation, which strategically circumscribes the role of popular persuasion in public affairs, conforms intentionally or otherwise to a concerted effort by contemporary liberal theorists to resist the rise of a rhetorical and thus potentially more democratic republic. Their resistance begins with objections proffered by Jeffrey Tulis and his colleagues specifically to the emergence of the rhetorical presidency and extends to promoting deliberative democracy as a rational antidote for demagoguery, thus reflecting an overriding concern, in James Fishkin's words, with "how to reconcile democracy and deliberation." The rise of the rhetorical presidency, they agree, is a sign of the republic in decline. Fishkin, in particular, complains that the nation has increased political equality over time at the expense of rational deliberation by adopting popular measures such as extended suffrage, direct elections, referendums, primaries, public opinion polling, simplified voter registration, and the like. Public persuasion, he warns, requires "simplified packaging" to move a mass audience, a degenerative practice that reduces governing to campaigning, forces policy to serve rhetoric, and promotes an "infection of violent passions" among a tyrannizing majority who would trample the rights of the political minority. Fishkin, like other liberal theorists, wishes to preserve the integrity of representative democracy against the threat of an unenlightened and unreflective mass public exercising direct authority. The rhetorical presidency therefore becomes a focal point of concern in the degree to which it presumably subverts rational deliberation by appealing directly to the general public over the heads of duly elected representatives in Congress. Such presidential manipulations of public opinion are taken as an ominous symptom of the nation's movement toward "a direct-majoritarian, plebiscitary model of leadership."[27]

Similarly, Tulis's influential critique of the deleterious effects of presidential oratory on republican government reflects the fear of the constitutional framers that "mass oratory, whether crudely demagogic or highly inspirational, would undermine the rational and enlightened self-interest of the citizenry which [the founders'] system was designed to foster and on which it was thought to depend for its stability."[28] Thus, presidents until the twentieth century generally restricted their deliberative messages to written communications with Congress and avoided popular oratory on matters of public policy. Theodore Roosevelt, Tulis argues, opened the presidential door to "blatant appeals to passion [and] demagoguery in its worst guises," and Woodrow Wilson transformed the bully pulpit into an instrument of popular leadership, believing presidential eloquence should articulate popular desires into public policy. Wilsonian inclinations toward presidential interpretations of the true sentiment of discordant public opinion confounded durable public interests with transient popular whims, according to Tulis, and presidential corruption of deliberative discourse became commonplace thereafter.[29] Gary Gregg even worries that this "cult of the presidency" might easily become a "presidential republic" that would surely supplant representative government and rational deliberation.[30]

A presidential republic, should it emerge, would amount to a horrendous setback for the cause of liberalism. Congress, Joseph Bessette has insisted, is the appropriate site for deliberating public policy—by design the "principal locus of deliberation in American national government." Indeed, "a government that empowers the majority but does not provide for appropriate institutional capacities may make sound deliberation, and therefore sound governing, impossible." The "crux of the tension between democracy and deliberation," in Bessette's view, is that Congress as the governing body becomes less able to deliberate soundly the more it "resembles the people themselves in number and type." Large representative bodies, like mass assemblies, cannot put "a premium on reason, order, information, commonality of interests, and farsightedness" as a deliberative check on the excesses of direct democracy to ensure the rule of deliberative majorities against the delusions of immediate desires, transient impulses, and unreflective popular sentiments. Thus, direct presidential appeals to the mass public on specific policy issues contaminate the congressional deliberative process and "the climate necessary for reasoned persuasion." In the American system of representative democracy, Bessette insists, the members of Congress must serve as "surrogate deliberators" for their necessarily uninformed and preoccupied constituents.[31]

Beyond the horizon of the rhetorical presidency and impending threat of a presidential republic lies an even greater calamity for deliberative democracy and representative government—the rhetorical republic. As Bessette observes, the framers of the Constitution thought rhetoric undermined "the formation of deliberative majorities." Although rhetoric theoretically can promote public deliberation under ideal conditions of "instructional or reasoned persuasion," where a president acts much like a "national schoolmaster" engaging in "civic instruction through rhetoric," experience confirmed for the framers "the dangers of conducting public policy on the plane of public opinion" where average citizens are "subject to misinformation, deception, prejudice, passion, and demagogic appeals." Madison and Hamilton believed that deliberative rhetoric could not prevail, or even hold its own, over demagoguery. Passion, not reason, was the threat to popular government. "Rhetoric was dangerous," Bessette reports, "precisely because it was the principal means of inflaming passions, of appealing to envy and prejudice." Passion was the infirmity of the people that made them slaves to the cunning of sophistry. "When orators rule," Bessette concludes, "it is because they are masters not of reason and argument, but of cunning, sophistry, and declamation." Even absent blatant demagoguery, deliberative rhetoric and reasoned persuasion are thought to be rare occurrences in public discourse, thus the framers' "injunction against popular rhetoric."[32]

Despite the framers' injunction, the rhetorical republic has arrived in our day of "discourses, imagery, interpretations, and desires attached to practices of representation," according to Dolan and Dumm. Much to the dismay and consternation of liberal theorists, our republic has become "a republic of words, which also means, necessarily, a republic of fantasies and images. The problem of governing the United States . . . is the problem of governing representations: of reinterpreting the phantasmagoric mix of images and tonalities, claims and counterclaims, that shape political discourse in the United States today." Thus, governing has become, by liberal standards, "an impossible project" of trying to predict and control meanings that have been "submitted to a community of interpreters." American politics are no longer shaped by "the grammar of a master discourse" but instead by a "plurality of public spheres."[33] This republic of words is a postmodern polity of the kind that liberalism, with its commitment to Enlightenment rationality and order, has always feared and attempted to prevent by monitoring difference as a sign of error and disciplining variation through deliberation, as if deviation were deviance and disagreement were discord bordering on disorder and disharmony.

What, then, is the prospect for democracy in a rhetorical republic if public deliberation is in decline? The idea of a postmodern polity is so disturbing to Farrell that it drives him all the way back to Aristotle in search of norms for an enlightened rhetorical culture—a culture in which the "triumphant murmuring of postmodernism" would be supplanted by a "judgment-centered" rhetoric that deploys practical reason to make civic institutions more responsive and participatory. "In presenting rhetoric as a genuine method of thought and action," he writes, "I hope to show that alternative historical outcomes are still available to us and that the triumph of the logic of disintegration is not yet assured."[34]

Yet, what Farrell calls the logic of disintegration appears to postmodern theorists as the disaggregation of democracy, in that the elements of the democratic imagination no longer fit neatly together in one monolithic way or common place. Liberalism, as Anne Norton attests, transformed itself over time from ideology into "the common sense of the American people," becoming "a set of principles unconsciously adhered to" and moving "beyond reason" to "the habits of everyday life" and "beyond thought to practice."[35] Postmodernism challenges these habits of mind and action and their totalizing metanarrative of political order that, reified as common sense, warrant a regime of privilege operating under a hegemonic conception of the public good.[36] The nation's democratic ethos, from this perspective, cannot be reduced to a single sacred institution, such as the Congress, or even contained within a single national border. Instead, democracy works affirmatively to contest identities and other "final markers" constituted historically or otherwise naturalized in the cultural and political discourses of a society. As William Connolly puts the matter, democracy unfettered "cultivates a politics of agonistic respect among multiple constituencies who respond differentially to mysteries of being while acknowledging each other to be worthy of respect partly because they are implicated in *this* common condition." The postmodern democratic ethos, in Connolly's view, "balances the desirability of governance through democratic means with a corollary politics of democratic disturbance through which any particular pattern of previous settlements might be tossed up for grabs again." The key to such a democratic culture is to maintain a "productive ambiguity" that balances the modes of government with a logic of "denaturalization of settled identities and conventions." Clearly, though, the postmodern mind perceives the greatest risk in failing to denaturalize commonsense attitudes and thereby allowing "state mechanisms of electoral accountability [to] become conduits of fascist unity."[37]

Thus, postmodern thought privileges a more direct or radical democracy than liberal democratic theory, an attitude that values democratic practice over republican institutions and strong democracy over thin or representative democracy.[38] In some respects, or at least some instances, this amounts to more of a shift of emphasis than a denial of all common ground with liberalism—stressing democratic participation and pluralism but not to the exclusion of liberal institutions and procedures aimed at preserving political order. But what are the consequences of this shift of emphasis for democratic deliberation? How does one deliberate in a rhetorical republic? Or does one?

Rhetoric and Democratic Deliberation

Democratic deliberation in a rhetorical republic is robust instead of distempered and open instead of contained. Farrell makes a similar observation about rhetorical deliberation, calling it "the worst fear of idealized reason and the best hope for whatever remains of civic life." It is, he says, "the collaborative art of addressing and guiding [public] decision and judgment." But Farrell, too, is attempting to "recapture" rhetoric as a theory of contemporary advocacy since it fell into disrepute as "reason's evil twin, the carnivalesque sideshow of figurative relativism." From the classical Greeks, he seeks to recover rhetorical norms of competence, performance, coherence, and the expression of difference, thereby revitalizing "the only art which evokes the capacity for practical reason from a situated audience." Thus, Farrell examines how rhetoric forms and frames appearances, opinions, and probabilities to achieve nontotalistic configurations of coherence that provide a sufficient sense of duration and legitimization of collective conduct without closing off further deliberation or eliminating interpretive tension. As he says, the practice of rhetoric entails "an invitation to struggle over the provisional meaning of appearances." He wishes to correct not only the postmodern turn toward complete rhetorical relativism but also a misreading of rhetoric based on the "rush to technical reason" and a "false sense of collusion between Aristotle's organon and the Enlightenment project of 'First Philosophy.'" Reasoning about particulars cannot succeed in monologue. Instead, especially in the context of participatory democracy, deliberation is a relational act involving the participation and adjudication of audiences. Rhetoric is concerned not only with contingency but also with community and, Farrell argues, emancipatory reason. Rhetorical audiences exercise agency on practical matters of public exigency, their decisions being key to achieving "some coherent, symbolic manner of securing collaborative public action." The public, from this perspective, is an accountable moral agent without whom reasonable and ethical judgments about configurations of appearances can be neither realized nor legitimized.[39]

Rhetorical deliberation that privileges the public as audience and relational agent participating in a sophisticated act of reasoning about contingencies and particulars is, however, beyond the pale of the liberal republic, at least according to theorists such as Bessette, who worry about "the tension between democracy and deliberation."[40] For Simone Chambers, following the lead of Jürgen Habermas, persuasion easily reduces to distorted communication and coercion except under idealized conditions of rational persuasion where citizens can participate in a "free and equal conversation."[41] Such a position raises once again old questions of practicality and whether the level of civic virtue is high enough among common citizens to realize the ideal of a convergence of rational opinion in a diverse, large, and complex polity. Politics in an ideal regime of rational deliberation labors under the mandate of serving truth, i.e., of discovering and respecting the common good through rational dialogue among informed and sincere equals, and thus strains under the pressure of mass participation where, it is commonly believed, passions will be aroused by rhetorical pleading that distorts the truth. The daunting question faced by those who would endorse broader and more direct public participation in rational deliberation (beyond just electing elites to a liberal regime of representation) is how to provide for the rule of reason and protect against the pull of passion and other distortions to which public communication is thought to be susceptible. Can rational deliberation become egalitarian?

This is a question addressed by political theorists writing about deliberative democracy and its common derivatives such as rational politics, discursive democracy, public deliberation, and reasonable democracy. A central aim of this body of scholarship is to improve public discussion of political and moral issues through reasonable argument that achieves consensus while respecting the diversity and complexity of the citizenry. Amy Gutmann and Dennis Thompson recognize the formidable task they have undertaken, writing that "neither the theory nor the practice of democratic politics has so far found an adequate way to cope with conflicts about fundamental values."[42]

Gutmann and Thompson's model of deliberative democracy prescribes a form of moral reasoning that features the key principle of reciprocity (defined variously as "acting fairly," mutual respect toward opponents, insisting on mutually acceptable resolutions of disagreements, using arguments "consistent with reliable methods of inquiry" and reasons that "could come to be shared by . . . fellow citizens," and, ultimately, citizens "considering what can be justified to people who reasonably disagree with them"). Reciprocity (fairness and rationality) is featured over impartiality or even prudence (enlightened self-interest in strategic bargaining among competing political interests) as an ideal. Gutmann and Thompson also argue for the value of publicity over secrecy and confidentiality in order to ensure reciprocity and for the principle of accountability to maintain the credibility of representative democracy. All of this assumes a constitutional foundation that protects liberty and opportunity. In short, they aim to enhance liberal democracy—that is, to legitimize republican government—by promoting open, fair, and rational expression of differences on otherwise divisive moral issues while maintaining the constitutional priority of liberty and protected privilege.

Short of a complete solution to moral disagreements, Gutmann and Thompson are satisfied if "citizens deliberate with the aim of justifying their collective decisions to one another as best they can." Such deliberation, they observe, "contributes to the legitimacy of decisions made under conditions of scarcity."[43]

The problem here is that commitment to this sort of "middle democracy" hardly amounts to more than a legitimation ritual rather than an exercise in participatory democracy. Its celebration of rational deliberation among constitutionally constrained citizens in civil society and governmental institutions under a regime of representative government is a mere gesture to diversity on volatile moral issues rather than an extension of egalitarian rule. Diversity still labors under the sign of error within this treatment of deliberative democracy, with moral disagreements subject to the discipline of rational justification, with rationality defined as arguments based on reliable modes of inquiry, with consensus among reasonable people the stated ideal, with decision making restricted to elected representatives and contained within a liberal constitution, and with the ultimate purpose of legitimizing an unequal distribution of scarce resources. Democracy is still lacking a way to address moral disagreement or to answer the question of how to extend rational deliberation from elite venues into public forums.

Yet, public deliberation of moral controversies in a vital, pluralistic democracy is the very problem James Bohman attempts to solve. "The challenge for a deliberative theory," he writes, "is to show how the core idea of egalitarian democracy—that legitimate laws are authored by the citizens who are subject to them—can still be credible in complex and pluralistic societies." He rejects a reduction of politics to either instrumental or strategic rationality because it is "crucial that citizens (and their representatives) test their interests and reasons in a public forum before they decide. The deliberative process," he continues, "forces citizens to justify their decisions and opinions by appealing to common interests or by arguing in terms of reasons that 'all could accept' in public debate." The measure of whether an outcome is considered democratic, according to Bohman, is "if citizens themselves are involved in the deliberation or if representatives make decisions that all citizens *would* agree to if given time, knowledge, a chance to be heard, and a disposition to make their reasons 'answerable' to one another." This is the counterfactual or regulative ideal for improving the quality of the public use of reasons in an egalitarian decision-making process where the better argument prevails through an exchange of reasons among competent speakers free of coercion.

To respond to skepticism over this ideal of public reason, where the social facts of pluralism seem to be at odds with the ideal of rational democracy, Bohman adopts a strategy of minimizing the normative assumptions necessary for the process of deliberation, thus siding more with John Rawls than Jürgen Habermas on the issue of constructivism while, at the same time, trying to avoid Rawls's commitment to liberalism. This is, almost needless to say, tricky business.[44]

Bohman attempts to negotiate this tricky ground both by building on what he takes to be the central achievement of the literature on deliberative democracy (which is to specify free, equal, open, and rational deliberation as the necessary condition of an ideal procedure for democratic deliberation) and by adopting the attitude of John Dewey toward developing "an account of how deliberation [actually] works—that is, a fine-grained analysis of how reasons become publicly convincing in deliberative dialogue." Thus, Bohman favors a dialogical over a procedural account of deliberation in order to make citizens conceptually answerable and accountable to one another and thereby prefigure their turns into the eventual outcome of the deliberation. A dialogical process is the key, he argues, to producing "publicly convincing reasons," agreements, and cooperation in and through actual deliberation. His goal is to improve the way in which deliberative majorities are formed rather than aim for a total transformation of society, to reform the practice of public reasoning while building on "the constitutional and institutional achievements of the past."[45]

By conceptualizing public deliberation as an interpersonal dialogue, which is an appealing metaphor for most people, Bohman attempts to capitalize on its entailments of a free and open discussion subject to public scrutiny and thus "likely to be epistemically superior." Dialogue and conversation, that is, imply dialectic, a time-honored mode of rational inquiry, over advocacy. Bohman's main criterion for deliberation is "dialogical uptake" rather than assessing an argument for its logical coherence or sufficiency of evidence, and he does not expect deliberation to achieve consensus. Instead, its success is measured by participants being "sufficiently convinced to continue their ongoing cooperation" because they "recognize that they have contributed to and influenced the outcome, even when they disagree with it." Rather than analyzing what kinds of arguments can or should be convincing, his "analysis of dialogue concerns how public interaction produces those practical effects on participants that make reasons 'convincing.'" Thus, "argumentation is deliberative only when it is dialogical."[46]

Dialogue as the give-and-take of reasons does not aim so much to produce "well-justified claims" but instead "to produce claims that are wide enough in scope and sufficiently justified to be accountable to an indefinite public of fellow citizens." Such dialogical deliberation does not require epistemic expertise but must be open to all citizens with a stake in the outcome and is measured by its uptake of various speakers' points of view into "the ongoing course of discussion." Thus, dialogical deliberation does not presuppose a singular norm of reasonableness or a regulative ideal of agreement that requires citizens to arrive at the same conclusion for the same reasons. Participants must agree just enough with one another, based on different reasons that have been made accessible in the same public sphere, to tolerate the decision and continue to participate and cooperate in the political process. Through dialogue, Bohman believes, we can achieve moral compromise democratically in pluralistic societies by insisting that everyone affected be provided with sufficient opportunity to participate and that the reason giving of the participants be taken into account by one another so that whatever arguments prevail meet the test of publicity. In this way, public deliberation develops its own norms of rationality rather than being held to some external standard. Achieving community is featured over seeking truth. Critical public reason exists to serve political ends. The point of political deliberation is to solve social problems, overcome conflict, and secure cooperation without suppressing diversity or disagreement.[47]

Bohman's way of making rational deliberation more democratic within liberal institutions—by characterizing it as an exercise in open dialogue that is likely to arrive at a reasonable agreement rather than as an exchange of arguments measured against a single standard of reason and evidence—is perhaps less idealized than Habermas's model of rational politics and more responsive to Dewey's criterion of accounting for actual practice. Nevertheless, it is an attempt to improve upon a democratic practice perceived as badly flawed and subject to the legitimacy crises of complex polities. Within Bohman's scheme, rhetoric remains problematic as a mode of strategic, justificatory rationality, or public advocacy, unless it somehow produces the unlikely result of dialogical uptake. Thus, rational public deliberation is for Bohman an unrealized ideal of open-ended conversation threatened by the reality of rhetorical manipulation that undermines the prospect of achieving democratic community. His ideal of dialogue on moral issues simply does not accommodate the actual practice of public persuasion or democratic eloquence, leaving democracy vulnerable either to alienation (for lack of sufficient accommodation to diversity) or to mass distemper (unless deliberation is contained within liberal institutions). If rhetoric instead of dialogue is the actual practice of public politics, does rhetorical deliberation pose a threat to egalitarian or rational decision making in the republic, or is it, as Farrell remarks, our best resource for reasonable public participation in civic affairs?

Farrell's answer to this question is that rhetoric is "inextricably linked with democratic civic practice." It "keeps the promise of the public sphere alive" and "guides deliberative action" by bringing practical intelligence to bear on matters of public judgment "in an open forum about uncertain matters." It is "argument in the service of judgment" regarding the business of civic life. As practical wisdom, it does not confuse reason with logic, some rarified faculty of rationality, or "the hegemony of reified reason." It recognizes that not all stories can be told at any given time—that judgments must be made and that political hierarchies are operative—but also remains responsive to the problem of alienation and exile. Rhetoric, in Farrell's view, is a partisan but permeable and egalitarian "mode of participatory reflection on cultural norms" that, through the invitation of the enthymeme (or implied premise), allows audiences to persuade themselves. Participation in a rhetorical culture provides opportunities both for the "invention and perpetuation of meaning" (innovation as well as continuity) to arrive at temporary closures in particular situations. Rather than a restricted elite code that makes audiences captive to a cultural hegemony, rhetorical culture is open to different and new interpretations of political contingencies and appearances; "although it always relies on what *appears*, as inflected by received opinions and convention," Farrell insists, "it may also recombine and individuate these so as to *interrupt* the quotidian of ordinary policy and practice," thereby confounding political orthodoxy to produce opportunities for emancipation.[48]

Farrell's revised Aristotelian conception of political rhetoric brings us closer to understanding democratic deliberation as rhetorical practice and nudges us nearer to overcoming an ingrained fear of the demos. Yet the challenge remains to understand how democracy, as a function of rhetorical culture, is concerned foremost with the politics of community, with public advocacy addressing the problems of identification and division through configurations of meaning that require public ratification in order to prevail, even momentarily, over alternative frames of acceptance and rejection. Reciprocity and uptake can be achieved only through a collaboration of advocate and audience, each accountable to the other. Together they construct political judgments in order to arrive at practical decisions on questions of public policy. The primary aim of rhetorical deliberation and democratic politics is not the quixotic, even tragic, quest to locate the common good in universal truths approximated through simulations of pure reason. Instead, as Kenneth Burke discerned, politics resides in the realm of the scramble, marked by fallibility and struggle, relying on a comic voice to resist the constant temptation of pursuing singular versions of truth or beauty all the way to the end of the line, over the edge, and into the abyss.[49]

Achieving a richer appreciation for the rhetorical enactment of democratic culture carries profound implications for the nation's post–cold war attitudes toward peace and war. If reason in political life is understood today to be neither context free nor culturally neutral, the classical republican expectation of the enlightened, virtuous citizen acting as an autonomous and pure knower who rejects rhetoric as cognitively and morally inadequate can be seen as itself a rhetorical strategy for containing democracy within elite institutions. This strategy, which may well have served the nation in an earlier era, nonetheless resists the further cultivation of freedom and equality for fear of releasing a contagion of democratic distemper. As Hanson has observed, there is "nothing intrinsically democratic about liberalism," which is "potentially incompatible" with popular sovereignty given liberalism's fear of mobocracy.[50] Hence, the dangerous irony of America's determination to impose a democratic peace on the post–cold war world order: how can a nation that distrusts the demos, indeed equates it with passion, tyranny, and chaos, hope to achieve global peace by setting about the task of democratizing the world? As Lloyd C. Gardner observes in a masterful understatement about the ideology of American foreign policy, "The desire to bestow self-determination on others is almost a contradiction in terms."[51]

Burdened by a historical distrust of the demos that ascribes deliberative rationality so narrowly to political elites, the nation's pursuit of a peaceful democratic order is motivated more by fear of the Other and a desire to contain diversity than any commitment to popular sovereignty. As Alan Nadel has observed, using "the story of 'democracy' to extend global hegemony" and "colonize the Other" is a continuation of the cold war culture of containment into the present. This "narrative of expansion," of "spreading democracy," is a story of democracy in name only, of democracy becoming "the name of the narrative it does not contain" and the policy that promotes democracy becoming "a narrative that does not contain it."[52] The enemy is the demos, the people both at home and abroad. As Tom Englehardt notes in his treatment of victory culture in contemporary American consciousness, "The enemy, horrific yet ill defined, lives in our shadow, threatening always to become us."[53]

Still, the global struggle for democracy remains America's proclaimed mission. In this Wilsonian tradition, the United States can never live securely except "in a steadfast concert for peace" maintained "by a partnership of democratic nations" or, in William Clinton's presidential words, by "securing democracy's triumph around the world."[54] The moment of opportunity has now arrived to "grasp" a democratic peace in the post–cold war world, according to Bruce Russett, by capitalizing on the end of communism and dissolution of ideological conflict and on "a surrender to the force of Western values of economic and especially political freedom," as evidenced by the replacement of "authoritarian regimes with democratic values and institutions in much of Asia, Eastern Europe, and Latin America." Stable liberal democracies, Russett argues, do not fight each other. Why? Because within a "transnational democratic culture, as within a democratic nation, others are seen as possessing rights and exercising those rights in a spirit of enlightened self-interest. Acknowledgment of those rights allows us to mitigate our fears that they will try to dominate us." In short, nations are safe when the people are contained universally by liberal institutions. Otherwise, liberal democracies must remain vigilant and suspicious of authoritarian regimes and even unstable democracies. Nations are not considered to be safely or really democratic unless they all adopt liberal "institutional constraints."[55]

Liberalism's ideological domination of democracy not only permeates American political culture, then, but by extension also penetrates its vision of foreign affairs, representing control of the Other as the key to national security and international peace. Yet, by any credible account, even Russett's, the United States lacks the material resources or authority to impose such regimes universally or to enforce such a peace globally. By the most optimistic accounts, it can only hope to assist in "the emergence and consolidation of democracy" while trying hard to resist the ceaseless temptation to engage in a crusade for democracy, including military interventions aimed at producing a new democratic world order.[56] Such patience is difficult to muster and temptation hard to resist, though, when democracy, so central to the national identity, is constituted ideologically as vulnerable to diversity and when diversity itself is equated with error and irrationality as forces of oppression and chaos. This legacy of thin democracy, which Benjamin Barber calls the "politics of zookeeping," renders democracy "fragile," "pallid," and "unaffecting" in its perceived devotion to liberty and ability to create or secure a culture of freedom, justice, and equality. So, as Barber observes, "liberal democracy's sturdiest cages are reserved for the People."[57]

The insufficiencies of liberal democracy can be traced to its deficient model of political reasoning, Barber argues, and represented as an anti-rhetorical conception of public deliberation, I maintain. It renders freedom and power as opposites and models political liberty as passive, in contrast to a notion of politics as an activity of exercising will and choice.[58] A strong, not thin or weak, conception of democracy, Barber insists, implies active citizens participating in the creation of political community and transforming rather than eliminating conflict. It "forestalls mob rule by developing internal checks rather than by developing a system of external limits on government," enjoining a "politics of self-regulation" in which "ongoing public talk and participation in public action induce in the people a spirit of reasonableness," judgment, and common will (instead of subjugating them to a regime of reason, knowledge, and truth). Political knowledge, then, "becomes its own epistemology," a "praxis" that is "provisional and flexible over time," "something made rather than something derived or represented," and "communal and consensual rather than either subjective . . . or objective." Democratic political talk "makes and remakes the world," for it "can invent alternative futures, create mutual purposes, and construct competing visions of community." It is the "art of engaging strangers" and stimulating kinship in them.[59]

Such is the attitude Barber advances under the notion of strong democracy where community is the product of public persuasion, interests are articulated, agendas are set, and commonalities are created among the myriad differences that otherwise set a people apart and at odds with one another. In a robust democracy, citizens address each other to coordinate and accommodate their differences; in a thin, predominantly liberal democracy, the people are deemed the irrational Other who must be contained, domestically and globally, in order to secure peace and prosperity, for diversity and difference are equated with error, chaos, loss of control, and thus insecurity and perpetual threat. Democracy too often is troped as a disease. Understood as an exercise in rhetorical deliberation, however, democracy is constituted as strong, healthy, indigenous, robust, and enduring. It does not require the subjugation or containment of the Other to ensure its own prosperity and preservation, nor is hegemony the price of liberty or freedom's fragility a reason for war.

An image of the savagery of the Other and corresponding fragility of civilized institutions of freedom, democracy, reason, law, and order has been

America's traditional motive for war and ideological incentive for imposing its version of democracy on an unwilling world.[60] This, in Smith's words, is "the American security interest in the spread of democracy worldwide" and the rationale of democratic internationalism to which George H. W. Bush appealed even in the unlikely case of the Gulf War against Saddam Hussein as the personification of dictatorial evil.[61] Moreover, it is the image that informed the Clinton administration's declared policy of "fostering democracy abroad for the sake of American national security." The stakes for expanding NATO into Eastern and Central Europe, that unstable domain of the former Soviet empire, were presented by Clinton as no less than "if democracy in the East fails, then violence and disruption from the East will once again harm us and other democracies."[62]

As represented in Clinton's public address, the emerging global democratic order was a fragile and vulnerable project that required American sponsorship and support to succeed and that must succeed in order to ensure national security. "Our mission is clear," he stressed on the fiftieth anniversary of the cold war's Marshall Plan. "We must shape the peace, freedom and prosperity [Marshall's generation] made possible into a common future where all our people speak the language of democracy. . . . We must meet the challenge now of making sure this surge of democracy endures."[63] NATO's enlargement, by this logic and according to Clinton, helped "to secure the historic gains of democracy in Europe," providing "a secure climate where freedom, democracy and prosperity can flourish." Most important, "the bottom line," according to the president, was that "expanding NATO will enhance our security" and "avoid repeating the darkest moments of the 20th century."[64] The horror of Bosnia was a case in point, Clinton argued, a war-ravaged place in "the very heart of Europe, next-door to many of its fragile new democracies." Bosnia required the leadership and help of "freedom's greatest champion" in order "to build a peaceful, democratic future," which is America's ideal and the aspiration of people throughout the "global village."[65]

This elitist and defensive attitude toward democracy and the global order reflects and reinforces a "traditional inclination" to see the United States as a target nation and thus sustains what Chace and Carr have documented as a deceitful dream and unattainable goal of absolute security through control of the Other.[66] Fear of the demos as the irrational Other within national borders, a legacy of America's liberal identity, works as a disincentive for peaceful relations with the Other outside its borders. Democratic deliberation in a rhetorical republic, however, is a robust practice of actively addressing and identifying with diverse others enough to achieve a working community of interests. It represents an alternative to attitudes that perpetuate a republic of fear and that motivate defensive wars of containment against alien influences at home and abroad on the assumption that freedom is fragile and democracy is easily distempered. In short, the concept of a rhetorically robust democratic practice is more friendly to difference and conducive to peace than is deliberative democracy in the liberal tradition.

If the give-and-take of rhetorical deliberation in the civic life of a pluralistic polity constitutes a courtship of internal Others that could well reduce inflated fears of external Others, then the nation's identity as a democratic people is made all the more problematic by its distrust of rhetoric, just as its apprehensiveness toward democracy is implicated in the futility and inevitable violence associated with trying to homogenize and control world politics consistent with American security interests. How, then, might Americans become more secure in their democratic identity? Is there a cure for democratic distemper? How can a robust democratic culture be enacted rhetorically?

One answer to these questions is that the rhetorical republic already engages in a more robust democratic practice than prescriptive models of deliberative democracy acknowledge or liberalism would wish to allow. Still, the need remains to develop, in the words of Thomas Goodnight and David Hingstman, new "strategies of democratic influence" through thoughtful critiques of actual democratic deliberation—critiques aimed at renegotiating "possibilities of shared life" through practices that mediate and construct complexly textured communities of opinion. These critical achievements must draw upon our "collective capacities of invention" and therefore cannot be taken for granted if the aim is to strengthen the bonds between communication and democracy by revising antagonistic social histories, redrawing problematic political boundaries, and transforming communication norms that promote victimization over reconciliation.[67] This is the importance Mouffe attaches to "recreating, in politics, the connection with the great tradition of rhetoric" by linking the return of the political to the value of addressing the Other rhetorically.[68]

Mouffe's gesture toward rhetoric, however, directs her reader to the work of Chaim Perelman, one of the sources on whom Farrell relies to make the case that, in my view, understates rhetoric's democratic potential. Perelman's overriding concern is with the question of justice in forensic or judicial discourse, rather than foremost with the problem of identification, tolerance, or community that marks political rhetoric specifically. He explores rhetoric as a theory of argumentation, or practical reasoning, looking into its many and varied resources for achieving adherence to claims of justice while holding arguments aimed at particular audiences to the standard of a fully informed, hypothetical "universal audience." The best arguments, in Perelman's view, are those calculated to gain the consent of an imagined universal audience. Such "argumentation addressed to a universal audience must convince the reader that the reasons adduced are of a compelling character, that they are self-evident, and possess an absolute and timeless validity, independent of local or historical contingencies."[69] And the kernel of Perelman's rule of justice is "equal treatment of essentially similar cases."[70] It is from this position that Farrell attempts to extend and modify Habermas's universal pragmatics so as to implicate audiences in "the world outside," a goal difficult to meet even with more appropriate materials. Moreover, when he turns to a more apt source, Farrell focuses on the "uniquely interactive notion of form" in Kenneth Burke's theory of symbolic action as a way of theorizing "audience engagement" and how "the normative pervades all symbolic action." Farrell's purpose in his appropriations of Perelman and Burke remains the same: to show that one can infer idealized normative content about the true, the right, and the just from everyday rhetorical performances, thus substantiating Habermas's universal pragmatics and discourse ethics "as powerful normative enticements, or goads, to the perfectibility of discourse practice." From Perelman, he argues, we gain a sense of the universal within the particular, from Burke an understanding of normative goading in the particularity of symbolic experience.[71] In neither instance, because of his focus on rational argumentation, does Farrell speak directly to the foremost concern of democratic politics, i.e., the problem of community, even as it is so thoroughly implicated in Burke's treatment of rhetoric as society's medium of identification. Thus, questions of truth and justice must be recontextualized, not ignored or dismissed, within a larger political framework that maximizes tolerance of otherwise always-threatening Others.

In anticipation of taking the next step toward a productive critique of democratic culture, a critique that addresses issues of truth and justice vis-à-vis the politics of tolerance and a rhetoric of identification, it is useful to summarize briefly the problem of chronic republican insecurity as it has been diagnosed in the foregoing discussion. My examination of the problem has highlighted the paradox of seeking national security in a democratic peace, that is, of promoting global democracy as a hedge against war even when the United States has been historically distrustful of the demos. Democracy in America is a weak tradition, a rhetorical tradition of liberal democracy that contains the power of the people within republican institutions of representative government by presuming that popular rhetoric subverts rational deliberation. Liberalism masks its own rhetoric under the sign of rational deliberation even while strategically reducing political rhetoric to demagoguery as the source and symptom of democratic distemper. The tragedy of American democracy in our time is that it fosters cynicism and alienation on a global scale that reinforces fear at home of the domestic and foreign Other. Thus, the nation's routinely exaggerated sense of danger is very much an effect of interpretation in which the cultural ideal of democracy connotes a contagion of irrationality and disorder. Traditional liberal anxieties over containing democratic distemper, intensified in twentieth-century America by the rise of the rhetorical presidency and imminence of a rhetorical republic, have prompted the nation to seek an impossible hegemony of liberal democracy over a disintegrating post–cold war world. In order to negotiate the prevailing forces of global fragmentation, the country must come to terms with its own demophobia, reconciling its troubled identity as a target nation by cultivating a more robust democratic culture, which requires in turn a revised sense of the relationship between rhetorical and political culture.

Rhetoric and the Politics of Community

The problem with continuing to think of deliberative democracy as a strictly rational mode of argument or a discussion-based ideal of politics, according to Iris Marion Young, is twofold. First, as presently articulated, the model of deliberative democracy assumes "a culturally biased conception of discussion" that can render certain groups of people mute and irrelevant. Second, it assumes inappropriately that arguments must begin with shared understandings and goals, which also has "exclusionary consequences." Her analysis of these shortcomings and how they might be ameliorated by what she calls an expanded model of "communicative democracy" is instructive, for it indicates the direction at least in which we can expect to find better answers about the democratic potential of political rhetoric.[72]

Young's preference for deliberative models of democratic practice over interest-based conceptions is rooted in her affinity for "reason over power in politics." However, deliberative theorists, she observes, focus only on bracketing economic and political power, overlooking the way power "enters speech itself." Thus, they miscalculate the condition of presumed equality when they disregard a people's "internalized sense of the right one has to speak or not to speak" or ignore the fact that some styles of speech are valued over others. Because of cultural differences and differentiations in social standing, people do not necessarily share the same ways of speaking and understanding; deliberation, in short, is neither culturally neutral nor universal. Even the norms of "reason" on which deliberative theorists rely derive from a specifically Western context, privileging speech that is assertive and confrontational, for example, over that which is tentative, exploratory, and conciliatory or speech that is formal, syllogistic, dispassionate, and general over that which is not. Young's communicative democracy would instead seek to encompass all styles, making argument only one such mode of communication and influence. Similarly, she would not idealize the achievement or presumption of unity and shared understandings as either a goal or a prior condition of deliberation, because diversity both does and should characterize contemporary plural polities and because the inappropriate assumption of unity "obviates the need for the self-transcendence" and transformation that otherwise occurs when people "revise their opinions or viewpoints in order to take account of perspectives and experiences beyond them." The basic fact of politics, she emphasizes, is that people find themselves stuck with one another and faced with the challenge of living together, creating a condition of interdependence that necessitates a minimal degree of mutual respect and procedural rules for "fair discussion and decision-making" that would enable them to speak "across differences . . . which are preserved in the process."[73]

Recognizing that argumentation and persuasion are necessarily interconnected and that rhetoric is either good or bad but never absent from political discourse, Young adopts a feminist account of "dialogical reason" to propose an expanded notion of communicative democracy consisting not only of the critical argumentation featured by rational deliberation theorists but also three additional elements: greeting, rhetoric, and storytelling—all elements that "recognize the embodiment and particularity of interlocutors" and thus respect the plurality of the polity. Greetings, leave-takings, smiles, handshakes, and other such rituals and courtesies "lubricate" the social and ego dimensions of dialogue by showing deference to particularities and politeness to individuals as opposed to coldness, indifference, and insult in contexts "fraught with disagreement, anger, conflict, counterargument, and criticism." Rhetoric adapts speech to audiences and situations, constructs occasions, invokes meanings and symbols strategically, secures attention, and colors arguments so as to "pull on thought through desire." Storytelling fosters understanding in circumstances of class, cultural, and other differences. It reveals the particular experiences of Others and "explains to outsiders what practices, places, or symbols mean to the people who hold them." All of this together helps to sustain a healthy plurality of perspectives and speaking styles as polities work to solve problems collectively.[74]

Although Young expands the rational model of deliberation into a wider conception of communicative democracy and thereby places rhetoric in a more favorable light, she nevertheless misses rhetoric's full significance, in part because she treats argument, greeting, and storytelling as distinctive elements separable from the rhetorical forms and functions of democratic politics and, perhaps even more important, because she divorces all four elements from interest-based power politics. A more inclusive understanding of political persuasion as strategic symbolic action would consider argument, greeting, and storytelling to be aspects of rhetorical discourse and would adopt a view of democratic deliberation that reconciles it with contested, interest-based politics. Working within the tradition of Isocrates, for instance, Scott Welsh observes that the prevailing cultural terminologies governing the meanings of a political collectivity are at the same time "sites of intense struggle" over contested preferences and plans of action. The "rhetorical tradition," he argues, "is uniquely equipped to move in this realm between identification and division" where rhetors compete with one another for the adherence of citizen-audiences.[75]

Rhetoric, as represented by Kenneth Burke, whom William Rueckert deems one of America's "great democratic critics," bridges political divisions by engaging private interests and aligning them with public motives. It manages the pervasive presence of power and hierarchy in human affairs and concerns itself with the overriding question of politics: how to live peacefully together without eliminating diversity or succumbing to the constant temptation of victimization and violence.[76] War, Burke observes, is a disease of cooperation that can be treated only by a kind of verbal sparring that cultivates comic correctives to the tragic inclinations of symbol-using (and symbol-misusing) beings. Human antics at their best are "a comedy ever on the verge of the most disastrous tragedy." Thus, Burke's philosophy of rhetoric promotes tolerance and contemplation by exploring how people in political communities might transcend themselves enough to observe their foibles even while acting strategically toward one another, that is, how they might act wisely together and toward one another with maximum consciousness by rounding out overly narrow perspectives. Human life is a continuous project of translation, composition, criticism, and revision in order to achieve or recover an ecological balance in political relations.[77]

Contrary to Burke's dramatism, however, the trend of democratic theory has been to bolster the rationalist foundation and universalist framework derived from Enlightenment sources, as Mouffe notes, to secure liberal-democratic institutions against the current tide of postmodern critique. This trend is reactionary, posing an "obstacle to an adequate understanding of the present stage of democratic politics," and it is misleading by implying that postmodernity represents a clean break with history and rejection of modernity's democratic potential. Rationalism, Mouffe argues, is premodern, not modern, in its essentialism, whereas democratic politics are antiessentialist. Hegemony occurs when power converges with objectivity to obscure the "logic of the constitution of the social." Because any social objectivity is ultimately political, "then the main question of democratic politics is not how to eliminate power but how to constitute forms of power that are compatible with democratic values" of freedom and equality. We cannot free politics from constructions of power, nor can we advance modernity's democratic project by masking it in an essentialist rhetoric of rational objectivity. Politics is not well modeled after economics, that is, as a market of rational individuals acting through instrumental reason to maximize self-interest in profit. Nor can a rational and universal agreement be achieved by relegating disruptive issues, antagonisms, and passion to the private sphere, for the political is "the dimension of antagonism that is present in social relations, with the ever present possibility of the us/them relation being constructed in terms of friend/enemy."[78] "A healthy democratic process," Mouffe argues, "calls for a vibrant clash of political positions and an open conflict of interests"—an "agonistic pluralism" over the "illusion of consensus and unanimity," accommodating "competing conceptions of our identities as citizens" and recognizing the contingency and ambiguity of identities over "the unified character of the subject." Rather than searching for ultimate foundations or succumbing to a postmodern fragmentation of the social, a healthy pluralistic democratic politics articulates fragments into contingent, pragmatic, relational identities, continually creating conditional unities in contexts of diversity, controversy, and contested interests through "metaphoric redescriptions" of social relations.[79]

The political dimension of human relations involves difference and divisiveness not only among but also within national identities, for political identities are themselves complex and conflicted (as well as situated and malleable). Their existence requires alien Otherness. Just as the internal-domestic is differentiated from the external-foreign by national boundaries, national identities contain boundaries of Otherness within. Any "we" cannot exist apart from a "them," and because the outside constitutes the inside, political communities are never fully inclusive. The challenge of democratic citizenship, Mouffe argues, is to exercise a "social imaginary" that manages the antagonisms of identity frontiers through a rhetoric of convergence. Rather than adopting an essentialist view of established identities that necessitates reified interest-group pluralism, rhetorically robust democratic communities transform existing subject positions into new identities that promote more "egalitarian social relations, practices and institutions." These articulations of convergence establish new hegemonies of democratic values with their own boundaries and constructions of Otherness; as political identities, they can never contain everything, never become completely inclusive or even undistorted by perspective and hierarchies of values. The question is not whether something remains alien or outside a democratic identity but whether any particular difference such as gender, race, ethnicity, or religion is an appropriate boundary between categories such as citizen and noncitizen, us and them, friend and foe and whether crossing such a boundary constitutes a significant enough threat to legitimize violence against a foreign (or even domestic) Other.[80] How, then, are boundaries negotiated rhetorically to increase and decrease perceptions of threat to a nation's democratic identity?

Burke's discussion of the rhetoric of identification, within the framework of his dramatistic theory of symbolic action, indicates a way of answering this question. The key to a Burkean critique of republican fear and American democratic culture is found in the intersection of drama and politics, specifically at the point of the agon. As Mouffe observes, the defining characteristic of political life is its "agonistic dynamic," and the problem of the political is how to create and maintain a pluralistic democratic order "based on a distinction between 'enemy' and 'adversary'" in a world fraught with antagonism. Democratic community in its healthiest form is achieved when opponents are routinely considered as legitimate adversaries to be addressed rather than as enemies who must be destroyed.[81] Opposition and antagonism mark human relations in Burke's view as well: "strife, enmity, faction," he says, are an "almost tyrannous ubiquity in human relations," but "identification is compensatory to division." The two coexist ambiguously together, never one without the other and never knowing for sure where identification ends and division begins. Individuals and groups are at once joined and separate, common and unique, allied and opposed. If individualities did not exist and people "were not apart from one another, there would be no need for the rhetorician to proclaim their unity." Thus, rhetoric "deals with the possibilities of classification in its partisan aspects; it considers the ways in which individuals are at odds with one another, or become identified with groups more or less at odds with one another" and how they can be made sufficiently "consubstantial" in a given time and place to act together and coexist peacefully rather than succumb to the depravity of war, for war is the "ultimate *disease* of cooperation" and "perversion of communion."[82]

The agon in human relations is as characteristic of Burke's dramatistic treatment of rhetoric as it is routine to politics. Rhetoric promotes social cohesion and induces cooperation by addressing adversaries who might otherwise be constructed as enemies. As the point of conflict between protagonist and antagonist, the agon is a site of "competitive collaboration" (or "cooperative competition") and thus a source of "agonistic development" that keeps a democratic polity from extending a singular set of principles or sole chart of meaning all the way to the bloody end of the line. Accordingly, Burkean rhetorical critique of symbolic action begins with the question of what versus what in order to examine "the development *from what through what to what*," thus observing a dramatic line of development in political relations that easily leads to tragedy and victimization unless a comic corrective strategically complicates the situation.[83]

Burke's notion of the comic corrective acknowledges that political relations are agonistic and recognizes that social cohesion and tolerance are promoted by people "acting rhetorically upon themselves and one another." It does not, however, assume that agonistic politics are inherently self-correcting or that their potential for realizing democratic ideals is easily fulfilled. Indeed, even as global conditions call for greater identification among all people, Burke observes, these same conditions have increased "the incentives to division," requiring a "sustained rhetorical effort, backed by the imagery of a richly humane and spontaneous poetry, to make us fully sympathize with people in circumstances greatly different from our own."[84] The comic attitude of respect for the complexities of political relations, effected rhetorically through strategic acts of identification, lessens the temptation to victimization and thus serves the primary goal of politics by muddling through differences enough to minimize violence against one another.

Comedy, in this sense, compensates for tragedy in the charting of human relations by shifting emphasis, as Burke puts it, "from *crime* to *stupidity*." Rather than picturing people as "*vicious*," he continues, comedy constructs them as "*mistaken*," in fact as "*necessarily* mistaken," for "*all* people are exposed to situations in which they must act as fools" and "*every* insight contains its own special kind of blindness." The trick is to adopt a wider, more well-rounded frame of reference in charting human motives, one that connects divergent people via symbolic bridges. This emphasis on the complexities of social relations makes the comic frame "charitable" but not "gullible." Its goal is to achieve an attitude and corresponding vocabulary of motives that could induce "humility without humiliation." The lesson of tragedy is hubris; the critique of hubris is comedy that adopts a "both/and" perspective to complicate "either/or" and "us/them" dichotomies, thus prompting better "ecological balance" in the political frames that "bureaucratize the [social] imaginative."[85]

By aligning rhetoric directly with the overriding problem of political relations, Burke's dramatism not only engages the question of tolerance and peace as its first priority but also recasts issues of rationality and justice within a framework of agonistic politics rather than consensus-driven deliberation. With this shift of perspective, rationality and justice are no longer divorced from the competition of interests or struggle for power that defines politics, nor are they dismissed as irrelevant or unimportant considerations. Justice instead becomes associated with the problem of victimization, and rationality becomes a question of scope, complexity, and proportionality of perspective. As perspectives become increasingly narrow and fixed, differences are transformed into struggles between good and evil, and injustices are performed in victimization rituals. The comic corrective aims to restore society to sanity and health, as William Rueckert notes, by enhancing a polity's symbolic equipment for living. Rather than killing, victimizing, and punishing one another, people in comic relations correct and connect with each other, thereby avoiding the reification of an absolutist frame that empowers a single point of view as exclusively correct and true. Thus, as Rueckert underscores, "many of the modifiers for the *comic* are terms that stress the need for a *wider* frame, a need to *broaden* one's terminology, a need for a *well-rounded* frame, one that is an *amplifying* device rather than a diminishing or reductive one; there is a need for a perspective that includes an awareness of *ambivalence* and *irony*, that promotes the ability to see double, to use and recognize metaphor, to see around corners, to take multiple approaches." Political reality, from the vantage point of the comic perspective, is neither static nor simple, but it is forensic, symbiotic, and ecologically interlinked. It requires a metaphorical over a literal-minded view of political relations, a linguistic skepticism that discounts reductionistic categories, symbols, and logic by cultivating a well-honed sense of irony. Although analytic, deconstructive, and skeptical, the comic perspective eschews a strong negative or cynical bias (it does not endorse sheer debunking, for example) and adopts instead an integrative, synthesizing, constructive attitude that tries to bring home "the complexities of modern relativism and pluralism." It stresses "getting along with people—rather than hating or vilifying or excluding or victimizing or killing them"—as the primary objective of "the good life" and emphasizes "peaceful social change" as "the way of democracy."[86]

Clearly, the comic critique of democratic culture represents a normative outlook and persuasive attitude on life in political communities, the forming of congregations, and the reforming of polities. As Barbara Biesecker argues, Burke's treatment of language as containing within it "the motive force of sociality" is an "intervention of rhetoric and history" that inquires into the "possibility of collective action." Rhetoric, by this view, is necessary "for the historical emergence of social formations," including robust democratic cultures. The rhetoric of identification does not create perfect egalitarian unities by any means, for estrangement, faction, and strife always remain in one degree or another, but identification is "the mode of production of the social." Unlike Habermas's universal pragmatics, which posits communicative understanding as a precondition to perlocutionary or rhetorical speech, Burke's dramatism posits, as Biesecker maintains, that "it is precisely the lack of complete understanding that keeps the desire for community alive," and "it is precisely because all human relations are vexed by the paradox of substance rather than underwritten by the logic of identity that any coupling, any community, is always already a project in the making, always already . . . an evocation rather than a yet to be actualized condition or foregone conclusion." By this reckoning, consensus cannot be a democratic goal or an ideal of political community.[87]

Rhetorical Critique of Republican Fear

A productive critique of America's liberal-democratic culture, focusing particularly on chronic republican fear of difference as an incentive for war, implicates rhetoric twofold: as a problematic tradition of political discourse and as a means of strengthening democratic culture. In the first instance, liberalism has masked its own elitism with rhetorical strategies that relate difference to menace and link popular persuasion to irrationality, thus insinuating the need to discipline diversity and contain democracy. This troublesome rhetorical tradition truncates rhetoric's democratic potential and exaggerates national peril. In the second instance, rhetoric is a cultural resource for effecting comic correctives to tragic republican fears. Through strategies of identification that address the Other, rhetorical discourse bridges divisions without suppressing differences or effacing the agon of political relations. Appropriating rhetoric in this second sense, as a comic corrective to republican fear, tempers the nation's antidemocratic rhetorical culture and nourishes its democratic imagination. By engaging a tradition of diminished democratic imagination, rhetorical critique fosters increased political consciousness as a disincentive to suppressing foreign and domestic Otherness.[88] Thus, instead of criticizing politics for being rhetorical and agonistic, a productive critique scrutinizes the existing rhetorical tradition in order to enhance its democratic ethos and allay a tragic sense of national insecurity.

Accordingly, the task at hand is thoroughly rhetorical in its objective, subject, and approach. As a critical investigation of U.S. predispositions toward war, it focuses on reconstructing the discourse of democracy that is key to developing attitudes more conducive to peace. I have known since my earliest study of presidential rhetoric that "democracy" is deeply implicated in the nation's motives for war,[89] and it has become apparent to me since then that a peculiar American identification with democracy promotes a republic of fear—that is, a republic that distrusts itself—which, in turn, prompts acts of war against others. The problem is to calm republican anxiety over democracy when the voice of the people evokes an image of chaos that is the enemy within. A critique of republican fear, then, must confront the daunting theme of democratic distemper, which is a basic tension deeply embedded in U.S. history and political culture.

Stephen Lucas has observed that although "democracy" is one of the few words in the nation's rhetorical pantheon today with sufficient authority seemingly to validate nearly anything identified with it, the partial ascendancy of the popular over the gentlemanly mode of public address during the early republic negotiated a recurring tension between elitist and majoritarian rule.[90] According to revolutionary Whigs, political authority rested on the consent of the people who nevertheless elected their betters to represent them; "government originates from the people," in the words of Jeremy Belknap, but the people "are not able to govern themselves."[91] The people, in this view, were spoken of by the colonial gentry as the "common Herd," an "unthinking Mob" whose emotions were preyed upon by demagogues. In contrast, the leveling rhetoric in Thomas Paine's *Common Sense* served as a precursor of the majoritarian vision of democracy. In its most extreme form, the majoritarian view of democracy equated the voice of the people with the voice of God. Yet, those Federalists who founded the nation remained wary of the people, doubting they possessed sufficient virtue to concern themselves with the good of the community as a whole and believing, therefore, in the words of James Madison, that "a republican remedy for the diseases most incident to republican government" must be adopted—a remedy that would protect the people from themselves and the nation from the pitfalls of direct democracy. Anti-Federalists believed these so-called remedies merely "masqued aristocracy" in the "suspicious garb of republicanism," resulting in "aristocratical tyranny." The Constitution attempted to manage this tension by incorporating the people as rulers indirectly through the medium of their elected representatives—representatives who, despite the fact that they were mostly rich, well educated, genteel, or otherwise privileged, became "the people."

Whether this constitutional remedy amounted to a leveling of social distinctions or a subversion of democratic rule has remained a contested issue. Lucas argues that it put to rest models of classical politics—"the last major rhetorical barriers to the triumph of the democratic, majoritarian ideology"—and thus allowed the principle of majority rule to be fully integrated into American politics over time. The new rhetorical order that emerged, according to Lucas, was completed with the election of Andrew Jackson in 1828. Yet, as arch-Federalists anguished over the growth of popular politics and a marked decline in the standards of public discourse, they complained of an uncouth excess of verbosity in which the gift of gab reduced the republic to a logocracy, or government of mere words and unmitigated mediocrity. Were these just the bitter barbs of sore losers? Or were they reminders that the meaning of democracy and the virtue of majority rule remained contested issues and problematic matters of political identity for the American republic?

In the course of his historical analysis of the democratic impulse in the United States, Hanson encounters various constructions of democracy that have rendered the term problematic. Consequently, he observes, "contemporary disagreements about liberal democracy lack coherence—they are confused" over the "contradictory implications" of a discourse that simultaneously embraces liberalism and democracy.[92] While liberalism concerns itself with the proper limits and scope of political power, democracy promotes popular rule. The convergence of liberalism and democracy in England and the United States is a remarkable but tenuous accommodation of competing forms of power talk that lacks closure historically and coherence in our time, thus yielding a profound suspicion and paradoxical distrust of democracy itself—a legacy, that is, of attempting to domesticate, tame, quarantine, and otherwise contain the democratic impulse in order to make it safe to practice. This legacy conflates power with reason in order to control the outcome of consensual decision making.

Democracy as an ideal possessed little normative value in the founding years of the American republic precisely because it referred to the rule of the commons, who ostensibly lacked sufficient virtue to protect individual liberty, minority interests, and the accumulation of personal property or to look after the commonweal. Such virtue was considered necessary to protect the nation against the internal threat of faction and the external threat of invasion. While Republicans contested Federalist elitism, the violent excesses of the French Revolution served to confirm deep suspicions of democratic rule and motivated Federalists further to contain the democratic contagion in America. Democratic societies in the United States were chastised in the Federalist press, for instance, as a "horrible sink of treason," "hateful synagogue of anarchy," "odious conclave of tumult," "frightful cathedral of discord," and "poisonous garden of conspiracy."[93] Accordingly, republicanism was preferred over the evils of "democratic distemper," "popular passions," and the "prejudices" of "mob rule." Yet, even a republican accommodation to popular sovereignty and political equality exposed the young nation to a potential corruption of its precious virtue, resulting in the threat of national degeneration, republican decay, and ultimately the decline of civilization itself.

Even the Jeffersonian Republicans who prevailed over the Federalists at the turn of the century did not immediately advance democracy as an alternative to republican government. When, after the War of 1812, Republicans began to promote democracy on behalf of popular over deferential politics, they attempted to discipline the popular impulse through a regime of political party rule. As Hanson states, "Civic virtue came to be identified with party regularity," and party regularity thereby became "essential to the health of the republic."[94] Without such discipline, regional and other kinds of factionalism would fracture the country, but partisanship itself proved also to be a source of corruption that threatened the health of the republic, thus leaving unresolved the problem of how to inculcate or otherwise ensure public virtue and thereby avoid the pitfalls of a "majoritarian tyranny" that would destroy liberty in the name of equality.

The problem of inculcating democratic virtue has been perpetuated in multiple permutations throughout nineteenth- and twentieth-century American history. Even the movement for women's suffrage relied largely on the argument of expediency over the argument of justice, thereby undercutting any radical conception of democracy that would have entailed the effective involvement of blacks, immigrants, and other marginalized groups. The argument of expediency justified women's suffrage on the grounds that middle-class women, who were most likely to vote, would raise the intellectual level of the general electorate and diminish the influence of riffraff, thus contributing to a desire for improved government by reinforcing the ingrained fear of a democracy of incompetent citizens.

Under the influence of Progressive reforms, democratic virtue became a function of managerial and administrative expertise and of extending the advantages of a liberal education to the populace at large. It did not take long, however, for opinion leaders such as Walter Lippmann to conclude that the Progressive faith in an enlightened public was a mere phantom, necessitating a greater reliance on experts equipped to look after the common good. In democracy, then, Americans have placed neither unqualified trust nor collective faith. It is a term fraught with ambivalence and ambiguity, a term that articulates a national identity infused with a sense of insecurity. The paradox of America's political consciousness is that it predisposes the nation to fear its own demise by depicting unfettered democracy as a dangerous disease of illiberal rule while rendering suspect any containment of democratic distemper as a violation of egalitarian ideals. Danger, in short, is a function rhetorically of representing democracy as a disease, a point developed at length in chapter 2.

Unable to resolve this conflicted trope internally, the nation has sought redemption and security externally in the vision of a democratic peace realized globally as an end to history and the final confirmation of America's exceptional virtue, a development examined closely in chapter 3. In the nineteenth century, the nation's historic mission as a beacon of liberty became its manifest destiny to expand the domain of democratic rule westward across the continent. More recently, following the end of the cold war and subsequent demise of the Soviet Union, the United States extended again the horizon of its democratic aspirations to embrace the bold vision of a new world order. The problem remained, though, of how to transform the image of democratic distemper into a healthy vehicle of peace when the prevailing tendency was to retreat defensively into a rhetoric of victimization and war.

Thus, a productive critique of republican fear must extend beyond the trope of democratic distemper, per se, to encompass the full range of metaphors and literalizing strategies that have converted democracy into a compelling motive for war in American political culture. The metaphor of disease participates in a rhetorical universe of decivilizing vehicles that constructs the Other in the image of savagery as a sign of extreme threat to freedom and civilization.[95] Within this rhetorical universe, savagery entails a set of contrasts between the threatening Other's irrational appetites and America's rational commitment to law, reason, and civilized order, between the brutal Other's affinity for coercion, force, and violence and America's steadfast regard for freedom, liberty, and peace, and between the hostile Other's willful acts of aggression and America's reluctant acts of self-defense against unprovoked attacks on the civilized world. This three-dimensional image is conventionally expressed in a number of types of metaphorical vehicles that concretize and literalize the struggle between savagery and civilization. These decivilizing vehicles construct the threatening image of an irrational, coercive, and aggressive brute by identifying the Other in terms of a menace of nature (fire, flood, storm, disease), a beast of prey, a barbarian, a machine, a criminal mind, a mentally disturbed or crazed adversary, a fanatic, an ideologue, and a satanic figure or profane instrument of evil.[96] Similarly, freedom as the symbol of civilization is portrayed as vulnerable and fragile, feminine, precious, and precarious. It is represented as an infant, tenuous experiment, a flickering flame or beacon in the stormy night, a hunter's prey in constant search of sanctuary, and a heroic struggle that might tragically fail.[97] These metaphorical vehicles and the images they convey are literalized beyond recognition as figures of speech by conventional usage and various other strategic constructions, including (1) plain, commonsense styles of presentation, (2) selected facts framed by a narrow point of view to verify threatening expectations, and (3) syllogistic or other logical signs of rational demonstration to insinuate certainty about the Other's evil character and hostile intentions.[98] All these literalizing structures discourage any recognition of metaphor as a strategic configuration, thus transforming tenuous similarities into practical identities and keeping them well below the threshold of legitimate dispute.

An attitude of ambivalence is implicated in this war-justifying ritual, not only by the dual representation of democracy as a disease and an object of desire but also by a corresponding discourse of containment. Equally significant, many of the decivilizing vehicles that justify war also share in the rhetorical universe that contains democracy. The Truman Doctrine speech, for example, the initial declaration of hostile relations between the United States and the Soviet Union following World War II, was deliberately designed to exaggerate the Soviet threat and American vulnerability. Images of fire, flood, and red fever were Truman's symbolic inducements to build political, economic, and military barriers between democracy and communism. Vehicles of disease, deeply embedded in the design of the speech, prompted arguments for aiding afflicted nations before an epidemic of communism could spread further. Moreover, the disease metaphor had been featured in the administration's internal communications preceding Truman's famous speech. Key figures such as Dean Acheson spoke of communist infection spreading globally, and even earlier George Kennan's influential "long telegram" had represented communist malignancy as a threat to the nation's health. Similarly, prior to and following the Truman Doctrine speech, members of Congress warned publicly that a red tide of global communism threatened to extinguish the lamp of freedom and that America lived in a feverish world with the virus of red fascism, already a blight on every hemisphere, threatening to take root in the United States itself. As the flames of a red fire seemed to be licking ominously at freedom's doorstep, democracy's presumed vulnerability to the disease of communist chaos seemed all the more apparent. Democracy and communism, that is, were simultaneously opposed to and identified with one another under the sign of infection and plague. Democracy was represented both as patient and contagion, requiring quarantine, containment, and rehabilitation in order to ensure world order, maintain the liberal-democratic system, and avoid darkness descending over civilization. Understandably, such a metaphor could be turned easily against the body politic itself, as in subsequent convulsions of McCarthyism.[99] Certainly, it configured the basic assumptions of policy makers and advisors such as Kennan, whose brand of fear-inducing political realism amplified the foreign threat by questioning the "health and vigor of our own society" while characterizing world communism as a "malignant parasite which feeds only on diseased tissue."[100]

The logic of this culture of containment extends to America's post–cold war project of achieving a "democratic peace," which aims to secure global order by enveloping the world in a universal web of stable liberal-democratic regimes. The goal is to eliminate difference and discipline diversity within a framework that maximizes America's international control. Clinton's foreign-policy rhetoric in particular perpetuated containment thinking through strong overtones of national vulnerability that envisioned U.S. security as a function of worldwide ideological and economic hegemony. His message was that the United States must grasp a fleeting moment of opportunity, building on the great victories of World War II and the cold war, to lead a bold adventure of securing democracy and prosperity American style throughout the global village. This vision was punctuated with frequent reminders of the threats facing the nation, including the risks even of extending democracy to the world. Everything about his message conveyed a sense of tenuous times, fragility, instability, uncertainty, and the compensatory need for control. Indeed, his words amounted to a national repository of democratic anxiety featuring allusions to epidemic, plague, purgation, nurturing, engulfment, containment, storms, darkness, crime, chaos, and a call for courage. His motif of a democratic peace imposed the agenda of liberal-democratic internationalism onto a fragmented world and disguised the critical fact that democracy is a contested term in such a world. Conflating democracy and capitalism not only strategically legitimized the economic agenda of the self-proclaimed guardian of world order, but also a vagueness of meaning was key to asserting that democracy is rapidly spreading throughout the world, that democratic nations do not attack one another, and therefore that peace is at hand. Ironically, the very proposition of a peaceful democratic world introduces yet another source of national insecurity and an additional incentive for war by focusing attention on achieving order and away from enriching democratic practice.

How, then, can republican fear be more productively addressed than by a discourse of disease and by attempting to contain democracy within an antiseptic environment only to promote war in the name of peace? What sources of comic corrective exist in the rhetorical culture for widening a tragic frame enough to develop confidence in more robust visions of democratic politics? And how might we stimulate this latent social imaginary to redress the current imbalance between liberalism and democracy in American political culture so that the nation might engage less defensively the tension of integration and fragmentation that inscribes the world at home and abroad? Obviously, there are no easy answers to these questions or quick fixes to the problems they indicate, but our analysis of the tropology of the problem suggests a direction in which to search for opportunities to transform the meaning of democracy. We need to explore how a frail republican constitution of deliberative democracy might develop into a robust democratic disposition of rhetorical deliberation, where diversity and difference are not associated so seamlessly with danger and error but instead are taken more commonly as healthy signs of articulating interests, addressing audiences, advancing strategies of identification, and transacting limited agreements through public persuasion and where rhetoric exercises and strengthens democracy by courting the otherwise threatening Other whenever possible to achieve some degree of consubstantiality between rivals. How might agonistic politics speak to the condition of antagonistic relations through the rhetorical enactment of democratic culture? This, in short, is the concern animating an explicitly rhetorical critique of the literalized republican representation of democracy as prone to demagoguery and disciplined by rational deliberation, a tragically flawed convention of representation in which the demos is either led astray by emotional public persuasion or led responsibly by elected representatives engaged in informed dialogue and dispassionate dialectic. Thus, the balance of the book examines critically, in search of suitable options, an overly reified discourse of democratic distemper, its pretense of universal peace, its perpetual war on terror, and, ultimately, its potential transformation into a more robust idiom of democracy.

2
Distempered Demos

The irony of democracy as a symbol of national purpose is that it alienates Americans from civic life and sets the United States at odds with the world outside its borders. Instead of the ideal of democracy promoting participatory politics domestically and internationally, it all too easily and often evokes potent rituals of republican fear that diminish the voice of the people while magnifying the threat of social disorder and global chaos. Political power is displaced from the public to a ruling elite by portraying the masses in the image of a primitive Other subject to the delirium of demagoguery, not unlike the barbarian beyond the walls of the polity. Such is the irony that reveals the significance of myth to a rhetorical republic and exposes the opposing forms of power talk in a liberal democracy where liberalism struggles to contain democracy's unruly impulse without entirely dissociating itself from the legitimizing ethos of self-rule. The very recognition of this irony would provide incentive to restore power to the people except for the mythic function of the metaphor of disease, which legitimizes liberalism's dominance over democracy by fabricating the image of a distempered demos. How, we might ask, does this image of a degraded people qualify as a fabrication? Is it not just a basic reality of political life that the multitude easily degenerates into an irrational mob?

Addressing the Demos

To answer this question we can turn first to the polis of ancient Athens, where a stable democratic culture emerged within a productive rhetorical tension between the demos and the elite, the very example the founders of the American republic more than two thousand years later used to impugn direct democracy. Yet, in Josiah Ober's judgment, the "Athenian example has a good deal to tell the modern world about the nature and potential of democracy as a form of social and political organization." Clearly, the Athenian polity fell short of contemporary standards, including its exclusion of women from citizenship, the prevalence of chattel slavery, economic disparity between a small wealthy class of landowners and the poor working masses of subsistence farmers, and an imperialistic militancy. Even with these serious shortcomings, it offers a corrective to the present belief that direct democracy is impossible. As Ober observes, the demos "was master of Athens" when rhetoric "was a key form of democratic discourse" that mediated between ordinary and elite citizens well enough to allow for "direct democratic decision making."[1] The contrast with U.S. political culture, where the masses are disciplined and rhetoric distrusted, is both remarkable and intriguing. Unlike democracy today, which is an insignia of good government but attenuated in actual practice, Athenian democracy was vigorously practiced for nearly two hundred years during the fifth and fourth centuries BC with only two brief oligarchic disruptions during the Peloponnesian War and another following Sparta's eventual victory over Athens. Finally, in 322 BC, the Macedonians forced an end to Athenian democracy but not without a continuing struggle thereafter to restore self-rule. The main distinction between now and then, Harvey Yunis notes, is the difference between pursuing principally private goals in the contemporary era and requiring mass political participation in the classical Athenian polis. In Athens, he writes, "the government essentially was the *demos*," and political rhetoric was the instrument of mass deliberation.[2]

Athenian democracy restricted the franchise to freeborn males but was direct rather than representative and thus lacked an "entrenched governing elite." Officials were usually selected by lot (with the exception, for example, of generals, who were elected annually for one-year terms) because elections were thought to privilege the elitism of fame over the egalitarian principle of democratic governance. Moreover, officials selected by lot were given short terms and limited duties, and their conduct in office was subject to judicial review by large panels of two hundred to two thousand citizens. The Athenian Assembly, which was accessible to all citizens, met often and regularly, as much as forty times per year, to deliberate and vote on matters of state. As the state's preeminent policy-making institution, the assembly typically drew six thousand of Athens's twenty thousand to thirty thousand citizens to the

Pnyx, where seating was egalitarian, attendance was encouraged by payment from the state, and deliberations beginning in the early morning consumed half the light of day.[3] A council of five hundred citizens over the age of thirty was chosen each year by lot to set the assembly's agenda. All citizens possessed the right to speak on the issues brought before the assembly if they could secure the attention of fellow assemblymen, who readily heckled boring or otherwise objectionable speakers. The decisions of the assembly, arrived at by majority vote, were accountable only to the people's court, itself composed of two hundred, five hundred, or more than five hundred citizens over the age of thirty who listened to arguments on both sides of a dispute in order to rule on matters both of fact and of law, rendering their decisions by a simple majority vote. Any rhetor who proposed legislation that the assembly passed on his advice could be, and often was, prosecuted in the people's court by another citizen should the recommended policy subsequently fall into disfavor. As Demosthenes exclaimed in 349 BC, while proposing a military expedition against Philip of Macedon, "I am not unaware, men of Athens, that if anything goes wrong, you often vent your disappointment, not on the responsible agents, but on those who happen to have addressed you last. I shall not, however, consult my own safety by keeping back what I believe to be for your true interests." In this way, elite politicians from Pericles to Demosthenes remained regularly answerable to the common people. The citizens of Athens, in Ober's words, who were the government, "possessed the political power in the state" at all levels.[4]

The institutionalized principle of egalitarianism required social and economic elites to become politically reconciled with the masses. Orators, especially Athenian upper-class political rhetors, were constantly faced with the challenge of accommodating to the norms of mass society while fulfilling an expectation of leadership under the constraint of the decision-making power of the citizen assembly and judicial authority of the people's courts. "Along with drama in the theater and gossip in the streets," Ober notes, "public oratory, in the courts and the Assembly, was the most important form of ongoing verbal communication between ordinary and elite Athenians."[5] Although only a small number of citizens could afford the time and the training required to serve effectively as rhetor-politicians, the role of the elite was not to rule but instead to address and advise the democratic mass; the function of ordinary citizens was to consider the advice of elite rhetors while exercising the authority of the majority to determine state policy. "I count it part of your good fortune that more than one speaker may be inspired with suitable suggestions," Demosthenes declared before the assembly, "so that out of the multitude of proposals the choice of the best should not be difficult."[6]

This dynamic between a decision-making demos and policy-advocating rhetors was key to the success of the Athenian experience with direct democracy. In Ober's view, self-rule and social harmony were possible because of "the mediating and integrative power of communication . . . especially between ordinary and elite citizens." The language of the public arena constituted the "discourse of Athenian democracy," a discourse of symbols and ideology, metaphors and signs, text and context, and topoi (commonplace themes and sources of arguments) and frames of reference shared by audience and speaker alike.[7] Orators had to adapt and deploy this medium of accommodation if they hoped to persuade. Accordingly, formal training in rhetoric became a necessity for elite politicians who wished to advance policy initiatives successfully by identifying with the terms of Athenian public culture.[8]

Although philosophers criticized rhetoric's centrality to Athenian democracy and condemned demagogues for appealing to emotion and prejudice, the Athenian citizen was neither exclusively logical nor simply irrational. "The successful orator," Ober argues, "was one who could consistently and seamlessly combine ideas drawn from mass ideology with moral principles and pragmatism in presenting a workable policy, a defense of his policy, or an attack on the policy of an opponent." Thus, the relationship of rhetor to demos was fraught with ambiguity and rich in complexity. The elite training and talent of the rhetor coexisted with a residual faith in the ultimate competency of the demos. Ordinary citizens were suspicious of the rhetor's powers of persuasion but expected from him entertaining oratory that instructed and influenced them on issues of public policy. Athenian political culture recognized the intelligence of citizens and the wisdom of their collective decisions but also conceded their vulnerability to deceptive persuasion. The orator in the Athenian democratic polity "was expected to express the unspoken will of the people, to defend the masses against their internal and external enemies, . . . to offer them sound advice," and even to assume a leadership role when circumstances warranted. The job of rhetors as elite political leaders was to articulate "real alternatives on important issues" for the mass of citizens to make real political decisions.[9] In this way, ancient Greeks achieved a discourse of democracy that assumed citizens were capable of ruling themselves.[10]

This democratic discourse negotiated social and political tensions between the ordinary citizenry and elite politicians without deteriorating into the dreaded factions of James Madison's worst nightmares.[11] Madison's view of factions as the source of democracy's sickness (an upcoming subject of discussion) was at odds with the Athenian experience. In a political culture where no ruling elite existed, politicians were unable to organize factions with reliable public support. Orators addressed the assembly alone, were held individually accountable for the advice they gave, and risked losing credibility if they appeared to be advancing special interests. Nothing like party politics existed in ancient Athens, where instead political groupings and alliances were fluid and the rhetorical relationship of elites to an empowered demos was the arbiter of influence and authority. In Ober's words, "The masses in the end, made and broke the politicians who constituted factions."[12]

Yunis, like Ober, challenges as caricature and ideological bias the received wisdom inherited from a long line of elitist political theorists who have reviled the "irrationality, immaturity, and irresponsibility" of Athenian mob rule.[13] Underscoring the productive tension between citizen decision makers and elite politicians, Ober identifies rhetoric as the integrating medium of Athenian democracy, a nexus of political communication and culture that provided for vigorous leadership in a context of self-rule. Yunis concurs but focuses on the efforts of elite Greek historians, philosophers, and politicians to fashion rhetoric into an instrument of responsible leadership, a means of taming the demos and preventing them from degenerating into an unruly multitude. This shift of perspective in Yunis's analysis is important to gauging the critique of rhetoric and democracy found in Plato and other classical sources.

Expected to advise a politically empowered citizenry within an institutional setting of personal accountability and through a democratic discourse of common images, metaphors, and topoi, orators "aspired to discover the kind of public speech that could effectively lead a mass audience toward realizing their best interests," that is, that met a standard of rationality for "instructing mature, autonomous citizens in the real choices, problems, and best interests of the *polis*," or what Yunis also calls "a rational, instructive political discourse, a discourse that applies human intelligence and will to make the citizen-community wiser, and therefore better." From the point of view of elites, orators needed to practice a rhetoric that would overcome the disabilities of the demos, including a "lack of foresight, concentration, and will" and thus, as in the case of Demosthenes, promote "a conscientious mode of deliberation" while trying to shape a "mature, responsible, attentive audience that is asked to respond favorably to [a rhetor's] candid, demanding, reasoned argument."[14]

Candor, indeed, was characteristic of Demosthenes, even when he chose for the first time in his political career to open a debate in the assembly rather than deferring as before to older statesmen. Delivering his first philippic on that day in 351 BC, he held nothing back by his own reckoning. Giving free utterance to plain sentiments, he began by telling the assembly that "your affairs are in this evil plight just because you, men of Athens, utterly fail to do your duty," and then he proceeded throughout the speech to castigate them for their "indolence and apathy," criticize their "carelessness" and willingness to be branded "a nation of cowards," and accuse them of carrying on a war with Philip "exactly as a barbarian boxes."[15] If this was flattery, it was the most perverse sort imaginable. Rather, leadership on urgent matters of state embraced even blunt rhetoric in the service of the public interest.

Ten years later, as he warned Athenians to combine forces with other Greek city-states against the Macedonian king's continuing advance, Demosthenes produced a consummate example of an immediately successful speech that synthesized shared notions and sentiments into a meaningful argument and public motive. As a practical matter, the argument required the assent of the demos in order to achieve the status of reason. In his words to the assembly he said, "I wish to tell you the grounds for my alarm about our condition, so that if my reasoning is sound, you may adopt it as your own . . . but if I seem to you a driveller and a dotard, neither now nor at any other time pay any heed to me as if I were in my senses."

To achieve the audience's assent, Demosthenes drew from selected topoi such as the conventional opposition between flattery and realistic advice, the distinction between words and deeds, and the boundary between Greeks and barbarians. Bad policy and Athens's "grave peril," he affirmed, were a function of listening to "those who study to win your favour rather than to give you the best advice," and, thus, "if, apart from flattery, you are willing to hear something to your advantage, I am ready to speak." Furthermore, Demosthenes asked, as a way of establishing the priority of his characterization of Philip's aggressions over Philip's professions of peaceful intentions, "is there any intelligent man who would let words rather than deeds decide the question who is at peace and who is at war with him?" And to underscore the basic divide between Athenian interests and Philip's motivation, Demosthenes insisted that Philip was "not only no Greek, nor related to the Greeks, but not even a barbarian from any place that can be named with honour, but a pestilent knave from Macedonia."[16]

As the last example reveals, the logic of a topos such as Us versus Them was embedded in a metaphor such as pestilence upon which the orator relied to make the case that Athens was in "grave peril." Accordingly, "Philip, like the recurrence or attack of a fever or some other disease," Demosthenes proclaimed, "is threatening even those who think themselves out of reach" while the Greeks "seem to watch him just as they would watch a hailstorm, each praying that it may not come their way." Not only had Greeks been "infected" with a "mortal sickness" that made "cowards" of them, but their lethargy placed their dearest values of freedom and liberty at risk. Metaphor, that is, informed the logic of the topos of the barbarian enemy, which entailed the symbol of slavery as the overriding threat to Athenian liberty and democracy. Demosthenes' Philip had "robbed" Greeks over the last thirteen years "of their free constitutions and of their very cities," setting up "tyrannies" in their place to "enslave" his victims.[17]

The topoi of offering realistic advice (not flattery) based on the actual record of Philip's actions (not his words) against the civilized world of Greeks (not barbarians) not only were articulated within the interpretive framework of a metaphor of disease that placed the preeminent value of Athenian liberty in peril but also were extended through a series of corroborating examples. Reasoning by example, that is, operated within a symbolic context of potent symbols and commonplaces. Thus, Demosthenes warned: "If we are going to wait for [Philip] to acknowledge a state of war with us, we are indeed the simplest of mortals; for even if he marches straight against Attica and the Piraeus, he will not admit it, if we may judge from his treatment of the other states. For take the case of the Olynthians." And later in the speech, Demosthenes advanced his inference in a burst of such cases:

For [Philip] says that he is not at war, but for my part, so far from admitting that in acting thus he is observing the peace with you, I assert that when he lays hands on Megara, sets up tyrannies in Euboea, makes his way, as now, into Thrace, hatches plots in Peloponnese, and carries out all these operations with his armed force, he is breaking the peace and making war upon you—unless you are prepared to say that the men who bring up the siege-engines are keeping the peace until they actually bring them to bear on the walls.

Nor did Demosthenes let stand "a foolish argument" from example that was advanced by opposing rhetors who tried "to reassure the citizens" by saying Philip was not yet as imposing as Spartans when "they were masters of every sea and land" and "enjoyed the alliance of the king of Persia." Even "when nothing could stand against [the Lacedaemonians]," the "foolish" argument continued, Athens "defended itself even against them and was not overwhelmed." The analogy between past and present was a false comparison, according to Demosthenes, because Athenians were "living today in a very different world from the old one," a world in which "nothing has been more revolutionized . . . than the art of war." Of significance, the changes in warfare to which he pointed were not technical improvements but matters of barbarity supplanting civilized behavior. The powerful Lacedaemonian Greeks against whom Athenians successfully defended themselves would fight only in the summer months before retiring home again and "were so old-fashioned, or rather such good citizens, that they never used money to buy an advantage from anyone, but their fighting was of the fair and open kind." Philip the barbarian, by contrast, gained his victories by bribery and deceit and by attacking during any season of the year.[18] Thus, the unity of Demosthenes' speech was apparent in its imagery and argument, each informed and reinforced by the other.

The point to underscore here is twofold. First, the assumption even among Athenian elites was that mass deliberation was the norm and rhetoric its necessary, even proper, vehicle. Rhetoric was not an instrument of propaganda but instead a means of proposing, deliberating, and deciding on public policy. The choice was between good and bad rhetoric, not between rhetoric and reason. Second, there was a tendency among the elite who studied and practiced political rhetoric to define good rhetoric as mass instruction for mass decision making, that which at its very best reasoned with the demos, appealed to their political intelligence and maturity, and explained policy well enough to persuade through understanding rather than mere flattery. Rhetoric of this sort was the key to achieving a rational political order, "the voice that kept the Athenians rational en masse and enabled them en masse doggedly to pursue [their] political goals" through democratic deliberation. The assumption was that ordinary people could be instructed and that they were responsive to reason, i.e., that "enlightened persuasion . . . leads to virtuous action."[19]

This rhetorical model of democratic deliberation cut two ways, however, not only underscoring the legitimacy and competency of an empowered demos to make reasonable decisions of state en masse but also postulating the tendency of the people toward irrationality—a weakness rhetors might either exacerbate or mitigate. Just as the model required an empowered citizenry to recognize and endorse rational arguments, it relied on elite orators to pro-duce good reasons and propose sound policy. Reason was the possession of the elite, something for them to identify, define, construct, and instruct the public to favor. It did not emanate from commoners, but it could be trans-lated into aphorisms, signs, and symbol systems comprising public culture. This tendency to defer to the elite for the production of rational options through rhetorical discourse constituted the citizenry as judges who voted after listening to experts deliberate. The masses in the assembly or people's courts did not deliberate among themselves but delegated that task instead to the competing orators among them. The role of the Athenian public in this political drama was that of an audience, judging the performance of op-posing speakers—not a passive audience by any means, but an audience nevertheless, determining by majority vote which rhetorical construction of political reality would prevail. Rhetorical deliberation, that is, not only ad-dressed the people as judges but also encompassed contested notions of re-ality and reason.

This was both the fact of democratic deliberation, Yunis argues, and its flaw that political thinkers from Thucydides to Plato and Demosthenes at-tempted to overcome by theorizing "the instructive potential of political rhetoric." What were the rhetorical means, these three critics asked, of "pre-venting an Assembly of deliberating citizens from degenerating into a mob"? How could the orator as political expert compensate for the disabilities of the demos, that is, for the limitations of mass deliberation in which prudence and understanding might succumb to flattery and emotional manipulation?[20] The answers Yunis derives from Demosthenes and from Thucydides' representa-tion of Pericles, in my view, are quite unlike the answers he finds in Plato, especially in the implications of the latter for fabricating the disparaging and overly pessimistic image of an innately distempered demos. Simply put, the first two of these political thinkers, one a practicing rhetor and the other a historian of Pericles' rhetorical practice, sought to adapt to the emotional tendencies of a mass audience, whereas the third wished to cure the disease of the demos. Demosthenes believed he could achieve his political goals in the assembly by relying on candor and reasoned argumentation to encourage mature responses. Similarly, Thucydides portrayed Pericles as explaining his position well enough for the people to adopt a proposed policy because they understood it. In both instances, political egalitarianism mandated rhetorical excellence; the demos were fellow citizens whom orators persuaded to make intelligent decisions not just by crafting rational arguments for the audience's consumption but also by reinforcing those arguments with appropriate emotional appeals. Thus, for example, Pericles might offset a prevailing sense of arrogance or indifference among Athenians with a strategic appeal to fear that bolstered his arguments for strengthening the city's defensive perimeter, whereas on another occasion he might wish to overcome their fear with a countervailing appeal to courage.[21] Attending to the emotional state of the audience was a condition of public persuasion, not a disease that turned the people into an irrational mob.

Plato, though, thought otherwise. His solution to the same problem was first to withdraw completely from the political process and then to construct alternatives that were outside the bounds of Athenian political institutions and democratic practices. In his *Gorgias*, Plato criticized rhetoric as a harmful flattery except, in his *Republic*, as a philosopher-king's tool to gain legitimacy and power in a utopian polis by persuading the masses that philosophers are the best rulers. Here he rejected rhetoric as a discourse for mediating political conflict. In the *Phaedrus*, Plato explored the question of how a knowledgeable leader might instruct the demos, i.e., what kind of rhetorical practice would serve the ends of truth and persuasion—answering that the true rhetor, guided by dialectical reasoning to know his subject and achieve the organic unity of his speech, also probed the nature and types of soul in order to adapt his message to the psychology of his audience. The implications of this concession to the possibility of instructing the masses were limited, however, to conditions well short of Athens's vigorous democratic culture, as underscored in the *Laws*, which was Plato's model of a second-best, less-utopian polis than that of the ideal *Republic*. The polis of the *Laws* granted absolute authority to a lawgiver who "addresse[d] the citizens rhetorically in the preambles to the laws" in order to give the people a basis for free consent short of actual deliberation. These rhetorical preambles, though delivered to the assembled citizenry when a new law was announced, were designed to be read and studied instead of debated; they were to be adapted to the psychology of the audience in the form of moral advice, much like preaching the received word to the flock.[22]

Plato's persistent disdain for rhetorical deliberation was grounded in a recurrent medical metaphor found throughout his writing on politics that articulated the goal, as Yunis observes, of "curing the *demos* of volatile behavior." In the *Laws*, the mass of citizens was compared to sick patients treated by a knowledgeable physician whose prescriptions they should readily accept and instructions freely receive in order to recover their rational bearings and political health. In the *Gorgias*, Plato attacked the rhetor for ministering falsely to the body politic without knowing what was good for it, of attempting to produce pleasure instead of right behavior, and thus of pandering to the animal desires and childish mind of the demos in order to produce an ignorant, impassioned mob. The rhetor's flattery was poison to a demented citizenry, just as unrestrained democracy was dangerously irrational.[23]

Had it prevailed in its own time, Plato's harsh critique of democracy based on the image of a diseased demos—an image that dissociated rhetoric from deliberation and reduced the empowered public to an ailing patient—would have undermined the productive tension that actually existed in Athens between elite rhetors and mass audiences. Moreover, Plato's medical metaphor expressed a clear and knowable distinction between truth and falsehood in politics that others, especially sophists, questioned and contested. Unlike Plato, who resisted democracy, "the sophists were all anchored in Athenian democracy," as Susan Jarratt observes. Protagoras advised Pericles, for instance, and Gorgias was an emissary from Sicily who most likely spoke before the Athenian Council even as he popularized epideictic rhetoric as a "vital instrument in the formation of political thought and cultural values." As teachers and commentators who shaped the Athenian political agenda, Jarratt concludes, "the sophists could be termed the first public intellectuals in a democracy." A common premise among the sophists was that phenomena were always in some degree of flux just as perceptions of reality varied from one individual to the next. Thus, contradictions, contraries, and competing views were the necessary order of the day in human affairs, and debating opposing positions to explore alternatives and test received wisdom was a corollary to democratic decision making. Preparation for participatory democracy included, therefore, cataloguing and studying topoi and commonplaces to expose and analyze "contradictions and inconsistencies in the matrix of accepted beliefs" and thus to reconstitute them into matters of reflection and choice.[24]

The sophists' holistic conception of political discourse fused aesthetic with functional considerations into a rhetoric defying the dualism of *mythos* and *logos* that has marked the prevailing historical understanding of "the rational revolution of the Greek enlightenment accompanying the birth of democracy."[25] As Jarratt argues in her rereading of the sophists, particularly Protagoras and Gorgias, myth and logic were not discrete categories in the classical period of Greece, just as the introduction of abstract, rational discourse did not involve a complete rejection of poetic, emotive discourse or a division of the psyche into separate rational and irrational domains. Eric Havelock observes similarly that sophistic rhetoric was not "the practice of unscrupulous persuasion upon the blind emotions of masses" but rather the complex process of "subtle currents of judgment which go to the making of the collective mind and the group decision."[26] *Nomos* (a critical consciousness of customs, habits of mind, social codes, norms, beliefs, and practices) served as the sophists' bridge between *mythos* and *logos*. Through narrative strategies, sophistic rhetoric organized belief, opinion, and value into guiding perspectives, thus creating political and social knowledge out of provisional and customary codes of behavior that spanned the Aristotelian distinction between *logos* and *pathos*. Because no particular ordering of the world was necessary, rhetoric was an act of invention and convention, and argument was a matter of probability. The world that existed beyond discourse could only be experienced through discourse. Human affairs were muddled and messy matters of interpretation and communication. Probabilities were not "a second-rate substitute for certainty" but instead a function of human experience, perception, and action in a world where no single truth could exist.[27]

Largely influenced by Protagoras and Gorgias, Isocrates stressed that the public orator combined wisdom with eloquence to negotiate the inherent uncertainties of political affairs while persuading the citizenry to follow his particular advice and adopt his proposed policy. In this regard, Takis Poulakos emphasizes, rhetoric was the art of politics in which the orator spoke as a citizen to an audience of citizens about "communal values, interests, and desires" in a collective deliberation over political ends and means. Rhetorical *logos* was an instrument of invention that could bring citizens together for their common benefit.[28] It involved much more than the Platonic view in the *Gorgias*, in Werner Jaeger's words, of "a purely formal technique of hypnotizing the ignorant masses with persuasive talk."[29] Instead of speech turning the demos into a beast, as Plato viewed the matter, deliberative speech by Isocrates' account enabled human beings to escape the life of wild beasts and to achieve the benefits of civilization through the power of persuading one another.[30] Rhetoric constituted politics and culture, the means by which citizens achieved community and enhanced their collective lives. Such deliberation, Poulakos notes, allowed experience to inform opinion, history to engage the present and the future, intellect to intermingle with imagination, logic to intersect with emotion, and reason to coordinate with desire.[31]

Even Aristotle, no friend of sophistry or democracy, recognized the deliberative function of rhetoric in the Athenian polis. Characterizing rhetoric as an offshoot of politics and counterpart of dialectic, he thought men were akin to wild beasts in their susceptibility to passion and considered radical democracy therefore vulnerable to demagoguery.[32] Yet he worked out a theory of rhetorical deliberation that constituted the demos as an audience, albeit a corrupted audience, to be addressed—rather than an Other to be suppressed.[33] In an ideal polis, the people would be educated in practical wisdom and socialized to desire the right things. In such a system, the need for rhetoric was minimal. But in the imperfect world of the actual polis, where issues were deliberated democratically and ordinary citizens acted as judges, rhetoric was politics. The successful orator's arguments had to be grounded in assumptions shared by the audience or, to borrow a phrase from Stephen Halliwell, in "the civic forms of life available within a community."[34] According to Aristotle, these "available means of persuasion" for arguing opposing positions included maxims, topoi, examples, signs, probabilities, fables, analogies, metaphors, a speaker's reputation, the power to stir emotions, and the like. Even the enthymeme, Aristotle's rhetorical proof most akin to a dialectical syllogism, was based on a probability known to the particular audience rather than the certainty of a universal truth. By exploiting popular morality, the practical wisdom of the rhetor achieved a "purchase on the minds of political audiences" that spoke to the public's advantage, benefit, and self-interest.[35] As Eugene Garver argues, Aristotle addressed the question of "whether there can be a civic art of rhetoric" in order "to show how the activities that are central to citizenship and human well-being can be subject to rational analysis and to presentation as an art." His *Rhetoric,* accordingly, provided "resources for arguing in situations of incommensurability and of conflicting goods" while "respecting the particularity and variability of practical circumstances."[36]

Overall, then, Athenians experienced participatory democracy through a medium of rhetorical deliberation that empowered the citizenry as audience and judge of political oratory. Within this framework, speakers advanced contested positions on public issues before a demanding, even recalcitrant demos, drawing deferentially and selectively from the community's various symbolic resources to earn the consent of a majority and thereby enabling political expertise to coexist in balance with an empowered public. Topoi, maxims, metaphors, probabilities, and the like were generative, heuristic sources of rhetorical invention, not a seamless ideology to which rhetors simply pandered nor a demagogues' cauldron for stirring people into a crazed mob. Despite Plato's demeaning trope, emotion was inseparable from reason in Athenian political discourse, which overall constituted a robust rather than distempered demos. How is it, then, that Plato's caricature of direct democracy prevailed among the founders of the American republic who, as George Kennedy notes, "deeply distrusted radical democracy as seen in Athens and were determined to avoid its excesses in creating the United States Constitution"?[37]

Diagnosing "Democratic Distemper"

Just as democracy in eighteenth-century America was reduced to a subordinate position in the constitutional design of the early republic, citizenship among the masses was demoted from the role of decision maker to that of bystander. During these formative years, a mythos of the demented demos was firmly established in U.S. political culture so that the revered fiction of the people no longer referred to the assembled populace but instead to their representatives elected and appointed from the political elite. By means of the metaphor of disease, the discourse of democracy was degraded so that it no longer presumed citizens capable of self-rule. Referring to what he called "the imprudence of democracy" and maintaining that even the people were beginning to tire of an "excess of democracy," Alexander Hamilton remarked before the Constitutional Convention on June 18, 1787, that "the voice of the people has been said to be the voice of God; and however generally this maxim has been quoted and believed, it is not true in fact. The people are turbulent and changing; they seldom judge or determine right."[38] Why? Because, as James Madison declared in *Federalist* 10, they lacked "a republican remedy for the diseases most incident" to popular government. "The instability, injustice, and confusion introduced into the public councils have, in truth," he continued, "been the mortal diseases under which popular councils have everywhere perished." Accordingly, Madison postulated in *Federalist* 55: "Had every Athenian citizen been a Socrates, every Athenian assembly would still have been a mob."[39]

What was this republican remedy Madison concocted for the disease of popular government? To overcome the threat of anarchy that he perceived in the weak and overly democratic governments of certain states operating under the Articles of Confederation,[40] Madison proposed a "proper cure" of substituting representative, or what he strategically called republican, government for the troubled regime of "pure democracy" or citizen self-rule that could "admit of no cure for the mischiefs of faction." This strategy of "guarding against the confusion of a multitude" by "the delegation of the government . . . to a small number of citizens elected by the rest" would "refine and enlarge the public views by passing them through the medium of a chosen body of citizens, whose wisdom may best discern the true interest of their country." The "public voice, pronounced by the representatives of the people," Madison surmised, would prove to be "more consonant to the public good than if pronounced by the people themselves."[41] Democracy, according to Richard Matthews, was to Madison "a fool's illusion"; cool reason could only be exercised by individuals in isolation because people assembled in groups stirred hot passions that overrode reason and justice.[42] Thus, as a safeguard against this "infection of violent passions," Madison observed in *Federalist* 63 that the "true distinction" between the pure democracies of ancient Greece and the proposed republic of the United States "lies *in the total exclusion of the people in their collective capacity*" from any share in government.[43]

What may be most revealing about Madison's stark dissociation of ordinary citizens from actual governance is that he declared it so emphatically and publicly as an obvious improvement over any system of self-rule. Indeed, his utter disdain for democracy was shared openly by fellow delegates to the Constitutional Convention. As the delegates debated the composition and authority of two branches of Congress, for instance, Edmund Randolph of Virginia argued that the "democratic licentiousness of the State Legislatures proved the necessity of a firm Senate. The object of this 2d. branch is to controul the democratic branch of the Natl. Legislature." James Wilson of Pennsylvania agreed that "a single legislature is very dangerous," suggesting that "legislative despotism" would result if the democratic branch went "unchecked or unrestrained by another branch." The "democratic body" was "already secure in a representation," Hamilton added, while warning that inclining too much toward democracy would quickly drive the country into monarchy and that the "preservation of our democratic governments" was the desire of European sovereigns who wished "to keep us weak." Gouverneur Morris of Pennsylvania elaborated on the threat of monarchy, saying that the object of establishing a second branch of the Congress was "to check the precipitation, changeableness, and excesses of the first branch. Every man of observation had seen in the democratic branches of the State

Legislatures, precipitation—in Congress changeableness, in every depart-ment excesses agst. personal liberty[,] private property & personal safety." Thus, "the aristocratic body should be as independent & as firm as the democratic." Without such a balance, the "rich will strive to establish their dominion & enslave the rest. . . . The proper security agst. them is to form them into a separate interest. The two forces will then controul each other." Furthermore, "we should remember that the people never act from reason alone. The rich will take advantage of their passions and make these the in-struments for oppressing them," reducing the people to "the dupes of those who have more Knowledge & intercourse" and resulting in "a violent aris-tocracy, or a more violent despotism." By checking the democratic House with an aristocratic Senate composed of men of "*ability* and *virtue*," he con-cluded, you "keep down the turbulency of democracy," secure "the *public good*," and achieve "stability in your government." Stability, in fact, was a primary goal of the delegates as a defense against "the turbulency and weak-ness of unruly passions." Whereas "democratic communities may be un-steady, and be led to action by the impulse of the moment," Madison af-firmed, "the government we mean to erect is intended to last for ages."[44]

The system Madison framed to last for ages had to anticipate that over time a rise in population would "increase the proportion of those who will labour under all the hardships of life, & secretly sigh for a more equal distri-bution of its blessings," thus by the logic of equal suffrage shifting power away from "those who are placed above the feelings of indigence." The trouble-some "symptoms of a leveling spirit" had already appeared in some quarters of the country "to give notice of the future danger." Madison's pessimism was deeply rooted, as he said, in the belief that "mankind in general . . . are vi-cious" and governed by "their passions," including prominently their "ambi-tion and interest." It would be a "great error" to "suppose mankind more honest than they are" or that they "act from more worthy motives." Hamil-ton was only marginally more optimistic than Madison, observing that the tenuous union among the confederated states was "dissolving or already dis-solved" but that the "evils operating in the States . . . must soon cure the people of their fondness for democracies." For Elbridge Gerry of Massachu-setts, "democracy" simply was "the worst . . . of all political evils." Thus, at the federal convention the people were reduced, in the words of Massachu-setts delegate Rufus King, to "those who are to be the objects of a Govt."[45]

Curiously, Madison never addressed the question of why even an assembly of citizens as wise as Socrates would succumb to "the confusion and intemperance of a multitude." He merely presumed that "in all very numerous assemblies, of whatever characters composed, passion never fails to wrest the scepter from reason."[46] The man who promoted an "Empire of reason," Matthews observes, based one of the principal premises of his "entire theoretical edifice" on "an unchallenged philosophic assumption not grounded in reason." One is left wondering, then, on what insight this pessimistic view of humanity was premised, especially when Madison's good friend Thomas Jefferson "conceived of citizenship as an ennobling activity" instead of a tyranny of popular passions that Madison identified as the mortal affliction of prior republics.[47]

Perhaps an answer to this question is suggested by Madison's personal fixation on disease. This man, who was the principal architect of the nation-building federal constitution, also was a secret epileptic and perpetual hypochondriac who dressed in black throughout much of his adulthood, anticipating imminent death. He lived to the age of eighty-five but thought of himself by age twenty-one as too "infirm" to "expect a long or healthy life." Throughout adulthood, according to biographer Robert Rutland, Madison regularly complained of "high fevers, diarrhea, or seizures." Another biographer, Irving Brant, has diagnosed Madison as suffering from the psychic trauma of hysterical epilepsy rather than any organic form of the disease. Thus, as Matthews observes, it should not be too surprising that "the use of medical language and metaphors to describe the sick and fatal republic is manifest" throughout Madison's public writing.[48]

If Madison's deity was Reason, his devil was Disease. Perhaps his greatest fear was letting a distempered demos loose in the delicately balanced republic he had so carefully designed to slow the inevitable, long-term decay of political order and to preserve the property rights and power of the elite minority against the tyranny of an irrational majority. "If men were angels," he wrote, "no government would be necessary."[49] In mass, they became demonic creatures infected by Passion when Reason should rule. Clearly, it seems to me, Madison was witness to a great struggle of mythic proportions in which storied deities such as Reason, Disease, and Passion were implicated in the founding of a nation and the constitution of a political cosmos. Madison's Calvinist universe, he knew, would ultimately fail, but he called upon Reason to postpone the inevitable decay.[50]

The mythos of the distempered demos, or demented demon, is of particular interest for what it illustrates about the mythic function of Madison's disease metaphor. If myth is the locus of creativity and innovation and an in-

dispensable cultural resource for apprehending the unknown,[51] then it operates in the realm of metaphor. As Turbayne suggests, myth consists of "extended or sustained metaphors" that are "taken literally" as the "correct" or
"best explanation of the facts" in an otherwise incoherent and disorienting
existence.[52] Thus, Northrop Frye argues that myth and metaphor are inseparable.[53] In each, similarities are expressed as identities and essences.[54]

Stephen Daniel, who treats metaphors as myths in miniature or, following
Giambattista Vico, as abbreviated myths, argues that just as "complexes of
metaphors . . . constitute myths," metaphors "serve as the elements of change
within myth." This creative function, this act of genesis, presents "a world
that only becomes meaningful in virtue of the account given in the mythic
expression," and that account exists only in the telling and retelling of the
myth. Experience, through the ritual of performing a myth, is organized "in
ways that validate claims, establish values, and identify problems."[55] Thus,
metaphors, such as Madison's metaphor of disease, fulfill the mythic function
of inventing a universe of meaning and interpretation, of providing the pre-
suppositions of any thought about political community and the origins of any
understanding of the people and their capacity for self-governance, indeed,
of generating the existence of such a world and even the possibility of its
being known. Each expression of such a metaphor re-creates a mythic world
and, in each unique or variant performance, the possibility and even risk of
realigning that reality. Rationality, including Madison's deity of Reason, does
not exist as the rationale behind the myth but instead is itself established in
the performance of a myth.[56] There is no origin of meaning beyond metaphor performing its mythic function. It is the irreducibly arbitrary antecedent
of historical understandings as well as new or emerging interpretations. As
such, Daniel concludes, metaphor and myth, in "their irresolvably creative
character," are "the indicators of the aboriginal character of a pattern of
thought."[57]

Moreover, when myth determines worldviews, as William Doty explains,
myth and ideology become synonymous. Even as myth "taps into the imaginative human propensities," it remains "a component of rational discourse,"
and when it is interpreted literally, it produces normative prescriptions.[58] The
metaphoric and mythic side of culture brings the connotative and analogical
dimensions of meaning into play with their denotative and logical extensions
to produce serious and authoritative stories that Bruce Lincoln compares to
"charters, models, templates, and blueprints"—mythic acts that evoke "the
sentiments out of which society is actively constructed."[59]

Disease as a charter or model of a distempered people deconstructed the democratic discourse of citizen self-rule and reconstituted the public as an unthinking, irrational mob whose emotions are preyed upon by demagogues, a common herd that lacks sufficient virtue to consider the good of the community. Madison's oft-repeated metaphors, which ritualistically rehearsed throughout *The Federalist* this legitimizing story for a republican constitution of representative or weak democracy, included references to a "proper cure" for "the violence of faction," "dangerous vice," "mortal diseases," and the "impulse of passion" to "convulse a society"; "curing the mischiefs of faction"; a "remedy" for being "inflamed with mutual animosity"; an "antidote for the diseases of faction," "the confusion of a multitude," "rage," "malady," "alarming symptoms," "the most dark and degrading pictures which display the infirmities and depravities of the human character," "the pestilential influence of party animosities [which is] the disease most incident to deliberative bodies and most apt to contaminate their proceedings," "a patient who finds his disorder daily growing worse," that which would "inflame the passions of the unthinking," "miseries springing from [America's] internal jealousies," a "defense to the people against their own temporary errors and delusions," and "the infection of violent passions." Others, including Hamilton, performed similar metaphorical rituals, referring in *The Federalist* to "a torrent of angry and malignant passions"; "domestic factions and convulsions"; popular assemblies being "subject to the impulses of rage, resentment, jealousy, avarice, and of other irregular and violent propensities"; faction as the "poison in the deliberations of all bodies of men"; and even "the contagion of some violent popular paroxysm." Other participants in the public debate over the Constitution regularly performed the myth of the distempered and incompetent demos by lacing their discourse with images of "the folly and blindness of the people," "haranguing the Rabble," the public becoming "dupes" to "those who wish to influence [their] passions," the threat of "popular rage," and the danger of "fits of passion" and "paroxisms."[60]

With these sentiments, a nation was constituted in the 1780s that, as Gordon Wood observes, was a peculiar kind of democracy—a democratic republic or representative democracy in which representation was engrafted upon democracy.[61] The principle of representation was the "pivot," in Madison's view, on which the American system moved, the redemptive source of rationality that the ancient Athenians had lacked.[62] All officials in every branch of the government, not just the elected representatives in the House, became agents of, and thus substitutes for, the people, thereby taking "the people out of the government altogether." Representation was the "healing principle" that would arrest the "decay and eventual death of the republican body politic" by allowing "the natural aristocracy" to "assert itself and dominate" a government that operated in the name of the people as if it was the people. These nation builders believed they had broken the cycle of history by telling the story of a people who "could diagnose the ills of its society and work out a peaceable process of cure," the story of "a constitutional antidote 'wholly popular' and 'strictly republican' for the ancient diseases" of a purely democratic polity. This story produced a constitution that "was intrinsically an aristocratic document designed to check the democratic tendencies of the period" with "an elitist theory of democracy."[63] The people, who could not be trusted to govern themselves because of their infirmities and intemperate passions, were reinvented as a national sovereignty transcending local government and dispersed throughout the federal authority. In short, Madison's mythic metaphor of a distempered demos legitimized the invention of a sovereign people who were disembodied and removed from self-rule through the fiction of representation, all of which was designed, as Edmund Morgan concludes, "to secure popular consent to a governing aristocracy."[64] This very achievement, "using the most popular and democratic rhetoric available to explain and justify [an] aristocratic system," Wood concurs, "created a distinctly American political theory" that impoverished "later American political thought."[65]

Madison's metaphor of disease, a truncated myth of the public's political incompetence, told a very different tale of Athenian direct democracy than Josiah Ober's more nuanced version of a robust citizenry assembled in ancient Greece to make genuine decisions on actual alternatives advanced in public oratory. Madison's performance of the myth of the demos altered its meaning and valence by varying its metaphoric expression. Orators were transformed from upper-class political rhetors who addressed the assembled citizenry to instruct, advise, and lead their deliberations into deceitful and fractious manipulators of popular prejudice. Madison's demagogue made "ignorance . . . the dupe of cunning, and passion the slave of sophistry and declamation"; the people, forever "subject to the infection of violent passions," could only be "misled by the artful misrepresentations of interested men." Accordingly, in Madison's mythic account, the people of Athens were incompetent to reason or judge the truth. They might have escaped their "bitter anguish" only by living in a republic instead of a "turbulent democracy," a republic guided by a principle of representation that removed the demos from the seat of power in order to protect the multitude from "the tyranny of their own passions" and the nation from "the violence of faction." Through the metaphor of disease, Madison derived the notion that men were not angels— a mythic creation for apprehending the unknown—and therefore that the people must be controlled by government rather than allowed to govern themselves.[66] Thus, he invoked the Enlightenment god of Reason as his ultimate constitutional authority.

A somewhat different story of the people might have been told if Thomas Jefferson had been invited to participate in the formative deliberations of the Constitutional Convention of 1787 instead of remaining in Paris as minister to France, for Jefferson's more favorable inclinations toward democracy were premised on a metaphor of life rather than death. Moreover, Jefferson seemed more outwardly in touch with the mythic rhythm of political life than Madison, whose mechanistic and instrumental Reason shrouded the myths he lived by in a veil of literal truth. In Jefferson's view, writing to Charles Thompson in September of 1787, "the moment a person forms a theory his imagination sees in every object only the traits which favor that theory."[67] Unlike Madison's liberal faith in the private individual, as Matthews points out, Jefferson was convinced that "man was a social, harmonious, cooperative, and just creature who, under the appropriate socioeconomic conditions, could happily live in a community that did not need the presence of the Leviathan," that indeed humans require one another's presence to make life meaningful, and that sharing the tragedy endemic to social life promotes healing. Similarly, Jefferson's mythic sensibility was reflected in arguments constructed self-consciously on first principles, which he labeled "self-evident," and in his commitment to the "moral sense" of man's heart, rather than the reason of his head, as the means of living in tranquility. As Matthews notes, the pastoral Jefferson relied on a "figurative, mythopoetic language [eschewing 'the sparse, arid, and analytic language of political economy'] to capture more adequately his image of a democratic society."[68]

One witnesses these Jeffersonian qualities in the creation myth of the People who, as he proclaimed in the Declaration of Independence, assume "the separate and equal station to which the laws of nature and of nature's God entitle them" and declare certain "truths to be self-evident: that all men are created equal; that they are endowed by their Creator with certain unalienable rights," including "life, liberty, and the pursuit of happiness," and that governments, "deriving their just powers from the consent of the governed," are "instituted among men" and also "abolished" by "the people" as necessary to secure their rights. The ideology evoked by this positive image of democratic revolution was averse to Madison's constitutional taming of the demos. Jefferson instead advocated a system of participatory ward politics, dividing counties into units small enough for citizens to act in person on matters related exclusively to them, and embraced the idea of a revolution every generation to renew the people's commitment to the laws by which they are governed. This mythic cycle of rebirth and renewal every two decades was an expression of faith in the resilience of the people and the perpetuity of the nation. Just as Jefferson felt deprived of a chance to participate in the drafting of the Constitution, he believed the continuing health of the republic required faith in a radical, revolutionary ethic that Madison, who imagined a fundamentally sick nation, was sure could lead only to anarchy. Where Madison's view amounted to "the rule of the dead from beyond the grave," Jefferson himself, as he told John Adams, preferred "the dreams of the future better than the history of the past."[69] Accordingly, Jefferson is the one founder "whose very name became a signifier of democracy."[70]

Ironically, Madison's rhetorical achievement amounted to nothing less than co-opting and displacing some of the existing appeal of democracy in the guise of creating a republic. As Isaac Kramnick has observed, the word "republic," which carried strong populist connotations in the eighteenth century, was appropriated by Madison to name what his Anti-Federalist critics called a new aristocratic order, an order of government in which popular participation was supplanted by a regime of representation. Not only was Madison adept at "stealing the concept from the Anti-Federalists while ridding it of the content that had endeared the label to these more populist opponents of the Constitution," but also he and his allies succeeded in appropriating to their cause the name "Federalists," which suggested a certain degree of respect for the sovereignty of the individual states, as opposed to the label "nationalists," which implied a diminishment of the states by the adoption of a strong central government. Thus, those who opposed the proposed constitution became known as Anti-Federalists, placing them at a tactical disadvantage while disguising "the centrist thrust" of Madison's "republic."[71] Already the ideological distinction between participatory and representative democracy—that is, a government of the people rather than a people governed—had begun to lose its critical edge in the public debate.

Even so, Anti-Federalist rhetors resisted the decline of popular participation by opposing the Federalists' favored "filter" metaphor with their own "mirror" alternative.[72] A regime of representation that included direct elections instead of legislative appointment of members to the "first branch of the general legislature," Madison noted at the Constitutional Convention, would maintain the "necessary sympathy between [the people] and their rulers" while happily "refining the popular appointments by successive filtrations" in other branches of the proposed government.[73] Again, in *Federalist* 10, he argued that the advantage of the principle of "delegation of the government" was "to refine and enlarge the public views by passing them through the medium of a chosen body of citizens, whose wisdom may best discern the true interest of their country and whose patriotism and love of justice will be least likely to sacrifice it to temporary or partial considerations." Size of the electorate was one of the key components of the filtering mechanism. The larger the number of voters involved in picking a relatively small number of representatives, the greater the likelihood of weeding out "men of factious tempers, of local prejudices, or of sinister designs, [who] may, by intrigue, by corruption, or by other means, first obtain the suffrages, and then betray the interests of the people." By this reckoning, "extensive republics are most favorable to the election of proper guardians of the public weal."[74]

Anti-Federalists understood, as indicated in the "Letters from the 'Federal Farmer'" (written most likely by New Yorker Melancton Smith), that such a filtering mechanism transferred power from the many to the few instead of mirroring the diverse interests of the whole polity. The value of the proposed system was "vastly lessened for the want of that one important feature in a free government, a representation of the people." Instead of power being "cautiously lodged in the hands of numerous legislators, and many magistrates," he argued, "we see all important powers collecting in one centre, where a few men will possess them almost at discretion." The "Federal Farmer" further allowed that

> the essential parts of a free and good government are a full and equal representation of the people . . . which possesses the same interests, feelings, opinions, and views the people themselves would were they all assembled—a fair representation, therefore, should be so regulated, that every order of men in the community, according to the common course of elections, can have a share in it—in order to allow professional men, merchants, traders, farmers, mechanics, &c. to bring a just proportion of their best informed men respectively into the legislature, the representation must be considerably numerous.

Instead of a large assembly reflecting the people in all their diversity, the proposed general government would "consist of a new species of executive, a small senate, and a very small house of representatives." Thus, it would make no "proper distinction between the few men of wealth and abilities . . . [who are] the natural aristocracy of the country, and the great body of the people, the middle and lower classes, as the democracy" in all their "different opinions, customs, and views."[75] In contrast to this Anti-Federalist call for large assemblies to mimic a gathering of the American polity, Hamilton argued in *Federalist* 35 that "the idea of an actual representation of all classes of the people by persons of each class is altogether visionary," that in reality "the natural representatives of all these classes" were "landholders, merchants, and men of the learned professions" who were "acquainted with the general genius, habits, and modes of thinking of the people at large and with the resources of the country."[76] Clearly, Melancton Smith disagreed, telling the delegates to New York's ratification convention that representatives should "resemble those they represent; they should be a true picture of the people; possess a knowledge of their circumstances and their wants; sympathize in all their distresses, and be disposed to seek their true interests."[77]

Just as the metaphor of the filter conformed to the mythos of a distempered demos and argued for consolidating the separate states under a national regime of checks and balances to ensure the ascendancy of cool reason over hot passions, the metaphor of the mirror placed representatives and their constituents in a more immediate and intimate relationship to one another that presumed the competency of the people and fashioned a contemporary analogue to Athenian self-governance. Whereas Federalists argued for less-frequent elections to preserve the "stability" and "energy" of the central government, Anti-Federalists favored frequent elections to hold representatives accountable as delegates.[78] "Brutus" (probably Robert Yates, a New York judge and delegate to the federal convention who opposed the proposed constitution) maintained that the vastness of the United States prohibited any such central government from functioning as a truly free republic, where the representatives of the people were numerous enough and sufficiently accountable to the public to "know the minds of their constituents" and to "speak the sentiments of the people." A free republic was not exactly a pure democracy in which the sovereign people assembled to deliberate and declare their will "by themselves in person," but it did derive its laws from the consent of the people through their chosen representatives whom they knew well and held to a high standard of integrity.[79] Correcting the defects of the Articles of Confederation, which was the original charge given the delegates to the federal convention, would suffice to meet the exigencies of the moment.[80] There was no need to create a consolidated government "ignorant of the sentiments of the midling [sic] class of citizens, strangers to their ability, wants, and difficulties, and void of sympathy, and fellow feeling," and there was no advantage in a distant central government undermining the sovereignty of the separate states where the people could be more numerously represented by the likes of a "neighbour" known to possess talents "sufficient to manage the business with which he is charged, his honesty and fidelity unsuspected, and his friendship and zeal for the service of his principal unquestionable."[81] The national House of Representatives, protested John DeWitt (an anonymous Anti-Federalist writing in the *Boston American Herald*), was merely an "apparent faithful Mirror" of the people that would amount to an "Assistant Aristocratical Branch" to the Senate of the proposed central government rather than "consisting of members chosen [annually] from every town," as they were in Massachusetts—men who lived "in the center" of their constituents and were subject to the "immediate control" of the people they represented and even "consult[ed] in their deliberations."[82]

In its closer approximation of direct democracy, the mirror image of representation afforded a more positive view of politics than the Federalists' negative filter. Attempts made to give voice to the "undistorted and uncorrupted will of the people," Ketcham notes, included unicameral legislatures, annual elections and rotation in office, town meetings, small districts and ward identities, local councils and committees, and referendums and recall, all consistent with a general commitment to maintaining the vitality of state and local government. This degree of intimacy between the people and their representatives was thought to foster trust and goodwill essential to wise public deliberations. Rather than seeking the power of empire and keeping government remote from the people, Anti-Federalists preferred a polity in which citizens managed their own affairs.[83]

"Degenerating" into Democracy

Although the Federalists prevailed in establishing a republican constitution that filtered the voice of the people out of the deliberations of their representatives, the impulse of democratic politics returned in force four decades later with the election of Andrew Jackson as the seventh president of the

United States. Jacksonian democracy, as Marvin Meyers and others have underscored, emerged when America was already departing from "the language of mob terror and elite guidance" that had characterized the Federalists as "a party of fear and resentment." The "popular voice" was the nation's "oracle," proclaimed George Bancroft in a Fourth of July address in 1826, "the voice of God." The Jacksonian party, in effect, became the symbolic vehicle for steering a democratic course against the Federalist currents of conservatism.[84] The notion of representation as a mirror rather than a filter of public persuasion would be extended within the existing federal system as a way of affirming the principle of majoritarian rule. Jacksonian Democrats not only championed the rights of the people but also valorized the public as wise and virtuous, insisting that "the will of the people must in all instances be obeyed by their representatives."[85] In his first message to Congress and consistently thereafter, Jackson advanced the principle that because the majority should govern, all intermediaries standing between the rule of the people and their government should be removed. Thus, the people should have the right to elect their own president directly rather than through an electoral college. Moreover, the Supreme Court, which was the body of government furthest removed from the people, should not be the final arbiter of the meaning of the Constitution. Instead, there should be a strict construction of federal and state constitutions, themselves subject to change only through the ballot box. The officers of government, Jackson wrote later, were the "agents" of the people—representatives who were subject always to instruction from the public and "bound to obey or resign." Appointed officers should be rotated in office every four years, and elected representatives (including senators and presidents along with members of the House) should be selected directly by vote of the people. Senators should serve for only four years, and presidents should be elected to a single term of four or six years. Even federal judges should stand for election, he believed.[86]

These innovations, aimed at placing ordinary citizens into the mainstream of politics on the premise that they were sufficiently intelligent to make good decisions, turned out to be largely ahead of Jackson's time and, accordingly, met with strong resistance from the Whig opposition. The very trust in the wisdom of the masses "to arrive at right conclusions," Whigs complained, was the source of civil disturbance and the reason "the *Republic has degenerated into a Democracy.*" Jackson's demagoguery, his "artful appeal to the passions of the poor and ignorant," was responsible for "the present *supremacy of the Mobocracy.*"[87] The Jacksonian persuasion had rekindled this orthodox fear of mobocracy by advancing the values of equality over privilege, liberty over domination, and honest work over idle exploitation, making the "Monster Bank" (reminiscent of Hamilton's first monster) into a hated symbol of federalism, of power consolidated into the hands of the privileged few, and of economic disparities and social inequities.[88] Most of all, Jackson's rhetoric stirred deeply embedded fears of a distempered demos exercising political power. Thus, Jackson himself became a symbol to elites of "a crude, unlettered demagogue who manipulated the people that he might mislead and even despoil them."[89] Whigs, believing their hand was forced by the democratic turn in national politics, resorted cynically to blatant demagoguery themselves in the "log-cabin" presidential campaign of 1840, where "even the godlike Daniel Webster," notes Barnet Baskerville, reluctantly but effectively "descended to the world of men to deliver some hard-hitting, colloquial stump speeches" on behalf of his party.[90]

Curiously, this apparent decline in the quality of political rhetoric occurred in the middle of a historical period, 1820–1850, commonly considered the golden age of American oratory, when the eloquence of Webster, Henry Clay, and John C. Calhoun dominated the great debates in Congress over vital issues of the era. Public speaking, which became a widely appreciated art form as well as a vital means of political persuasion, was reported verbatim and analyzed in detail by elite and penny newspapers, with full texts of speeches often reprinted from press reports and even used as campaign pamphlets. Delivered in the classical style of oratory and lasting two, three, four, or more hours, sometimes even carrying over from one day to the next, such speeches could pack congressional galleries and gather huge crowds at public events around the country. Yet, despite great moments of political eloquence, the standard quality of deliberative speaking was often judged poor—that is, as characteristically diffuse, inflated, pointless, gratuitous, and irrelevant to the issue at hand. Baskerville attempts to explain why congressional oratory in the golden age could be uncommonly great, yet generally deficient by suggesting that men strove for an ideal of eloquence appropriate to a modern democracy, but because they were not properly equipped with "taste, learning, nor a sense of the appropriate," they "succeeded only in pleasing audiences with similar limitations, while making themselves ridiculous to people of discernment." Congressmen, he concludes, too often pandered to their immediate constituents instead of deliberating intelligently on the burning issues confronting the nation. Similarly, beyond the floor of Congress, stump speaking had developed into a sporting event of partisan politics in which "flights of fancy were more effective than rational argument for scoring points and winning personal advantage. . . . Speakers were performers; oratory was drama, diversion, spectacle, the manner of expression more admired than the substance."[91]

Baskerville's analysis of the democratic dark side of golden-age oratory features a different sort of contest than Kenneth Cmiel sees in the rhetorical tumult of the Jacksonian era. Instead of first and foremost a low-brow battle between partisan spellbinders, the fight was predominantly at a cultural level, he argues, over the kind of political discourse most capable of sustaining a "healthy democracy." The issue was whether the elegant taste of the gentleman orator in the neoclassical model would prevail or whether a "middling" style would emerge, combining refined and vulgar speech into a more inclusive mode of public debate. Whereas the neoclassical canons of rhetoric, which carried forward from eighteenth-century republican politics, presumed a select audience deliberating rationally, the middling style, which developed out of the more boisterous nineteenth-century democratic persuasion, merged politics with popular culture. In one regard, "course stump speaking and 'vulgar' conversational informality were part of meeting the *demos* on their own terms," Cmiel observes, but even as the democratic sentiment of the period encouraged "rough, familiar speech," it also continued to admire refined speech and began to push for more widespread education among the masses, thus eroding traditional divisions between high and low culture while fusing reason and emotion into a discourse of impassioned rationality as the preferred model of democratic eloquence. Not a development exclusive to Jacksonian Democrats, the middling style was also eventually adopted by Whig orators such as Abraham Lincoln to reason with popular audiences on their own terms, so that by the 1840s it was the accepted style of mainstream politics in America. Jackson's presidency was the turning point, in Cmiel's estimate, when in 1832 his message vetoing the Second Bank of the United States directed its blunt appeal at the public rather than respecting the aristocratic tastes or prerogatives of Congress.[92]

By conveying the sense of an empowered people (even as the citizenry were restrained by a federal regime of republican representation and disciplined by a national system of two-party politics), this new democratic style for influencing public opinion exasperated a recurring conservative fear that the gentleman-orator's ruling ethos would succumb to the vulgar demagogue's persona of political leadership.[93] In James Morone's view, the Jacksonians stimulated the democratic wish for greater representation and raised popular expectations for direct political participation while actually extending an administrative apparatus that further restricted "the voice of the common man in the affairs of the republic." The "pageantry of the common man," he argues, "simultaneously amplified and muffled the popular voice" by obscuring the ways in which the political parties defused grievances and controversial issues.[94] Thus, the overall difference in income between the rich and the rest of the country increased while industrial capitalists undermined traditional crafts and created a large class of urban wage laborers.[95] Wealth dominated both political parties even as refined political and cultural critics believed that decorum, civility, and principled conduct had been victimized by a discourse that aimed only to please the crowd. "Catering to the *demos*," in this view, had "replaced moral probity" and "was smothering the very possibility of moral rectitude in public affairs," thereby undermining the health of the polity.[96]

Indeed, this Jacksonian turn set in motion a long slide toward diminished confidence in political rhetoric and popular rule. E. L. Godgin's *Nation* complained relentlessly about the "bastard eloquence" of contemporary politicians and claimed in 1866 that there was a growing impression throughout the land "that Congressional debates are farces intended to amuse or befog the country people." Political rhetoric had been reduced to a state of verbosity, irrelevance, and display, others regularly agreed. Rank oratory, according to Frederick Hedge, smelled of "extravagance, exaggerated statement, hyperbolic imagery, overdone sentiment, counterfeit enthusiasm, superfluous verbiage, riotous invective, and all that straining after coarse effect commonly known as 'sensation.'" For the next twenty-five years, throughout an era of industrialization and urbanization, accumulation of wealth became the nation's preoccupation and the principal business of party politicians who, by Baskerville's account, engaged in the "oratory of obfuscation," deploying demagogic appeals to sectional hatred in order to divert public attention from vital issues of declining natural resources, increasing levels of crime, deepening poverty and unemployment, and rampant political corruption. While the Republican Party sustained its hold on national power by "waving the bloody shirt" of Civil War antipathies, its Democratic counterpart exhorted southerners to "vote as you shot."[97]

This negative trajectory in nineteenth-century democratic America from deliberative rhetoric to partisan demagoguery culminated, at least from one perspective, in yet a further distancing of citizens from political power. As progressive politics challenged the hegemony of business and industrial interests, a new style of stump speaking, exemplified by Teddy Roosevelt and referred to generically as spellbinding, epitomized mainstream turn-of-the-century political communication. Compared to neoclassical orators, spellbinders gave short, colloquial, typically extemporaneous presentations laced with slang that flattered and interacted with audience members who might interject comments or heckle the speaker at one point or another. Roosevelt exhorted such audiences into heightened states of emotion with striking turns of phrase rather than just reasoning with them in the mode of public debate. Spellbinding was a casual style for communicating with the masses instead of deliberating and deciding on issues, a style that Cmiel thinks "dulled critical faculties instead of exercising them." It, like the simultaneously emerging preference for professional jargon and technical expertise and the soon-to-follow partiality for the plain style of letting the facts speak for themselves, was an antipolitical theory of discourse that worked to "submerge civic contention" and to sap any remaining will for spirited public debate. Following this trajectory, U.S. politics at the beginning of the twentieth century was poised, under the direction of experts and technocrats, to emulate advertising, propaganda, and mass persuasion more than participatory democracy.[98]

As Michael Sproule observes, mass-mediated forms of political persuasion had largely replaced more direct modes of influence by the turn of the century. The oratorical model of rhetorical deliberation and strategic argumentation had given way to a new curriculum of informative composition in which the ideal of public communication was represented as the "technical transfer of information." Consistent with a modern faith in objective rationality, technical expertise, and the scientific ethos, propaganda critics such as Walter Lippmann warned that urbanized mass public opinion was susceptible to symbolic manipulation, stereotypical thinking, manufactured consent, and other mental weaknesses. The solution, it seemed to many, was for scientific elites to manage the public in order to protect it from its own infirmities, supplanting the problem of participatory politics with a progressive commitment to top-down administration and social control. In the spirit of elitist, expert democracy and "driven by a vision of an irrational citizenry helpless before clever propaganda," paternalistic critics such as Lippmann distrusted the people to the point of doubting that even better education or more information could salvage a democratic public. Less-pessimistic straight thinkers and scientific semanticists argued that educating the people in logical skills and the rational use of words would help to protect the public from itself. "Theirs was an education in Thinking 101," Sproule concludes, "rather than a project to alert members of an already competent public." Even this minimalist gesture to public participation in democratic politics gave way later in the century, under the pressure of hot and cold war, to government-sponsored programs of "engineered consent" and propaganda *for* democracy aimed at saving the republic from its internal and external enemies.[99] Thus, the myth of democratic distemper sustained liberalism's containment of participatory politics not only throughout a history of republican fear but also up to the moment of post–cold war trauma.

From a different perspective, however, the nation's experience with democratic persuasion is suggestive of the public's potential for spirited and responsible self-rule. Bruce Ackerman argues, in fact, that America's uniquely "dualist democracy" constitutes the people as the ultimate source even of their own political rights, i.e., that the Constitution puts democracy first in the most basic of ways by not entrenching even the Bill of Rights beyond the reach of the public to amend it. Thus, transformation and reform through sustained popular struggle are built into the political system and have culminated in significant achievements such as repudiating slavery. Despite the risk of demagogy, a traditional discourse of dissent and struggle has prevailed over radical and revolutionary voices. The public has won a degree of equality and sustained a history of constructive reform through "energetic debate, popular decision, and constitutional creativity."[100]

A look back at the protest rhetoric of popular reformers in the final decades of the nineteenth century, for instance, underscores the prudence of a people prodded by strong emotions and the stability of a political culture anguishing over democratic initiatives. The rhetoric of this troubled period was neither devoid of reason nor lacking in vision or constructive influence. Moreover, its demagogic excesses proved relatively harmless and unpersuasive in their own time, as well as over the long haul. Even under the acute duress of economic displacement, industrial abuses, and political corruption, widespread popular participation in civic affairs neither culminated in mythic chaos nor "degenerated," according to the republican nightmare, into vulgar democracy. Yet, the popular protests of late-nineteenth-century Americans were decidedly democratic in spirit and style. Their rhetoric of dissent included a variety of causes from women's rights, especially suffrage, to unionization of urban workers and financial relief for severely distressed farmers. Their politics ranged, as Robert Gunderson has remarked, from Daniel DeLeon's Marxist socialism through Eugene Debs's democratic socialism,

Ralph Bellamy's utopianism, Henry George's single-tax program, various schemes for work relief and monetary reform, and a third-party initiative from the People's Party. Through speeches, letters, pamphlets, petitions, cartoons, marches, songs, and novels, they protested the exploitation of wage laborers; the crush of agrarian indebtedness; the unregulated power of trusts and railroad monopolies; the legal, political, and social diminishment of women; and the chronic apathy of the Republican and Democratic Parties. As a whole, in Gunderson's words, this outbreak of popular agitation was "devoted to political democracy" and "opposed [to] political corruption because it subverted the democratic process."[101]

Moreover, the populist persuasion, as Michael Kazin calls it, constituted a language of populism that conceived of ordinary people as a "noble assemblage" opposed by self-serving and undemocratic elites. Throughout U.S. history, with deep roots in the nineteenth century that extend into contemporary times, populist speakers on the left and the right have deployed this language to voice "a profound outrage with elites who ignored, corrupted, and/or betrayed the core ideal of American democracy: rule by the common people." Their protest rhetoric has been impassioned, optimistic, and idealistic but short of revolutionary intent or effect in its reliance on "traditional kinds of expressions, tropes, themes, and images to convince large numbers of Americans to join their side or to endorse their views on particular issues." This traditional discourse has enabled them to protest deep inequities robustly without calling into question the basic political system itself. Populism migrated in the middle of the twentieth century away from liberal causes and toward the political right of ardent anticommunism, tax revolt, white opposition to immigration and a backlash against black activism, and the moral majoritarianism of resurgent religious fundamentalism only when leftists and liberals lost their faith in ordinary citizens and stopped talking to the demos in a populist dialect.[102]

To be sure, the democratic style of protest politics has always been marked by passionate but conservative "moral suasion." As a rhetoric of dissent, it is neither detached nor objective in its sense of urgency, expressions of exasperation, faith in humanity, or commitment to democratic ideals.[103] Agrarian "calamity howlers," such as "Pitchfork" Ben Tillman of South Carolina, "Sockless" Jerry Simpson of Kansas, and Harrison "Stump" Ashby of Texas, were notably animated, provocative, and colorful in their oratorical endeavors to "set aflame the tinderbox of discontent" and to redress the injustices of rural poverty.[104] These prophets of gloom and distress vigorously denounced moneylenders and railroad barons in "homely, pungent, collo-quial speech which came straight from the cow barns and grist mills of rural America." Their language was occasionally profane, laced with ribald humor, frequently violent, and deeply religious. "Bloody Bridles" Davis H. Waite, one of the most vituperative orators of the populist crusade, was branded a dan-gerous anarchist by establishment newspapers and party politicians (even while he served as governor of Colorado) because of his public profanity, they claimed, but primarily because they feared his attacks on political corruption and his ideas for economic reform. Public oratory was the mark of agrarian protest during the decade of the nineties, among rural men and women alike and at local, regional, and national levels. This oratory came not just from prominent speakers, such as "Harpy" Mary E. Lease, a Kansas lawyer and mother of four who agitated tirelessly throughout the West and South, but also from farming husbands and wives regularly engaged in local speech making throughout rural America. Local farm organizations typically elected as one of their officers a "lecturer" to speak and distribute pertinent materials to other speakers. Study groups were formed as well to supply an army of speakers with sufficient materials on key points of protest.[105]

Like their agrarian counterparts, flamboyant orators such as Carl Browne in "silver-dollar-buttoned, buck-skinned, sombreroed attire" spurred on Jacob Coxey's ragtag army of unemployed industrial workingmen by sermonizing against poverty and injustice while castigating "argus-eyed hell-hounds of the subsidized press" and "hydra-headed" public officials who had tried "to arrest the triumphant progress of the Commonweal of Christ" in its march on Washington, D.C.[106] The spellbinding oratory of labor agitator and three-term mayor of Scranton, Pennsylvania, Terence Powderly, was blunt and emotional in its commitment to the Jeffersonian ideals of freedom and equality and its concern for the welfare of exploited workers.[107] Similarly, women suf-fragists, from the severe Susan B. Anthony to the ever-tactful Lucy Stone, who made determined appeals to the revered value of liberty, were often dis-missed as "noisy" and "turbulent" advocates of sexual anarchy and other radi-cal reforms against nature.[108]

The emotional intensity and urgency of these egalitarian protests for so-cial justice, so strongly resisted by entrenched political elites, seldom lacked a supporting rationale solidly grounded in the nation's political ideals and icons. Indeed, innovative appropriations of traditional conceptions and styles of political reasoning were abundant. Suffragists, as Frances McCurdy has observed, routinely invoked the authority of the Constitution and Declaration of Independence on the question of equal rights; quoted throughout their speeches the words of George Washington, Benjamin Franklin, Thomas Paine, Samuel Adams, Thomas Jefferson, and James Madison; and argued the injustice of women being taxed without representation while "denied the ballot along with criminals, idiots, and the insane."[109] Likewise, "in the course of human events," the content and cadence of the Farmers' Declaration of Independence expressed the "self-evident truths" of the Granger movement's protest against the sins of the railroads and the failure of Congress to redress the "tyranny of monopoly," proclaiming farmers free and independent of past political connections and pledging to each other their lives, fortunes, and sacred honor.[110] Farmers and industrial laborers alike continued to work with and within the two major parties as much as possible, even through third-party candidates for local and national office jointly endorsed by Democrats or Republicans. At rallies, picnics, and debates, they embraced the traditional values of individualism, honesty, thrift, hard work, reason, patriotism, and peaceful reform in the idiom of Christian brotherhood and equality. Populist orators intertwined logical refutation of monopolist practices with emotional appeals for fair prices, relying on the evidence of statistics and the testimony of authorities to support their case. Similarly, suffragists attempted to educate the public and political leaders by means of statistical and logical justification through letters, pamphlets, and speeches that associated their cause with natural rights, religion, temperance, purity, and peace. Agrarian protesters, believing in popular control of local institutions and expecting the federal government to act only as an honest umpire among contending interests, remained opposed to the notion of a welfare state administered by centralized authority. Even Coxey's ragtag army of unemployed workers sought to maintain good discipline and reputable conduct on their march to Washington in order to refute charges that they were tramps prone to violence.

Overall, the democratic uprising not only operated reasonably within the broad framework of political culture but also was constrained by widely endorsed proscriptions against systematic violence and economic revolution. Even while resisting the injustices of the establishment, as Gunderson concludes, determined political reformers believed they could achieve their ends through persuasion. "They had faith in education and in the basic goodness of mankind and in the human capacity to learn. They had a romantic notion that even powerful institutions might be changed by their agitation."[111] Afflicted masses ignored or abandoned would-be leaders who did not share this faith. When violent language and intolerance of disagreement became the standard of extremists such as anarchist Johann Most and Marxist Daniel DeLeon, they failed to mobilize a reliable following.[112] Moreover, the same laborers who were taken with Terence Powderly's eloquent expressions of concern for exploited masses ignored his radical economic proposals to abolish the wage system, replace capitalism with workers' cooperatives, and discard the concept of land as private property. Populist reformers were at once nostalgic for an idyllic agrarian way of life and progressive in their quest for legislative and regulatory relief. Even though the public at large remained skeptical of the specific proposals advanced by such avid reformers, the dissent was sufficiently compelling to make it increasingly difficult for political realists to ignore the economic plight of farmers and wage earners and the civil injustices suffered by women. "Under construction here," observes Kazin, "was a moral community of self-governing citizens, not a conflict of economic classes." Even the good Marxist and president of the American Federation of Labor, Samuel Gompers, altered his mode of persuasion by the mid-1890s from radical expressions of class consciousness to old-fashioned appeals to Americanism and democracy.[113]

In addition to the intensity of late-nineteenth-century popular protests against economic and political inequities, the desire to achieve a more democratic public was also evidenced in the early-twentieth-century innovations of urban progressives who were working to establish local citizen forums for deliberating pressing civic issues. Tom Johnson, mayor of Cleveland, Ohio, took a page from populist history to establish periodic tent meetings for public debate of important political problems. Under the roof of these egalitarian tents, citizen audiences listened to politicians express their views, sometimes heckled them, and then engaged in give-and-take discussion during question-and-answer sessions. Johnson encouraged open argumentation and did not fear the expression of radical views, even allowing Emma Goldman to speak in the city's public square. Similarly, the People's Forum, which was initiated by the People's Institute of New York in 1897, began to focus regularly scheduled lectures and discussions on current public and legislative questions, resulting in resolutions sent to city council members. In this setting, an audience of mostly working-class immigrants listened to and interacted with elected officials, public intellectuals, and political activists, holding speakers accountable, through lively question-and-answer sessions and a certain amount of heckling, to advancing cogent and persuasive arguments on issues ranging from tenement housing to U.S. imperialism. The forum movement spread throughout New York City, then to the Ford Hall Forum in Boston, and eventually to the country at large until by 1916 there were about one hundred active forums, most clustered in the northeastern region and others in western and southern states. The Cooperative Forum Bureau became its national clearinghouse for recruiting speakers chosen by the leaders of local forums. Yet, as Kevin Mattson points out, the format of these forums, with emphasis placed on asking questions of political elites, fell short of giving control of the deliberative process directly to the people.[114]

A more citizen-controlled, social-centers movement began in 1907 in Rochester, New York, and spread to Ohio, Indiana, Minnesota, Oklahoma, and throughout the Southwest until there were 101 cities involved by 1912. It developed nationally into a robust expression of "true democracy" before it was eventually transformed in 1917 by federal authorities into an instrument of war propaganda. This movement, which Mattson deems "the most important attempt to create a democratic public during the Progressive Era," experimented with formats that actively involved everyday citizens in political deliberations. Common citizens, not experts or professionals, met in public schools during the evening hours to decide what they would debate, who would do the debating, how to organize forums, and what political actions to undertake based on their deliberations. Social centers were founded by a wide range of local groups, from nativists on the right to suffragists in the liberal middle and socialists on the left, all finding common ground in lively democratic forums where controversy was indulged rather than discouraged. Debates covered local and national issues such as housing conditions, city parks, public libraries, school systems, public transportation, municipal utilities, direct primaries, women's suffrage, labor unions, race relations, immigration, and the Philippines. Speakers on all sides of such issues were invited to participate, and citizenship was transformed from a habit of conformity into an act of critical participation in matters implicating the community, society, and nation. Rather than mobocracy, social-center democrats promoted widespread and lively citizen deliberation through which elected representatives could become increasingly accountable to the publicly pondered and vigorously debated opinions of their constituents.[115]

Before they could reach full potential, the citizen forums of the social-centers movement were co-opted by the state for purposes of war propaganda and thereafter subjected to a regime of public opinion management through mass communication. Yet, in the course of their first ten years, these popular forums demonstrated the validity of the impetus for self-rule that defines

American political culture no less than liberalism's continuing determination to contain this recurring impulse under the fearful sign of democratic distemper. Despite the trend toward expert democracy and corresponding representations of an ignorant and irrational public by political pundits and liberal intellectuals alike, as chronicled by Michael Schudson, an emphasis on mobilization and national unity through two world wars, a regimen of communist containment and perpetual red scares, the emergence of mass society and consumer culture, and a host of other inducements to political conformity and public passivity, the nation's democratic imagination, although weakened, proved ultimately irrepressible throughout the remainder of the twentieth century.[116] Even as the masses increasingly became privatized consumers devoid of political interest or initiative, citizens "continued to organize themselves within their local communities," Mattson observes, "often setting up forums to educate themselves about current political problems." The "renaissance of citizen activism" that became the civil rights movement, for instance, emerged from a democratic public fostered within black churches opposed to racial segregation.[117]

This practical expression of what Jeffrey Isaac refers to as "localist democracy" continued to take many forms short of totalizing or singular ideological programs of social reform and transformation. "The Algebra Project," founded in 1982 by a former leader of the Student Nonviolent Coordinating Committee, aimed to establish a network of teachers, parents, administrators, and community leaders dedicated to assisting at-risk students lacking basic learning and math skills. This exercise in community-based participatory democracy, which focused on a specific educational goal for a targeted population, spread to more than one hundred schools in the United States. Additional examples of localist initiatives extending beyond narrow geographical or political boundaries include community-based organizations through which citizens have acted together to address problems of crime, urban decay, or poor housing; to establish shelters for battered women and rape victims; to improve local schools through parent-teacher associations; and to form broad-based and wide-reaching networks of ordinary citizens mutually concerned with a variety of environmental issues. These constitute, in Isaac's view, oases of meaningful participation in the desert of liberal democratic mass politics—flickering beacons of hope under the deepening shadow of political alienation, environmental crisis, and economic challenge that marks a dark time for liberal democracy even after its celebrated victory over Soviet communism.[118]

Alienating Democratic Identity

Here, in the heart of darkness, is where we presently find the consequence of republican fear of the demos and the immediate challenge facing a faltering regime of liberal democracy. In Isaac's words, "Both the promise and the fragility of democratic politics today are obscured by a perspective that seeks to fit the developments since 1989 neatly into a narrative about the ideological triumph of liberal democracy." This, he believes, is a narrative that needs to be challenged "in the name of a robust and yet chastened conception of democratic praxis that may contribute to the reinvigoration of liberal democracy." Simply put, liberal democracy is in decline, proving itself "increasingly ineffective and decreasingly legitimate in the eyes of . . . citizens." Liberal democracy cannot respond effectively to the socioeconomic crises jeopardizing the lives of ordinary people largely because its political institutions do not provide for public participation. Without some way of democratizing liberalism, the prognosis for politics in the near future is bleak, ranging from "a descent into increasingly fractious and violent forms of exclusion and conflict" to, at best, "a persistent and noxious immobilism characterized by insecurity, meanness, and a deterioration of anything remotely resembling a genuinely democratic political culture or civic equality." Liberal representative democracy is at risk of squandering its remarkable achievement of civil liberty and governmental accountability within a stable political system by succumbing to its tendency toward bureaucratization, rigidity, and elitism. Without "channels of healthy civic participation" it alienates the people from the republic and leads to antiliberal sentiments, reduced faith in government, bad policy, and administrative gridlock.[119] Noting that opinion polls repeatedly demonstrate the presence of "deep-rooted political alienation" among the citizenry, Mattson warns that the public has been reduced to "a disengaged and passive television audience jaded by images and sound bites" that sell politics like any other commodity and supplant active deliberation with the meaningless substitute of shopping for candidates.[120]

The kind of participatory politics Isaac envisions as a necessary adjustment to current realities—that is, the dual reality of liberal democracy both as the prevailing politics of our time and as a political formation in decline after the fall of communism—celebrates, along with Hannah Arendt, "the average citizen's ability to think, deliberate, and act." He, like Arendt, does not think in terms of mass democracy, for the mass public is not an active democratic public, but instead in terms of self-selecting citizens who address political issues and act in concert with other citizens, using their rhetorical skills in localist initiatives to pluralize political space and decentralize political authority in ways that supplement and complement existing structures of representative government. Moreover, he resists what he calls the "rationalistic fallacy" of progressives who divorce reason from power in their belief that they can accurately depict the world and that subscribing to the truth will set us all free. Like any ideology or totalizing vision, he argues, this way of thinking is not only antidemocratic but also a grandiose substitution of oversimplified conceptions for a "healthy sense of moderation" in human affairs. Following Arendt, Isaac's key criteria for political discourse, therefore, are that it respect "equality, participation, plurality, reflexivity" in creating "open, revisable, contestable political associations and communities."[121] This is the very attitude of humility endorsed by Kenneth Burke in his comic corrective and rhetoric of identification, an attitude of addressing the Other realistically rather than in caricature.

A key to overcoming the alienation of caricature and achieving a more robust democratic culture, as we have seen, is in recognizing the mythic function of Madison's pessimistic image of a distempered demos. The mythos of this recurring image constitutes the people as an unthinking mob whose emotions are preyed upon by demagogues and who lack sufficient virtue to consider the good of the community, and it instantiates Madison's republican remedy of a privileged governing elite that anguishes over episodic outbreaks of popular politics and declining standards of public discourse. This tradition of a fearful, elitist discourse of democratic distemper aims to tame the popular passions aroused by the rhetorical republic in order to preserve the integrity of representative liberal democracy against the threat of an unenlightened and unreflective public exercising direct authority, or at least being appealed to directly by a demagogic president over the heads of Congress in an age of mass communication. When policy serves rhetoric instead of reason, according to this mythic construction, it infects the majority with a tyrannizing passion to trample the rights of the minority elite. This debilitating caricature of the madding mob in an ungovernable rhetorical republic persists as a bizarre assemblage of self-destructive forces undermining the very prospects of liberal democracy in the present era.

Whether the mythos of the demented demos is rehearsed in the scholarly works of political theorists and philosophers who decry the poor state of public deliberation as they call for a reasonable and rational democratic practice, or takes the form of popular culture on daily television talk shows and news programs that repeatedly dramatize in so many different ways the standard story of an ignorant, distracted, and fickle public, such ritualized performances sustain a fiction of the people that discourages serious experimentation with participatory politics, for who would want their fate determined by rogues and fools?[122] The difficulty is not in discerning the main implication of this way of thinking, which is that engaging the people directly is to risk political dysfunction and social disorder, and that, accordingly, the domestic Other has to be controlled—transformed and embodied symbolically as a governing elite—rather than addressed and asked to decide on matters of public policy, no less than the foreign Other has to be disciplined by the financial, moral, and military superiority of the United States in its capacity as the only remaining superpower and sole essential nation. "Realistically," that is, Americans must remain as frightened of the world at large as they are accustomed to fearing the unruly domestic multitude.

That much is clear so long as the myth remains reified in U.S. political culture. The difficulty of seeing this "reality" as a reified myth, and in general the problem of discerning the myths we live by, is compounded by the distinction we routinely make between history and fiction. The stories we tell about ourselves from within a culture are taken as historical fact; the stories we observe at a distance in exotic cultures and report as outsiders are understood as figurative and fictional musings about the mysteries of "life, death, divinity, and existence."[123] This latter group consists of "crucial 'framing stories' that are *treated* as 'true' by the people who tell them" in order to "provide justification for a social structure" through appeals to "a great hero [who] can conquer evil." Such myths occur "outside of normal historical time" and "outside of the normal world" while relying heavily on archetypal language.[124] Primary myths, interpreted literally and internalized as ideology, remain invisible to us even as they determine our own worldview, our ethics, and our sense of the rational. For how can children of the Enlightenment recognize themselves as akin to "Odysseus, sacker of cities, the sceptre in his hand, and by his side flashing-eyed Athene, in the likeness of a herald" as they, too, rise to speak to the multitude and conquer the barbarian?[125]

What reveals to us our own ironic history of mythically invoking the god of Reason to dispel the curse of mass hysteria? The answer to this question is that our myth is recognizable in the form of a condensed metaphor that associates the public with vehicles of disease and that the story it tells is the arbitrary origin and now conventional narrative of an alienating and debilitating fear of participatory politics. The point is not that we can hope to escape the world of metaphor and myth but that we must become alert to its presence in our everyday reality to the extent that pernicious appropriations of a particular mythic construction can be contested in order to yield more viable visions of democratic practice. In this regard, the peculiarly American mythos of the distempered demos is suspect in its origins because it rests on Madison's singular quest for order and his corresponding antipathy for democracy, as reflected in his unflattering representation of Athenian direct democracy in order to legitimize his "republican" alternative of indirect, representative governance by political elites who substitute for and assume the identity of "the people." Athenian democracy was neither the unstable nor irrational polity Madison depicted. In fact, it endured despite its flaws for nearly two centuries of ordinary citizens empowered to judge the rhetorical arguments of competing political elites and to decide on questions of policy as well as issues of justice. Not only did Madison and his political allies fail to appreciate this achievement but they adopted Plato's trope of disease to reconstitute the American people as a mob in need of a rational cure for its supposedly volatile rhetorical behavior. Although this mythic construction prevailed and has persisted into the present, it did not go uncontested by Anti-Federalists in its time of origin or by democratic voices throughout two centuries of protest, reform, and experiments in self-rule. This national legacy of resistance is rich enough at least to demonstrate the cultural validity of envisioning a more robust democratic ethic for an ailing liberal republic that otherwise will continue to project a democratic identity that alienates the people by failing to provide adequately for their participation in political deliberations and decision making.

Alienating the people from their democratic identity is a suspect outcome of a flawed rhetorical practice. It caricatures the complexity of the public by reducing the demos to the threatening image of an irrational mass or disorderly mob infected with the germs of political chaos—a disease that must be contained by rational elites to ensure the safety of the republic from internal and external dangers. Such a rhetoric inhibits vigorous political exchange within and between diverse polities and transforms the Other into an alien, even evil, enemy. To the extent that the people themselves are supposedly vulnerable to unenlightened influences, the danger of exposing them to an alien orientation is increased. Similarly, the degree to which democratic practice is deemed risky in domestic spheres corresponds to the level of fear in engaging foreign Others, except to control them. The problem here is in the kind of rhetoric practiced, not in the choice of rhetoric over reason. The antidemocratic mythos of Madisonian rhetoric calls upon the authority of Reason beyond the grasp of a distempered demos, which amounts to a rhetoric of war rather than a commitment to lively give-and-take. The better alternative is a democratic rhetoric of identification that deploys reason to build bridges between otherwise warring communities both at home and abroad. The possibility of achieving a more democratically robust rhetorical culture, although implicit to the historic struggle of liberal democracy for political hegemony, is conditioned largely by our cognizance of the ways in which democracy has been fashioned into such a potent and paralyzing symbol of fear, which, as we will see, extends both to America's quest for a democratic peace and its open-ended war on terror.

3
Democratic Peace

The United States entered the twenty-first century on an impossible mission of achieving perpetual peace through global democratization—a quixotic quest sanctioned by politicians and scholars alike. Indeed, the idea of a democratic peace quickly became a truism of the post–cold war era. Derived from a spate of scholarship in international relations, the alleged "fact" that democracies do not fight one another easily morphed into a commonplace of presidential rhetoric and a centerpiece of U.S. security policy. The irony of locating democracy at the intersection of war and peace, however, was that it rehearsed an old attitude of insecurity, an exaggerated fear of domestic as well as foreign Others.

The rhetoric of democratic expansion, aimed at dispelling international anarchy and taming the forces of chaos, transposed rather than supplanted the cold war discourse of containment. "Containment was the name of the privileged American narrative during the cold war," Alan Nadel notes. It was a story that "derived its logic from the rigid major premise that the world was divided into two monolithic camps, one dedicated to promoting the inextricable combination of capitalism, democracy, and (Judeo-Christian) religion, and one seeking to destroy that ideological amalgamation by any means." It named both a "foreign and domestic policy" as well as "the rhetorical strategy that functioned to foreclose dissent, preempt dialogue, and preclude contradiction."[1] As before, protective boundaries after the cold war were drawn and redrawn in the name of freedom and consistent with the aims and privileges of elites to keep virulent outside sources of ideological contamination from infecting and inflaming latent inside tendencies toward distempered democratic egalitarianism. Because the delicate ecology of liberal democracy inside the polity must be maintained by reducing its exposure to alien influences, according to this reconstituted logic, the domain of liberal democracy must be pushed forward in order to drive ideological foes into an ever-narrowing perimeter. Just as liberalism would contain democracy, democratization would expand the size of the liberal container to promote a pristine and peaceful community of nation-states sharing a single regime type—or so the theory of a democratic peace nervously prescribes.

The continuity of republican fear achieved in the transition from containing communism to expanding democracy is remarkable but largely obscured by a discourse that conflates science with politics or, more specifically, that advances an appeal to the universal in circumstances that require an ability to cope with the diversity of particulars. Thus, as the theory of democratic peace moves toward universal truth, it moves away from democratic practice and promotes war in the name of peace, as we shall see by scrutinizing the scholarship and the politics of the theory.

Idealizing Universal Peace

Bruce Russett, author of *Grasping the Democratic Peace: Principles for a Post–Cold War World*, made the standard case in 1993 for the theory that democracies do not fight each other. This norm of international relations, he argues, developed toward the end of the nineteenth century, became harder to ignore in the 1970s when the number of democracies increased to over three dozen, and was widely recognized by the end of the 1980s, that is, by the end of the cold war. The empirical evidence for this pattern of peace among democracies is, in his words, "extremely robust, in that by various criteria of war and militarized diplomatic disputes, and various measures of democracy, the relative rarity of violent conflict between democracies still holds up."[2]

Russett's account of this empirical finding not only anticipates an inclination among theorists to advance a theorem of democratic peace but also exhibits the difficulty of such rarified thinking about a subject as complex as international relations. He acknowledges, for example, that the empirical finding does not mean democracies are necessarily peaceful in their relations with nondemocratic states or even less likely to experience civil war. Curiously, even the standard of what counts as a democracy in this research is quite relaxed, keying on criteria such as "a voting franchise for a substantial fraction of citizens, a government brought to power in contested elections, and an executive either popularly elected or responsible to an elected legislature" but not necessarily guaranteeing civil or economic liberties. The case also rests on the assumption of a democratic regime's stability, excluding the belligerence of fledgling democratic states. Moreover, Russett's discussion of marginal cases of democratic nations fighting one another reveals that a key factor is whether one nation sees the other as democratic or not, as in the case of the Spanish-American War of 1898 when U.S. decision makers and public opinion perceived Spain as tyrannical even though it was a nation that practiced universal male suffrage and had a bicameral legislature to which the executive was somewhat accountable.[3]

Russett also acknowledges that the empirical relationship of democracies remaining at peace with one another (assuming we accept that such an empirical relationship exists given the questions of definition indicated above) requires a strong theoretical account to make a compelling case for domestic regime type determining foreign relations. He rejects the notion taken up by others, for example, that democracies are inherently less war prone than nondemocracies, arguing instead that powerful norms within democracies operate as restraints on violence against other states perceived as sharing such norms of legitimate decision making. Self-governing people, by this account, do not believe other self-governing people are easily misled by self-serving elites into aggressive acts toward other states, and on those rare occasions of democracies fighting one another, usually at least one of them is politically unstable.[4]

The theory, it would seem, stands on shaky grounds, even when advanced by one of its strongest proponents. The empirical argument is subject to a questionable definition of democracy, sometimes excluding civil liberties but requiring a condition of stability. Instances of war between democracies are dismissed as a function of political instability and of perception. Democracies are prone to violence against nondemocracies and cannot feel secure until the unlikely time when all nations become stable democracies. Russett himself acknowledges that when one democracy threatens or uses force against another, its justification for war emphasizes the instability of the enemy regime; moreover, the theory of democratic peace could even have the unfortunate consequence of encouraging wars against authoritarian regimes, the great majority of which are not aggressive, for the purpose of creating a peaceful democratic world order. "A crusade for democracy," he warns without foreknowledge of the U.S. invasion of Saddam Hussein's Iraq ten years later, is a dangerous way to deal with even "the most odious dictators."[5]

Despite such concerns, questions, and conundrums, the tendency to declare a law of international peace persists, in part because the ideal of a universal theory conforms in spirit to Immanuel Kant's "definitive articles for perpetual peace among nations," the first of which is that "the civil constitution of every nation should be republican." That is, constitutions that promote peace specifically cannot be democratic, according to Kant, for "*democracy*, in the proper sense of the term, is necessarily a *despotism* . . . in which all citizens make decisions about and, if need be, against one," placing the general will in opposition to freedom. Through the principle of representation, however, citizens of a republic are able to constrain their leader sufficiently to prevent war: to wit, "the consent of the citizenry is required in order to determine whether or not there will be war [and] it is natural that they consider all its calamities before committing themselves to so risky a game." In contrast, war is "the easiest thing in the world" to declare under a "nonrepublican" constitution, where the ruler remains immune to the ill effects of war. A skeptical reader might perceive some conceptual slippage in Kant rejecting democracy on the grounds that it is a form of despotism while at the same time attributing the peaceful nature of a republic to the citizenry's wish to avoid suffering the calamities of war, but clearly Kant premised perpetual peace in 1895 on eventually achieving a community of republics, rather than democracies, that accommodate one another's commitment to freedom and justice. Moreover, "if good fortune should so dispose matters that a powerful and enlightened people should form a republic (which by its nature must be inclined to seek perpetual peace)," it would provide "a focal point" for a federation of republics ultimately to "include all nations and thus lead to perpetual peace."[6] The relative number of such republics determines the size at any given point in time of what Michael Doyle calls "a liberal zone of peace." This is a pacific union of "liberal states," by his reckoning, because the defining criteria of Kant's republic are met by the "set of rights [that] forms the foundation of liberalism," including the so-called negative rights that protect individuals from arbitrary authority by guaranteeing equality under the law, freedom of speech, and the right to hold and exchange private property.[7] Thus, Kant set in motion a vision of universal peace in which all nations would become liberal republics ensuring freedom and justice against democratic and other forms of despotism within and among nations through the constraint of representative government.

Contemporary theorists conventionally refer to Kant's universal as a democratic peace, by which they mean pacific relations by, and especially among, liberal democracies, but still this preference for a name, especially among proponents of the theory, is notably ironic given Kant's explicit condemnation of, and liberalism's continuing ascendancy over, democracy. One encounters early in R. J. Rummel's treatment of democracy and nonviolence a revealing vestige of the shifting name for Kant's universal peace based on a particular regime type. In an endnote to the introduction for Part I of *Power Kills*, Rummel observes that his early work deployed the term "libertarian" instead of "democratic" to refer to peace between "those nations that assure civil liberties and political rights" because, he continues, democracy is a "blurred" term that can stand for "dictatorship" and technically does not stand for political rights and liberties but instead for majority rule, which can threaten minority rights and liberties, the "very rights and liberties that create the conditions reducing the likelihood of collective violence." Yet, to avoid "ambiguity and confusion," he now adopts the label "democratic," which is the "settled term" among those scholars and practitioners who argue "freedom promotes peace."[8]

Not only is the ideological imperative behind this line of scholarship apparent in the desire to associate peace with freedom, rights, and liberty but also a political strategy is implied in the move to place the entire cluster under the sign of democracy on the grounds of promoting clarity. Why, we might ask, has democracy become the "settled term" among scholars as well as politicians? Again, Rummel's text yields an important clue when he asks, "How did we fall off the classical liberal path to peace [revealed in Kant's *Perpetual Peace*] and fail to find it again until recently?" The most important reason, he observes, is that intellectuals lost faith in the liberal view when capitalism fell under the scrutiny of socialism for fostering exploitation and war. But, and here is where Rummel is particularly revealing of the relationship between ideological motive and political strategy, the 1980s witnessed "a conservative resurgence of classical liberalism" exemplified by the rise of Ronald Reagan and Margaret Thatcher with "their often-expressed views on the positive role of free institutions for peace. . . . With the end of the cold war those in the social sciences and peace research communities also began to entertain what just a decade or so previously they would have considered right-wing propaganda." The "peace-making effects of democratic freedoms" could once again be acknowledged now that capitalism was no longer an object of attack and that "freedom" and "democracy" had become interchangeable terms, as evidenced in Rummel's own writing.[9] One might infer from all this that, in a manifestation of the spirit of the universal, the politics of referring to a democratic peace is an assertion of the end of ideological struggle, or what Francis Fukuyama has declared the end of history.[10]

Moreover, the science in Rummel's narrative, with which he tests this ideological insight and establishes the "fact of our time" that "democracy is a method of nonviolence," is itself a symbolic medium of universal truth. Through a series of five chapters, Rummel reviews "the empirical research supporting this fact" that democracies do not engage in war with one another, that the severity of violence between regimes decreases as they become increasingly democratic, and that the most democratic regimes are the least prone to violence of any kind, including internal violence against their own citizens. In an odd but revealing endnote, Rummel offers certain evidence of "the final acceptance of the inherent peacefulness of democracies as being obvious" in the recommendation of an anonymous reviewer against publishing this book on the grounds that it presents "nothing new." What may not be new, but makes Rummel's work notable, is the degree to which he pushes empirical findings into the purest theoretical form possible. His one ultimate truth or general principle, that democracy is a method of nonviolence, is elaborated into a set of formal propositions, referred to sequentially as "the interdemocratic peace proposition," "the democracy/dyadic violence proposition," "the democratic/foreign violence proposition," "the democracy/internal collective violence proposition," and finally the "democracy/democide proposition."[11] Along the way, he filters out empirical impurities as well as theoretical reservations and limitations, dismissing persistent issues about statistical significance, for example, by rejecting David Spiro's contrary findings as "deeply flawed" and based on a "statistical approach [that] is problematical."[12] Similarly, he sets aside what he acknowledges to be "the prevailing wisdom among students of war" (i.e., that democracies are as war prone as any other regime type except in their relations with one another) by arguing that "when properly measured, democracies are less violent than nondemocracies."[13]

This propensity to establish absolutes and to frame formal principles carries into the second part of Rummel's book, where he develops "first-level," "second-level," and "third-level" explanations of why democracies are nonviolent by placing types of regimes on a continuum from "cross-pressured" to unchecked power, that is, from libertarian-democratic "exchange societies" through authoritarian-monarchial "authoritative societies" to totalitarian-communist "coercive societies." This progression takes him to the ultimate and unattenuated truth that "power kills" whereas "freedom promotes non-violence." The greater the power, the more the killing. In a free society or nation, what Rummel calls an exchange society, power is checked by cross pressures, which comprise "a field of continuous *nonviolent* conflict" among "constantly interacting individuals and groups, all pursuing their own interests" as naturally as the pacific operation of "the free market of goods and services." Without such checks and balances, human nature makes democratic people "prone" to murder, genocide, and war. "*Just reforming regimes in the direction of greater civil rights and political liberties,*" Rummel stresses, "*will promote less violence.*" Accordingly, he concludes, "democracy is a method of nonviolence because democratic freedoms create a spontaneous society whose culture promotes negotiation and compromise; and whose social, economic, political, and cultural diversity and cross-cutting bonds inhibit violence. . . . *Power kills; absolute Power kills absolutely.*"[14]

By extension, the spirit of this universal truth brings Rummel to the ultimate political conviction that "we" should advance the domain of freedom, by which he means the spread of liberal democracy, preferably by plebiscite, referendum, or democratic election instead of by force, toward the end of achieving a "wholly democratic world."[15] Rummel's "we," I should add, places the United States in the subject position of a disinterested party assuming the role of Kant's powerful and enlightened republic that would become the focal point of an expanding federation of peace. Moreover, in its purest form, Rummel's prescription for peace is liberal, even libertarian, not democratic. Like Kant, he fears the tyranny of democracy, and like other democratic peace advocates, he appropriates the symbol of democracy to imply the end of ideological struggle and to advance a liberal zone of perpetual peace. His republic, like Madison's amended constitution, would contain the "democratical" impulse within a liberal system of checks and balances, guaranteed rights, rule by elected elites, and the like.[16]

Rummel is not alone among proponents of a "democratic" peace in his quest for a perfect container of tyranny—including the tyranny of democracy itself. The teleological tug of universal truth inspires such work as the rule rather than the exception to standard practice. For example, Russett insists that "it is impossible to identify unambiguously *any* wars between democratic states in the period since 1815," and Jack S. Levy concludes that "the absence of war between democracies comes as close as anything we have to an empirical law in international relations."[17] But nowhere is the claim advanced more absolutely and with such sweeping scope as in Spencer Weart's appropriately titled book *Never at War*. As a rule of history, he concludes, *"well-established democracies have never made war on one another."* Weart's rule of history is no less universal and timeless in its certainty than the problem it is intended to address and the question it purports to answer. "In the long run," he observes, "we may not survive unless we avoid all wars—not just among some states, but among all of them; not just for the next couple of decades, but for all time." Weart then asks, "What international order can achieve so much?" His answer, of course, is that democratic republics never have and never will fight one another; thus, if we can "achieve universal democracy," then we will "at the same time attain universal peace."[18]

The trick, Weart argues, is to achieve "genuine democracy" within and among all nation-states without succumbing to the temptation, so difficult especially for the United States, of "crusading for democracy." By genuine democracy he means stable republics in which at least two-thirds of adult males possess voting rights, enjoy political freedom, and live under the rule of law in a regime that has tolerated dissent for at least three years. By comparison, an oligarchic republic restricts such political rights to a third or less of adult males and is ruled by an entrenched elite. Well-established oligarchic republics, he argues, seldom fight one another, although they do engage actively in war against other regime types, including democracies, and suppression of a significant body of their domestic population who constitute an internal enemy. It is this latter characteristic, the ruling elite's suppression of its own common people, that puts oligarchies at odds with authentic, liberal democratic republics—even to the point of motivating open warfare. Thus, universal peace requires ultimately the global reign of liberal democracy. While pushing democracy toward this ideal, Weart cautions that "we" (that universal "we" again) must employ "more short-term methods of avoiding war, not excluding alliances with despots and the other tools of realpolitik," but always remembering that "peaceful negotiation is dependably practiced only among such people" as those who share an authentic republican culture. Other recommended interim measures, short of military crusading for freedom and democracy, include "nonviolent pressure, negotiation, and mutual concessions" such as "economic sanctions to push other nations to change" and fostering local efforts in nondemocratic countries to develop "a free civil society." Although necessary to avoid the threat of catastrophic war, achieving democratization through "small, cautious steps" is tricky, frustrating, and even dangerous work. Toward that end, "we" must cultivate a "tolerant politics . . . as part of the liberation struggle itself." Still, the key to republican war and peace is political culture, and the political culture of true republics mandates peaceful interchange only among people like "us" rather than "them," thus turning the demonizing of rivals into a default condition and making a nonviolent transformation into a state of universal peace difficult to imagine.[19]

In sum, framed as a universal by Rummel, Russett, Weart, and other "democratic peace" theorists, the pursuit of perpetual peace among liberal democratic republics appears to be as suspicious of democracy, per se, as it is of any authoritarian, totalitarian, or even oligarchic regime that compromises or otherwise threatens individual rights and political freedom. Moreover, the very form and spirit of the universal entails a second troublesome tendency toward perfection—the quest for a perfect peace—that becomes itself a potential motive for war. Given such an ironic and unsettling possibility, one might wish to question the degree of certainty conveyed in the works of these democratic peace proponents. Are their findings sufficiently unequivocal and absolute to establish a law of international relations, especially a law that could doom humanity to interminable war?

Complicating the Liberal Ideal

Apparently not. Two recent books challenge, respectively, the certainty of a liberal zone of peace and the wisdom of expanding any such zone. I do not mean to suggest here that these are the first two works to question the findings of democratic peace proponents. In addition to Spiro's previously mentioned challenge on the grounds of statistical significance, for example, Christopher Layne has argued that the theory has little explanatory power compared to realism "as a predictor of international outcomes."[20] Joanne Gowa's *Ballots and Bullets* and Alexander Kozhemiakin's *Expanding the Zone of Peace?* provide further reminders that such issues are not yet resolved so conclusively as Rummel and Weart indicate.[21]

Gowa's study conceptually and empirically challenges many of the theoretical underpinnings of a democratic peace, including the pacific role of democratic norms, and she argues that realistic considerations of interests and alliances account for outcomes that "do not conform to the predictions of the democratic-peace hypothesis." Most interesting, however, she disaggregates the data commonly used by democratic peace proponents to discover for the years 1816–1980 that "war and other militarized disputes between democratic states are relatively rare only during the Cold War." In periods prior to the cold war, pairs of democratic states are as likely as any other pairs to fight one another. Accordingly, she concludes, "the most unambiguous and important message" of her book "is that the democratic peace is a Cold War phenomenon . . . limited in time to the years between 1946 and 1980" (which is the period of a bipolarized world of nuclear-armed, ideological antagonists), that it "does not exist in the pre-1914 world," and that it "cannot be extrapolated to the post–Cold War era." Thus, she advances a serious challenge to the purity of a democratic peace, which reduces its status from that of an established law (or even probability) to an unconfirmed hypothesis, and reinforces the complicating suggestion of a competing explanation. Moreover, Gowa raises the stakes of the debate higher by warning against continuing to base U.S. foreign policy on the flimsy notion that security can be purchased by propagating democracy. Such a strategy of enlargement is "potentially explosive," she argues, at a time when the United States would be better advised to build bridges to existing regimes rather than to construct new democracies.[22]

Similarly, Kozhemiakin complicates matters on the issue of democratization, which he argues can readily decrease international security and increase international conflicts. In that illiberal, liminal moment when democratic institutions and procedures have been adopted but not consolidated, he suggests, elections and increased executive accountability become conduits for "hawkish domestic preferences." This is a particularly problematic result that has been all but ignored by proponents of democratization at a time when so many regimes are in transition and "democratizing states are disproportionately likely to fight wars." In fact, he observes, only a "tiny minority" of third-wave democratizing states has "so far managed to consolidate successfully the nascent democratic institutions and norms" crucial to pacific relations, while the "vast majority" are either still struggling or have already reverted to authoritarianism. It is during this problematic attempt to transition toward democracy, Kozhemiakin stresses, "that international security is most likely to be threatened"; thus "democratization as such is *not* a reliable recipe for international peace." Except in those instances where a struggling nation had no prior history of initiating international conflict, all other cases of problematic transition examined by Kozhemiakin led to more belligerence under the stress of democratization. Russia, he observes, is a particular example of how the mere adoption of democratic forms such as free elections does not neutralize a cultural legacy of imperialism but instead makes government leaders more susceptible to popular hawkish appeals and nationalist pressures that work against international cooperation. Given that democratization is difficult to achieve and risky to attempt, Kozhemiakin cautions the West to proceed slowly and carefully, strengthening liberal-democratic culture where possible over the long haul while otherwise deploying a mix of traditional security strategies to cope with immediate challenges and individual circumstances.[23]

The complications of particular cases are most thoroughly revealed in *Paths to Peace,* a carefully crafted volume of essays under the general editorship of Miriam Fendius Elman, who characterizes the authors as "gatecrashers at the democratic peace party." The basic point of the book, substantiated in a wide-ranging set of qualitative case studies, is that "democratic peace proponents have overstated their case" by focusing too exclusively on regime type, which "is not the only—nor typically the most important—variable" influencing foreign policy decisions. The purpose here is not to throw out the theory entirely, but instead to recognize its limitations and to take into account many other factors and contingencies or, as Elman says, to "forswear grand theories and simple dichotomies, and instead . . . develop contingent generalizations that identify the interactions among a greater number of domestic and international variables."[24]

From the many specific limitations and particular contradictions uncovered by the different authors, some of whom are more favorably disposed toward the democratic peace hypothesis than others, Elman draws together certain common themes that indicate the types of reservation and degree of uncertainty that should supplant Rummel's and other such theorists' bent for a universal liberal truth and definitive law of international relations. She observes that various case studies suggest, for example, the large influence of material capabilities on the conduct of democratic states during periods of international crisis as well as instances in which domestic democratic politics is not always a benign force. Furthermore, contrary to the notion that regime type determines outcomes, these cases indicate that changes of leadership within a democratic regime can affect war and peace decisions and that not all democratic systems constrain leaders equally "in their capacity to wage unpopular wars." Moreover, a number of case studies reveal instances where pairs of democracies threaten each other and prepare to engage one another militarily, and other cases "suggest that democracy is not the cause of peace among democracies" and that "ideological preferences typically do not determine democracies' relations with nondemocracies."[25]

One overriding conclusion of particular importance permeates this revealing collection of diverse cases. Studies of war and peace between democracies include Christopher Layne's analysis of realism in Anglo-French relations 1830–1848, Stephen Rock's scrutiny of the role of liberal values and democratic institutions in Anglo-U.S. relations 1845–1930, John Owen's investigation of the limits to liberal peace in the Mexican-American and Spanish-American wars, and Elman's probe of Finland's status as a democracy on the wrong side of the divide in World War II. Studies of whether democracies are generally more pacific consist of Lawrence Freedman's analysis of how the democratic process affected Britain's decision to reoccupy the Falkland Islands, Sumit Ganguly's investigation of hostilities between India and Pakistan, Elman's review of Israel's 1982 invasion of Lebanon, and Arie Kacowicz's examination of two sets of militarized crises in the third world, one between Peru and Colombia and the other between Senegal and Mauritania. Studies of war and peace between nondemocratic regimes include Martin Malin's analysis of the role of autocracy in relations between Iraq and Iran 1975–1980, Kurt Dassel's inspection of the relationship of domestic instability and internal military strength to pacific adjustments of Indonesian foreign policy 1956–1971, and John C. Matthews III's investigation of the role of strong political parties in Turkish and Hungarian foreign policy during the years between two world wars. The one conclusion integrating this diversity of studies is that democratic peace proponents overemphasize universal arguments and thereby further U.S. ideological interests more than the prospects of global peace.

Elman notes that this pattern involves a strong tendency to "dismiss exceptions to the peace-proneness of democracies," even though "social science theories are rarely either universally applicable or completely invalid." It may not be as applicable, for example, in situations where "a state faces extreme external threat," may apply best to decentralized as compared to centralized democracies with leaders who "see force as a legitimate tool of foreign policy," and is more likely to hold for stable democracies than "new democracies with weak party systems and strong nationalist movements." The very simplicity of the democratic peace theory, Elman concludes, is both the heart of its appeal and its central weakness, given that "the vast complexity of war and peace decision making cannot be explained by reference to a single variable." Yet, it does apply best to great powers generally and accounts most for U.S. inclinations specifically because great powers face fewer severe security threats than small states, "their survival is rarely at stake, and they have more leeway for action"; thus they can afford to let ideology influence their conduct. More than other great powers, and presently as the sole superpower, the United States uses ideological criteria to sort friend from foe. Rock's study of past Anglo-U.S. relations, for instance, in which liberal values applied in some limited degree primarily to U.S. (not British) policy and public opinion, concludes with the larger observation that "democratic peace theory may be little more than an artifact of the peculiarly American worldview of those who have proposed it." What is the cost, one might ask, of representing a particular ideological motive as a universal truth about peace in order to reduce exposure to illiberal influences?[26]

Constraining Democratic Practice

The answer perhaps is that this expanding liberal hegemony diminishes the place of democracy too much to enhance the prospects of peace. The issue here is one of proportion, of redressing an imbalance, and is not a question of democracy displacing liberalism. That, at least, is the attitude of Alan Gilbert's response to the engaging question posed in the title of his book *Must Global Politics Constrain Democracy?*[27] Gilbert's vision of democratic internationalism conforms to "an explicit liberal democratic political theory" and thus entails a full commitment to liberal rights and values, including those "primary liberties" of "freedom of conscience, speech, association, and the vote."[28] Just as Elman credits democratic peace theorists with establishing the relevance of domestic politics to decisions at the international level, Gilbert argues that realism, even neorealism, does not necessarily "disengage international from domestic politics" even though it professes the need "to shield 'professional diplomacy' from 'popular diplomacy.'"[29] Realist Hans Morgenthau, for example, endorsed the Vietnam-era antiwar movement, a popular resistance to elite policy and rampant anticommunism, as consistent with national interests. This democratic initiative collapsed the wall between realist internationalism and domestic politics from the bottom up, a point Gilbert develops throughout a chapter focusing on realist criticisms of the Vietnam War. Typically, as in this case, the main direction of influence is "the *destructive feedback of international rivalry* on democracy at home." The prevalence of such "*antidemocratic feedback*" in the United States and elsewhere, Gilbert argues, is decisive but need not always remain so if we recognize the compatibility of democracy and realism in domestic politics and international affairs, make some immediate reforms, and undertake a "nonviolent social revolution." In short, his optimism is restricted in the same degree that democracy itself is constrained to *envisioning* peace as a function of a more robustly democratic internationalism.[30]

What does this vision of democratic internationalism entail? And how would it provide a genuinely democratic balance to the liberal hegemony? Its justification and feasibility rest on two enabling arguments. One is the claim that liberal democracy is corrupted and ultimately lost through the hubris of imperial expansion. The other is that democratic movements in one country can positively influence developments in other countries. For the first argument, Gilbert draws initially on the moral perspective of ancient Greek realism, which "aimed to avoid the hubris or pride that crazed politicians and destroyed them and their causes." Politicians who "pretend to know" are inclined, for lack of humility and moderation, to "kill others." For the second argument, Gilbert begins from Marx's analysis of transnational solidarity among oppressed classes to build a case for the "possibility" (as distinguished from any present reality) of achieving "*liberal* moral insights" through democratic movements within states that would address suffering abroad short of using violent means.[31] Thus, democratic internationalism would buffer and redress the worst tendencies and egregious harms of great power rivalries via the process of citizens organizing from below, primarily within countries, to realize the common good.

In what ways might citizens deliberate for the common good and "make contemporary oligarchy more democratic"? Conceiving of deliberation mainly as a "*conscience-sustaining regime,*" Gilbert considers a number of possibilities for reform. The idea of democratic internationalism, by itself, alerts citizens to the likelihood that their leaders will "intervene against democracy abroad," as they have often before, while deploying "fierce ideologies of anti-radicalism, racism, and sexism that stigmatize others as 'enemies.'" Expressing little faith in the deliberative potential of public reasoning and pointing to the deliberative deficit in election rituals that have been reduced to personality contests, bogus issues, and negative campaigning, Gilbert looks to civil disobedience as "an instigator of deliberative democracy" because, for example, "the democratic deliberations on which the American regime prides itself— those leading to abolition [of slavery], women's suffrage, unions, unemployment insurance and social security, civil rights, and the like—stemmed mainly from nonparliamentary protest from below, not from electoral activity." Thus, today's comparable issues might be raised through strategies of obstruction, including "temporary violations of property rights," and tax resistance. Given the fact of globalization, Gilbert points also to examples of transnational movements from below as ways of representing the common good on particular issues "such as outlawing land mines, curtailing the emission of greenhouse gases, barring the use of children as soldiers, and founding an international criminal court." Genuine democratic practice, by Gilbert's reckoning, is so thoroughly constrained by oligarchic regimes (and I would add by the antidemocratic ideology of universal peace) that "struggle from below" is the "*driving force* in democratic deliberations." Deliberation is mostly an outcome of nondeliberative pressures rather than a productive means of redressing social injustices. Yet, Gilbert remains faithful to the idea that "a society of genuinely democratic states would be more peaceful than current regimes" and maintains some cautious hope that global politics will not always so constrain democracy.[32]

The role of political communication may very well be crucial to achieving a genuinely democratic peace that remains faithful to liberal values without succumbing to republican fear of diversity. The perhaps overly cautious hope surviving Gilbert's assessment of antidemocratic feedback in contemporary global politics exists in the narrow political space of nondeliberative struggle because, at least in part, communication is reduced there to the status of diversionary and ersatz display instead of being credited with potentially constitutive force. As I have argued in chapter 1, prevailing models of deliberative democracy are insufficiently rhetorical to support robustly democratic politics that engage differences constructively and productively without becoming, as Chantel Mouffe would say, universalistic and rationalistic in the extreme.[33] Benjamin Barber, too, has traced our distrust and underestimation of the potential of strong democracy to a deficient model of political reasoning.[34] Thus, we need to attend to the ideological work of political rhetoric, probing more deeply the question of how political communication can empower democratic practice within liberal environs.

This is not a matter primarily of testing for instrumental force, identifying effective strategies of persuasion, and the like, but instead a question foremost of how to rethink political communication's constitutive role in redressing the liberal democratic imbalance. Instead of policing universals defensively, can we develop an understanding of political communication that entrusts democracy to engage differences constructively and therefore constitutes democracy as a sign of freedom's strength rather than a source of liberal republican fear? How might democracy be reconstituted within political culture as less threatening and distempered? And how might liberal values be reappropriated to support democratic practice rather than taken necessarily to require democracy's constraint? Such a model of political persuasion, in a world where division is a recurring incentive for identification and identification a constant temptation for what Kenneth Burke calls victimage, must test the limits of rhetoric before we will know the full potential of democratic peace.[35]

The current rhetorical tendency, however, is to subordinate the term "democracy" to the ideological purposes of liberalism and the promotion of private enterprise. Unless this facade of democracy can somehow be transformed into a more meaningful commitment to collective self-rule, the expectations generated by such a misleading political posture, especially following the fall of a communist empire, may ultimately exacerbate international tensions and reinforce chronic U.S. insecurity. Yet, democracy connotes disorder and chaos within American political culture more than trust in the rule of the people. We must wonder, then, whether we can overcome the rhetorical legacy of the cold war (and before) in order to constitute a more democratic (and peaceful) world order. The challenge facing us is indicated not just in the universalizing tendency of "democratic" peace theories but also in the legacy of cold war presidential rhetoric and its perpetuation by William Clinton's quest for a democratic world order.

Crusading for Democracy

The decisive moment for the fate of democracy, according to Tony Smith, was the "defeat of fascism in 1945 and the American-sponsored conversion of Germany and Japan to democracy and a much greater degree of economic liberalism." Those were the "glory days," the "moment of triumph," he argues, "of American liberal democratic internationalism," that is, the realization of tenets advanced by Franklin Roosevelt and Harry Truman that had been brought to the fore of the national agenda in this century by Woodrow Wilson. Thus, when William Clinton, like his immediate predecessors, made democratization the linchpin of his foreign policy, he perpetuated a twentieth-century tradition of linking American national security to the hegemony of one form of government. Although the classic period of the cold war focused on containing communism, even when that meant supporting noncommunist authoritarian regimes as a tactical measure, the leitmotiv of U.S. foreign policy remained constant throughout even the Vietnam debacle. This resulted in what Smith acknowledges to be "a bid for international hegemony," that is, "a form of anti-imperialist imperialism, aiming to structure other countries economically, socially, and politically so that they would presumably be part of a peaceful world order congenial to American interests" and security. "The dominant logic of American foreign policy," he continues, "was dictated by concerns for national security; and the dominant way Washington saw to assure this security in terms of the construction of a stable world order congenial to America's way of life was that democratic governments be promoted worldwide."[36]

Even the promotion of human rights abroad, as illustrated in Jimmy Carter's response to post-Vietnam malaise, remained true to cold war objectives while advancing traditional Wilsonian principles within a rhetoric of ideological conversion. Breaking with Henry Kissinger's increasingly criticized version of amoral realism, Carter censured the Soviet Union for its illtreatment of dissidents, put South Africa on notice for its apartheid policy, and distanced the United States from repressive military regimes. The soul of his foreign policy was a crusade for human rights consistent with the predilections of a born-again Christian while aimed at containing Soviet expansion and insuring national security.[37] In fact, the continuity between Carter's and his predecessors' images of U.S.-Soviet relations was sufficient to renew the quest for security in terms that reinforced a cycle of fear.

The source of Carter's rhetorical continuity with, and extension of, other cold war presidencies was the conceptual metaphor guiding his particular construction of how to achieve peace and security. Truman had promoted visions of disease, fire, and flood to evoke a sense of emergency in postwar Greece, Turkey, and Western Europe to inaugurate the containment doctrine.[38] Eisenhower in turn relied on an image of Soviet brutality blocking the road to true peace in his campaign to legitimize a perilous crusade of nuclear deterrence.[39] But Carter's rhetorical signature was religious imagery, often thoroughly secularized.[40] Intently against making any bargains with the devil, Carter's rhetorical ministry was devoted to achieving peace and freedom by converting the Soviets through moral suasion and, when that failed, by punishing the Communist infidels for their transgressions. The president himself, Gaddis Smith's claim to the contrary, never underwent a personal conversion from a pre-Afghanistan "philosophy of repentance" to a post-Afghanistan commitment to cold war realism.[41] His goal was to persuade the Soviets, whom he knew to be evil, to repent and convert to the ways of freedom—a goal he maintained until it became apparent they were beyond repentance and still continuing their evil ways.

If freedom could not be worshiped universally, Carter assumed, it was vulnerable everywhere and would have to be defended wherever it came under attack. The vehicles of Carter's religious imagery expressed a "quiet confidence" that "democracy works" and that "democracy's example will be compelling" without succumbing to the "tempt[ation] to employ improper tactics" akin to the "flawed and erroneous principles" of the communist adversary. The fire of communism would be quenched with the water of renewed faith in democracy by a "politically awakening world."[42]

As circumstances unfolded, the president concluded that the Soviets remained immune to moral suasion and unwilling to convert to the democratic faith. Thus, after Afghanistan, he no longer spoke of converting the enemy but of punishing the Soviets for their transgressions. The Soviet Union's decision to use military force "to subjugate the fiercely independent and deeply religious people of Afghanistan," Carter told Americans in this 1980 State of the Union address, would be "costly to every political and economic relationship it values."[43] The Soviets had proved by their behavior that they remained infidels against all religious peoples, Muslims as well as Christians.

Carter had never believed in a détente that meant cooperating or coexisting with the Soviets in an undemocratic world, anymore than he would ever accommodate to evil. His confidence in the nation's quest for a moral peace merely added to the heavy burden of national insecurity by a people already unable to accommodate themselves to an imperfect peace in a world of conflicted motives. Carter, as characterized by a senior aide, was a "Christian warrior" who sought to make American power an instrument of moral suasion.[44] Confident of democracy's superiority and communism's ultimate demise, he set out to transform and convert the Soviets to democratic ways through a rhetorical ministry of candid persuasion, negotiation, and cooperation while at the same time preaching the sermon of human rights. He understood himself to be in a "struggle with evil" and believed that peace ultimately depended on fulfilling the world's spiritual requirement for freedom.[45] Power was exercised on behalf of a moral agenda. Having reinforced the premise that peace would be achieved through strength, Carter's moral quest paved the way for Ronald Reagan's crusade against communism, giving the nation one less reason to support anything short of total security backed by military might and realized in ideological hegemony. As Barry Gills and others have observed, "The Carter administration policy on human rights can be viewed as the direct predecessor of the more overt U.S. policy of democratisation that followed under President Reagan."[46]

Ronald Reagan announced his administration's "crusade for democracy" in 1982 while addressing the British parliament, a crusade that economically subordinated the third world through "austerity measures, debt servicing, privatisation, economic liberalisation and structural adjustment, promoted by the U.S. via the IMF, the World Bank, and the Group of Seven Industrialised Countries."[47] Simultaneously, the Reagan administration began abandoning beleaguered dictatorial regimes in the Philippines, Chile, Haiti, and Paraguay in order to forestall revolutionary movements in those countries while also attempting to overthrow revolutionary regimes in Angola, Afghanistan, and Nicaragua. The purported purpose was to establish new democratic governments by supporting "freedom fighters" and funding the National Endowment for Democracy while contesting the Soviet Union's "evil empire."[48] Reagan's foreign policy, more aggressively Wilsonian than that of any of his predecessors, was based on the premise that the best hope for peace was a world of democratic nations. In his words, "History has shown that democratic nations do not start wars."[49]

George H. W. Bush, who inherited Reagan's crusade, witnessed the breakup of the Soviet empire and announced the emergence of a new world order in which "great nations of the world are moving toward democracy through the door of freedom . . . [and] toward free markets through the door to prosperity."[50] A new world order such as Bush's version of Wilsonianism, Amos Perlmutter has argued, "is mission oriented, seeking stability in the name of a hegemonial ideology that is intended to dominate the world system."[51] Thus, "beyond containment lies democracy," proclaimed Bush's secretary of state, James Baker. America's mission, he told the World Affairs Council in 1990, was the "promotion and consolidation of democracy."[52] And when the Bush administration failed to pursue this mission with sufficient fervor, it caught a blast of criticism from challenger Bill Clinton, who proclaimed that national security required an American-led global alliance to secure "democracy's triumph around the world."[53] Yet, as Perlmutter notes, the melting of the Soviet glacier has resulted in the growth of very little democratic grass where tribal, nationalistic, and ethnic forces have trampled the ground. The present trend, he believes, is actually against a new world order that would ensure peace and security. "The world is not ready for democracy," in Perlmutter's judgment, nor is democracy necessary for international order and national tranquillity.[54] Nevertheless, the quest for a new democratic world order remained unabated in President Clinton's foreign-policy rhetoric.

Democratizing for Peace

Clinton's rhetoric of a democratic world order is important to examine not only for its perpetuation of cold war themes but also for the imagery in which those themes are embedded, revealing strong overtones of national insecurity and vulnerability that drive the desire to dominate others. His message, in brief, was that the United States must grasp a fleeting moment of opportunity, building on the great victories of World War II and the cold war, to lead a bold adventure of securing democracy and prosperity in the global village, all the while recognizing the substantial threats facing America, including the risks even of extending freedom and democracy to the world. Everything about this message conveyed the sense of tenuous times, fragility, instability, uncertainty, the compensatory need for control, and thus the fear of democracy itself. The president's words were a national repository of democratic anxiety.

Clinton's myriad variations on the theme of democracy's endangerment and fragility ranged from allusions to epidemic, plague, purgation, nurturing, and renewal through suggestions of instability, engulfment, containment, storms, darkness, crime, and chaos to invocations of bold journeys, marching, frontier spirit, and civil courage. Such imagery permeated his foreign-policy discourse from the beginning of his first term, effectively recovering the narrative of the cold war as the tragic plotline of America's heroic mission in a new world. The prevailing threat and unspoken implication of heroic courage throughout Clinton's text was one of ultimate defeat and failure to secure the peace in the end. Thus, we might reasonably ask whether democratic hubris is America's tragic flaw—if that, indeed, was the unintended lesson of Clinton's rhetoric. His actual words are revealing.[55]

Clinton's first inaugural address, delivered "in the depth of winter" on January 20, 1993, "celebrated the mystery of American renewal" that would once again "force the spring," a "spring reborn in the world's oldest democracy, that brings forth the vision and courage to reinvent America." The nation's founders knew, he continued, "that America, to endure, would have to change." Each generation must learn to "march to the music" of the nation's timeless mission, and "today, a generation raised in the shadows of the Cold War assumes new responsibilities in a world warmed by the sunshine of freedom but threatened still by ancient hatreds and new plagues." The nation's economy, although the world's strongest, had been weakened in an age of global communications and commerce, with such profound and powerful forces "shaking and remaking our world" and raising the "urgent question" of "whether we can make change our friend and not our enemy." Ominously, the nation had "drifted" in the face of "fearsome" challenges, and such drifting had "eroded our resources, fractured our economy, and shaken our confidence." Americans, always "a restless, questing, hopeful people," must therefore recover "the vision and will of those who came before" them to rebuild the "pillars" of their history and "foundations" of their nation, to make democracy the engine of their own "renewal." To renew America, Clinton proclaimed, "we must revitalize our democracy," meeting challenges abroad as well as at home, for "there is no longer division between what is foreign and what is domestic." The world's problems affect us all, and "the new world is more free but less stable" than before, for "communism's collapse has called forth old animosities and new dangers." The United States must "shape change, lest it engulf us."[56]

The "imperative of American leadership," the president told an American University audience one month later, was to meet "the great challenge of this day" in "the face of global change" now that "democracy is on the march everywhere in the world" following the end of the cold war. But, he reported, people across America were "raising central questions about our place and our prospects in this new world we have done so much to make," this "new global economy, still recovering from the after-effects of the Cold War" in which the prosperity of the whole world depends upon ensuring the prosperity of America. Government must break free of "the death grip of gridlock," avoid "repeat[ing] the mistakes of the 1920s or the 1930s by turning inward," and follow the example of "the successes of the 1940s and the 1950s by reaching outward." The world "remains a dangerous place" of "ethnic hatreds, religious strife, the proliferation of weapons of mass destruction, [and] the violation of human rights flagrantly." Even though "democracy is on the march in many places in the world," it "has been thwarted in many places, too." Thus, American leadership is crucial to foster "the world's new and emerging democracies" upon which U.S. security and prosperity depend: "If we could make a garden of democracy and prosperity and free enterprise in every part of this globe," Clinton proclaimed to the applause of his audience, "the world would be a safer and a better and a more prosperous place for the United States and for all of you to raise your children in." But, he quickly cautioned, "democracy's prospects are dimmed" by slow global growth and trade barriers. We must "strengthen the bonds of commerce" if we "believe in the bonds of democracy." Moreover, to overcome the perils facing Russia's fledgling democracy, the United States should be willing to invest at least a tiny fraction of the trillions of dollars it spent to ensure communism's defeat in the cold war, never forgetting that the global economy is "unruly," a veritable "bucking bronco that often lands with its feet on different sides of old lines, and sometimes with its whole body on us." We must "harness the whole horse" if we are "to ride the bronco into the next century" and continue to expand "the frontiers of democracy."[57]

In April, Clinton spoke to the American Society of Newspaper Editors about the nation's purposes in the world, continuing to juxtapose promise with risk and the constant threat of failure in assuming "the ennobling burdens of democracy." Following the collapse of the Soviet empire, the world now faced "the proliferation of demonic weapons" and "resurgent ethnic conflict," undermining U.S. security in a "global village" where "there is no clear dividing line between domestic and foreign policy." Thus, U.S. policy must focus on "relations within nations," i.e., on "a nation's form of governance, economic structure, and ethnic tolerance" that influences how it treats its neighbors, because "democracies are far less likely to wage war on other nations than dictatorships." We must learn, he observed, from the "triumph of Truman's era" that "we cannot stop investing in peace now that we have obtained it." In particular, "the danger is clear if Russia's reforms turn sour—if it reverts to authoritarianism or disintegrates into chaos." The hope is that "Russia's transition can continue to be peaceful" and that its progress toward democracy and free markets will not be "thwarted."[58]

In July, the president took his message to Seoul, declaring that "Korea proves that democracy and human rights are not western imports" but instead "universal aspirations" that "flow from the internal spirit of human beings." The "struggle for freedom and democracy," as the "guardian of our security," is a "marathon," a race nations must somehow run but are not sure to win.[59] At the United Nations in September, Clinton observed that Boris Yeltsin was leading Russia on its "bold democratic journey" in a "new era of peril and opportunity." The "habits of democracy are the habits of peace," the president proclaimed, but "as we work toward this vision we must confront the storm clouds that may overwhelm our work and darken the march toward freedom," for "the end of the Cold War did not bring us to the millennium of peace. . . . Indeed, it simply removed the lid from many cauldrons of ethnic, religious, and territorial animosity." Thus, the challenge was to "ensure that the tide of freedom and democracy is not pushed back by the fierce winds" of ethnic hatred and dangerous weapons.[60]

Clinton's theme in the May 1994 telecast of a "global forum" continued to stress "an era of change and opportunity and peril [in which] America must be willing to assume the obligations and the risks of leadership." The world's "oldest democracy," a "unique nation," he said, must remain the "beacon of strength and freedom and hope," continuing its "most daring experiment in forging different races, religions and cultures into a single people," "promoting the spread of democracy abroad," and confronting "an epidemic of humanitarian catastrophes" in this "pivotal moment" for expanding "the frontiers of freedom."[61] In July, visiting Poland, Clinton warned of "oppression's fatal grip" and against "would-be dictators and fiery demagogues [who] live among us in the East and in the West, promoting ethnic and racial hatred, promoting religious divisions and anti-Semitism and aggressive nationalism." The president called on his audience to "sustain the civil courage" it takes to stay on track with "free markets and democracy [which] remains the only proven path to prosperity and to peace."[62]

Back at the United Nations in September 1994, Clinton pushed hard the theme of democracy's fragility. Telling the General Assembly they were meeting in a "time of great hope," he observed nevertheless that the world faced a contest "as old as history" between "freedom and tyranny." It was this generation's task to "secure the peace" and to assume the "sacred mission" of building a new world that is more democratic and prosperous, for "terrible examples of chaos, repression and tyranny . . . mark our times" and challenge "the very institutions of fragile democracy."[63] Thus, as he told the nation in October, America was working for "a post–Cold War world of democracy and prosperity."[64]

The theme of a struggle for American leadership against the forces of isolationism punctuated Clinton's address on March 1, 1995, at the Nixon Center in Washington, D.C., arguing that the idea of an open society remains as much under attack today as it was previously by fascism and then communism and thus that democracy still must be "nurtured" with investment and support given to "fledgling democracies." Democracy was a "trend," not an inevitability, nor would it be easy to "establish or shore up fragile democracies," he stressed.[65] In May, the president visited Moscow State University, urging faith in Russia's "young, fragile democracy" but observing as well that "the more open and flexible our societies are, the more our people are able to move freely without restraint, the greater we are exposed to [new security] threats," such as the bombing of the World Trade Center, the tragedy of Oklahoma City, bombings in the streets of Israel, the gas attack in a Tokyo subway, and the problem of organized crime—a point he later reiterated in his State of the Union address on January 27, 1998.[66] Democracy itself, and the free flow of information it permits, was a source of global insecurity. As Clinton stressed in October 1995, the United States possessed a special obligation of leadership for the "cause of democracy, freedom, security and prosperity" in a "Technology Age that can mean simply breaking open a vial of sarin gas in a Tokyo subway. It can mean hooking into the Internet and learning how to build a bomb that will blow up a federal building in the heart of America. These forces, just as surely as fascism and communism, would spread darkness over light, disintegration over integration, chaos over community."[67] Thus, in his second inaugural address, the president declared that "America stands alone as the world's indispensable nation"; the "world's greatest democracy will lead a whole world of democracies," sustaining its "journey" and striving to keep an "old democracy forever young."[68]

Besides the pervasive theme of democracy's fragility, then, Clinton's rhetoric featured the motif of a democratic peace—the premise that peace and security depend on spreading democracy globally. Typical of his cold war predecessors, Clinton legitimized America's economic agenda of world capitalism by placing it under the sign of a quest for democracy.[69] Moreover, the vague meaning of democracy as the key term in the logic of such a peace—the claim that democratic nations do not attack one another—conflated the apparent increase in the number of democracies throughout the world (Samuel Huntington's "third wave" of democratization in the late twentieth century) with the reality that (1) this trend represented only one relatively weak variation on the theme of democracy, (2) the extension of democratic regimes had not necessarily improved the quality of people's lives, and (3) increases in the number of democratic states had not increased democratic practices among and between nations.[70] Furthermore, as democratic theorists have argued, "the theorem of 'peace among democracies' is a dangerous one" because it "almost suggests that by using any means to force autocratic regimes into submission, including war, the best of all possible worlds can be achieved," thus lending "ideological ammunition to the strongest states . . . to defend their interests in the international realm regardless of the interests of weaker parties."[71]

All of this should be cause for concern when we take into consideration the Clinton administration's emphasis on achieving national security through a democratic peace while at the same time stressing the fragility of fledgling democracies; the continuing threat of totalitarianism, dictatorship, authoritarianism, and terrorism; and in particular the claim that "the growth of cooperation between the United States and the Russian Federation . . . is rooted in democracy," which of course is a weak foundation for a relationship in which one of the partners is the oldest democracy in the world and the other is characterized as a "young, fragile democracy."[72] Indeed, the proposition of a peaceful democratic world order is a dangerous source of national insecurity and a strong invitation to war. Moreover, it focuses attention on achieving "order" and away from enriching democratic practice itself, which within the American tradition of liberal democratic internationalism is a thin concept at best reflecting a basic distrust of the demos. The question we should ask, then, is whether the United States can break its cold war habit of using democracy as an ideological tool to perpetuate a crusading sense of national insecurity and begin to develop a more robust democratic culture to promote responsible international participation without requiring global domination. How might the nation alter its understanding of democracy to accommodate better to the post–cold war forces of integration and fragmentation?

Reconstituting Democracy

The problem indicated by the question of reconstituting democracy is not subject to a quick, easy, or definitive solution. The cultural, rhetorical, and institutional dimensions of the problem, however, point in the direction we might search for answers before the post–cold war enthusiasm for a more democratic world dissolves completely into rampant fear of terrorism and international disorder. In particular, we need to attend to an imbalance in the nation's tradition of liberal democracy and to ask how its frail republican constitution might develop into a healthy democratic disposition. America's long but thin democratic legacy, as Benjamin Barber, David Held, and others have argued, is increasingly problematic in an era that has made democracy the standard of political legitimacy.[73] "While we cannot do without democracy," Held maintains, "it is increasingly bankrupt in its traditional shape and, thus, needs fundamental reform."[74] Within this tradition of thin, liberal democracy, the people are marginalized by overdeveloped institutions of elite representation that act as a disincentive for participatory politics. Individual rights, in particular property rights, the marketplace, economic growth, and social stability, are given priority over the rule of the people.[75] The historically contested premise that democracy and free-market capitalism are inseparable has been maintained, albeit with some difficulty, by diminishing the vitality of democracy while protecting special economic interests.[76]

According to liberalism's prevailing logic, which equates democracy with demagoguery rather than rational deliberation, exercising democracy vigorously increases the risk of mobocracy and political distemper. Where democracy promotes popular rule, liberalism concerns itself with the proper limits and scope of political power, conflating power with reason in order to control the outcome of political decisions while attempting to contain the democratic impulse enough to make it safe to practice. Historically, then, Americans have placed neither unqualified trust nor collective faith in democracy despite its status as a god term of national ideals and mission. It inspires more awe than faith or trust, engendering feelings of fear and dread combined with wonder and veneration and fraught with ambivalence, ambiguity, and a chronic sense of insecurity. The paradox of American political consciousness is that it predisposes the nation to fear its own demise by depicting unfettered democracy as a dangerous disease of illiberal rule while rendering suspect any explicit repudiation of egalitarian ideals. Such paradoxical danger is a function, rhetorically at least, of representing democracy as a political disease. Unable to resolve this conflicted trope domestically, the country has sought its redemption and security in a vision of democratic peace realized globally as an end of history and a confirmation of national virtue, its historic mission as a beacon of liberty evolving into a manifest destiny to expand the domain of liberal democratic rule across the continent and into a global order. Spreading democracy globally, however, has not resolved the problem of transforming an image of popular distemper into a healthy vehicle of international peace and security. The concept of democracy as presently constituted remains a calcified discourse that reinforces national anxieties in a decidedly risky world and perpetuates a war mentality by exaggerating perceptions of national peril.[77] In short, an excess of liberalism has diminished the nation's faith in its democratic imagination and undermined its ability to respond confidently to popular movements.

This legacy of anemic, thin democracy (Barber's "politics of zookeeping") renders democracy fragile and weak, contained like a deadly virus.[78] In a thin democracy, where the caged commons are deemed the irrational and threatening Other—an Other that must be restrained domestically and globally in order to secure the peace and ensure prosperity—diversity and difference are equated with error, disorder, and danger rather than taken as normal, healthy signs of rhetorically articulating interests, addressing audiences, developing strategies of identification, and transacting agreements through public persuasion that values agonistic politics over antagonistic relations.[79]

Consistent with the rhetorical enactment of a healthy agonistic political culture (as discussed in chapter 1), an extension of democratic institutions could also help to redress the imbalance of liberalism in American politics and foreign affairs. Held's work on "cosmopolitan democracy," for instance, points toward worthwhile possibilities of institutional change along these lines. As he emphasizes, the cosmopolitan model of democracy represents a "direction of possible change with clear points of orientation" short of a detailed plan that can be realized immediately with all conceivable objections answered satisfactorily.[80] His is an indication of ways to respond more democratically in venues other than just the nation-state.

Held's model responds to the condition of globalization and its erosion of national barriers to create interconnections among diverse peoples at several levels of governance. He aims to maximize the degree to which the people affected by a policy decision are able to participate in its formulation and deliberation. Furthermore, he recognizes that the "dynamics and logic of the inter-state system would still represent an immensely powerful force in global affairs" even if more regional parliaments were created and strengthened, international referendums were conducted on transnational issues, and participatory democracy was intensified at local levels to complement deliberative bodies at the global level. A democratic world order organized vertically and horizontally into a cosmopolitan community that accommodates "diverse and distinct domains of authority" and respects a plurality of identities would not presume the integration of cultural and political diversities into a single consensus of beliefs and values but would rely on a continuing democratic practice to deliberate competing narratives and address conflicted values.[81] These, at least, are the kinds of practices that have to be considered and confronted, Held concludes, if the emerging world order is actually going to become more democratic at a time in history when "the locus of effective political power can no longer be assumed to be national governments," that is, when "effective power" increasingly is "shared, bartered, and struggled over by diverse forces and agencies at national, regional, and international levels."[82]

Held's argument is not to supplant liberal values with democratic practices but instead to articulate an overarching democratic public law, or legal order, within various structures of political action that entail a cluster of rights and obligations with which to meet the contingencies of "overlapping communities of fate," contingencies such as transnational health issues, nuclear energy development and waste management, the degradation of rain forests and depletion of nonrenewable resources, instabilities of global financial markets, the proliferation of weapons of mass destruction, and the scourge of international terrorism. These are the kinds of challenges that raise questions about who constitutes the proper constituency, what is the appropriate realm of jurisdiction, and what forms of political participation should be adopted. To meet these challenges and advance the politics of self-determination, Held envisions the development over time of a transnationalized community of democratic communities, bound by a democratic public law that holds state, economic, and cultural power accountable. In such a world, democratic deliberation and decision making would move beyond national borders when groups significantly impacted by an issue constitute a cross-border constituency and when national or lower levels of political authority cannot manage the problem well or legitimately. Thus, nation-states would be "articulated with, and relocated within, an overarching democratic law," and sovereignty would no longer be associated with fixed borders. Instead, people would "come to enjoy multiple citizenships." The unhappy alternative of maintaining the existing system of rigid nationalism while many of the most compelling problems and forces transcend the boundaries of nation-states, Held argues, is that the world will fall prey to new forms of fundamentalism and tribalism, "all asserting the a priori superiority of a particular religious, or cultural, or political identity over all others, and all asserting their sectional aims and interests."[83]

Yet, there are dangers also to be considered in pursuing Held's cosmopolitan vision too far down the road of a transnational democratic polity. Like the argument for universal democratic peace, the notion of a transnational community of democratic communities could too easily be perverted and co-opted by those who would justify war now as a necessary means of democratizing the world later, that is, as a prerequisite to creating a world safe for the development of a community of democracies. Moreover, as Will Kymlicka argues, Held's perspective too easily overestimates the impact of globalization on citizenship to the point of "undermining the meaningfulness of participation in domestic politics" and underestimating the requirements of "collective deliberation and legitimation," which include "some degree of commonality amongst citizens" in order to understand and trust one another in the process of democratic self-government. Whereas Held cautions against ignoring the huge impact of globalization but recognizes the continuing role of nation-states, Kymlicka acknowledges that globalization constrains national polities and legislatures but warns against exaggerating the loss of national identity and sovereignty or understating the potential of globalization for enriching the meaningfulness of domestic citizenship, for "decisions by national collectivities to integrate into transnational institutions are, in part, decisions about what kind of societies people want to live in." And, Kymlicka stresses, "democratic politics is politics in the vernacular." By this reckoning, it would be difficult to meet the criterion of participatory democracy in the vernacular under a condition of transnational democratic citizenship.[84]

Just as Kymlicka cautions against overestimating the negative impact of globalization on domestic politics, Ian Shapiro warns of the danger world government would pose to achieving democratic justice. Again, the difference between Shapiro and Held (as between Held and Kymlicka) is largely one of emphasis. Where Held envisions moving to higher levels of crossnational decision making when domestic forums cannot cope adequately with problems that impact their constituencies and those of others, Shapiro emphasizes the need to remain at national and local levels as much as possible in order to avoid distancing and disenfranchising citizens by moving precipitously to a transnational level of deliberation and decision making. Both, however, share the goal of maximizing democratic practice. For Shapiro, contrary to the liberal view of a private sphere, "no domain of human interaction is beyond politics," and yet, unlike the communitarians, he does not ground democratic justice on the assumption of bonds of intimacy and affection within closely circumscribed and traditional polities of commonality. Traditional societies are subject to change, boundaries of politics shift, and political struggle is a constant possibility under the condition of inevitable human innovation. Relations of conflict and power make politics ubiquitous to human affairs, meaning to Shapiro that "a suitably developed account of democracy offers the most attractive political basis for ordering social relations justly."[85]

If Kymlicka is perhaps guilty of minimizing the reality of dissensus in politics (a variation on the problem of universal reason afflicting theories of deliberative democracy) by stressing the importance of a shared language and other commonalities in smaller rather than larger polities, Shapiro's corrective of a suitably developed account of democratic practice recognizes that "one person's consensus is often another's hegemony." Dissensus in politics, he argues, is a sign of health and vigor, not valueless anomie, when managed appropriately without presuming that broad social agreement is practical and desirable. Thus, democracy is both a foundational and a subordinate good to which there is no practical alternative for shaping "the terms of our common interactions without thereby determining their course." That is, democracy is the best way to pursue competing, conflicted wants—an "antidote to exclusion and domination" toward which we should evolve civil institutions on the assumption that decisions achieved relatively more democratically acquire comparatively greater legitimacy. Both the stability of a democratic regime and the likelihood of justice are enhanced by the possibility of opposition, which enables people to "challenge prevailing norms and rules with the realistic hope of altering them." Moreover, democracy is meaningless without the backing of indispensable civil rights and freedoms of speech, press, assembly, and so on. Accordingly, Shapiro concludes, "the presumption is against undemocratic ways of doing things. . . . The burden of persuasion should always lie with those who would limit democracy's operation." We should be especially skeptical of anyone who "claims to know how to get to democracy undemocratically" and of any "missionary quest" deploying "invading armies" in the name of democratic justice.[86]

Under present circumstances, the challenge of balancing the post–cold war forces of integration and fragmentation will be difficult to meet. Reconstituting and strengthening America's democratic disposition along the general lines suggested by the likes of Held, Kymlicka, and Shapiro might very well be a key to achieving a better balance, whereas the liberal appropriation of democracy is becoming increasingly problematic and quite possibly self-defeating by repeating the myth of democracy's fragility and perpetuating the cycle of national paranoia. The unfortunate legacy of cold war discourse, as illustrated in Clinton's foreign-policy addresses, is a republic of fear holding fast to a vision of the new world order that is more democratic in name than practice. That legacy need not prevail, however, if we explore ways of rhetorically enacting a strong democratic culture instead of persisting in the defensive and fearful attitude of prosecuting an aggressive war on terror. Even the penetrating insights of democratic theorists, including those who are rightly critical of consensus theories of democratic deliberation and universal theories of democratic peace, have failed so far to take into account the full potential of a rhetorical perspective on democratic culture and practice. Held, for instance, seems to presume that only people existing in demo-

cratic communities and abiding by an overarching democratic law can interact democratically with one another. Kymlicka stresses the importance of
shared identities and underlying commonalities for the legitimate deliberation of public issues to occur within a given polity and linguistic community. Shapiro grants the presence and vitality of disagreement and dissent
in democratic culture but does not consider how agonistic relations are addressed within democratic polities or between democratic polities and nondemocratic Others short of deteriorating into antagonistic relations of coercion and warfare. Even Mouffe, who points to the tradition of rhetoric as
a means of preventing opponents from becoming enemies, presumes that
agonistic relations can be managed democratically only by those who accept
the rules of the game and share in the democratic ethos, which amounts to
a kind of minimalist sense of reciprocity with a corresponding commitment
to a complex ensemble of discursive practices and "a shared adhesion to the
ethico-political principles of liberal democracy: liberty and equality."[87]

Whereas some rhetorical practices can aggravate an endemic fear of the
demos and foreign Others to prompt an attitude of belligerency, other rhetorical practices can manage agonistic relations of adversaries less anxiously
and antagonistically, whether those relations occur within a democratic polity
or between democratic and nondemocratic Others. That is, rhetoric is the
mode of discourse in the realm of political relations for good or ill. It can
undermine or enrich democratic culture by the way it addresses the human divide, either by calling for the obliteration of a sacrificial Other in a
ritual of victimization that would rid the world of an evil threat and redeem
a troubled but otherwise virtuous people or, alternatively, by articulating
enough points of consubstantiality between adversaries to prevent them from
becoming sheer enemies. In this way, rhetoric can call a frantic nation to war
or speak more confidently of peace in the idiom of democracy, as we shall see
by examining the manner in which Americans have been called upon to
fight a prolonged war against a troublesome caricature of terrorism.

4
Fighting Terror

On August 5, 1945, the United States dropped an atomic bomb on Hiroshima, then another within three days on Nagasaki. A third bomb was readied to explode over Tokyo when, on August 14, Japan finally capitulated to America's demand of "unconditional" surrender. The axis of fascism was defeated; freedom had prevailed; world order was restored, civilization secured. In announcing that "an American airplane dropped . . . the largest bomb ever yet used in the history of warfare," President Harry S. Truman observed matter-of-factly: "The Japanese began the war from the air at Pearl Harbor. They have been repaid many fold." Justice was served; evil was obliterated by righteous fire. The nuclear age thus began, in the president's words, as "a new and revolutionary increase in destruction." It was an innovation in the mass destruction of civilian lives made possible by "harnessing the basic power of the universe," but it was also a continuation and an escalation of the established practice of firebombing urban populations from Dresden to Tokyo for the purpose of undermining enemy morale. This new kind of bomb had been aimed first at the center of a city of 350,000 people and was used again to destroy a second city with a population of 270,000. In Truman's view, Americans should be "grateful to Providence" that decent people acquired this weapon to defeat an evil enemy.[1] The United States had emerged triumphant, powerful, and proud in its war against fascism, but not without setting in motion a new cycle of terror even as another was brought so violently to a close.

Since 1945, the United States has bombed and otherwise engaged in hostilities with a long string of countries from North Korea, China, Cuba, Vietnam, and Cambodia to Grenada, Libya, Panama, Bosnia, Yugoslavia, Somalia, Afghanistan, and Iraq. Its arms industry has developed and sold the world's most sophisticated weapons to clients around the globe. In Vietnam and Cambodia, it prosecuted a war against an elusive enemy by resorting to Agent Orange, napalm, and carpet bombing, which devastated the civilian population.[2] "In Cambodia alone," writes John Pilger, "600,000 people died beneath American bombs."[3] A CIA-led coup in Chile instigated the infamous murder of democratically elected president Salvador Allende. Ruthless dictators have been supported by the United States in Haiti, the Philippines, and Iran. The Reagan administration funded death squads in Honduras and aided terrorizing "contras" in Nicaragua while training Central American military leaders in the art of torture at its School of the Americas in Georgia. Since World War II, a triumphant America has "terrorised or backed terrorists in Nicaragua, Brazil, Uruguay, Cuba, Guatemala, Indonesia, East Timor, Zaire, Angola and South Africa."[4] Tens of thousands of Iraqi civilians were killed in America's first Gulf War, and others died in the aftermath from an epidemic of cancer in southern Iraq where depleted uranium shells littered the land.[5] Civilian deaths have been dismissed as "collateral damage"— the unfortunate but necessary consequence of legitimate force used in self-defense by a virtuous democratic state and its allies—while those who have resorted to force in opposition to the United States and its allies have been branded terrorists. As Noam Chomsky observes, the word *terrorism* means in actual practice "the violence that *they* commit against *us*—whoever *we* happen to be."[6] While the self-serving and violent United States of America is a terrorist state in the eyes of its victims, it is a peace-loving victim of terrorism in the minds of most Americans.

Terrorism today, regardless of America's myopic innocence, is firmly rooted in a violent history of empire since World War II. Terrorist attacks throughout the world are *Blowback: The Costs and Consequences of American Empire,* as Chalmers Johnson maintains in a book by that title. Johnson is referring to an "unacknowledged" and "informal" empire, for the most part, an "imperial project that the Cold War obscured" but the by-product of which is "reservoirs of resentment against all Americans . . . that can have lethal results." America's determination "to dominate the global scene," to project its military power and extend its social, political, and economic system throughout the world, is a "triumphalist" act and attitude, Johnson argues, for which the United States and its citizens will continue to "pay a steep price" unless and until Americans reassess their global role and become more conscious of how they look to others who hate them for their arrogance and hegemony.

Even as Americans worry about how to defend themselves against "rogue states," they must consider "whether the United States has itself become a rogue superpower." The United States has declared itself the world's "indispensable nation" and the architect of "a new world order." Now Americans must confront the likelihood that when it comes to understanding terrorism, "empire is the problem," at least to a significant degree.[7]

Yet, the United States is an exceptional nation that persistently turns a blind eye to its own imperialism. Its unacknowledged empire exists in a political culture that has schooled itself in the image of a reluctant power, a great nation that fights only under duress and then on behalf of peace and democracy against oppression and imperialism. "*Empire*," observes Clyde Prestowitz, "remains a word that for Americans means conquest and subjugation of foreign peoples against their will. It represents the antithesis of the ideals on which America was founded." Thus, even as President George W. Bush advanced a new doctrine of U.S. world supremacy and preemptive warfare, he assured West Point cadets that "America has no empire to extend." The reach of American military might, economic influence, and cultural impact is so great that it would make the world its condominium without declaring itself emperor, except to proclaim in Jeffersonian overtones an "empire of liberty." Americans perceive themselves to be an exceptional nation, a chosen people, destined to extend the fruit of freedom to an enslaved world. Their mission is to uplift humanity unilaterally if necessary and by exercising supreme leadership at a minimum. America is nothing if it is not an ideology of liberty and equality for everyone, a civil religion, "a chosen people laboring in God's vineyard to create a new, perfect society." Americanism is for everyone, and everyone is a potential American. Accordingly, every contest is a moral crusade, a just war of absolute good against absolute evil in which victory must be righteous and complete.[8] Moral exceptionalism, notes Seymour Martin Lipset, means that Americans must always be on "God's side against Satan."[9] And God's chosen people do not see themselves as imperialists. They lead coalitions of the willing to salvation, from the blighted world of turmoil and tyranny to a democratic promised land of peace and freedom.[10]

Instead of reflecting carefully and judiciously on America's global presence, then, considering how the United States might play its post–cold war role more adeptly—less fearfully and arrogantly—the nation's first impulse after 9/11 was to close ranks in patriotic fervor, declare war on international terrorism, and vow triumph over evil. By succumbing to this great temptation in a time of crisis, Americans risked falling ever more deeply into what Jeffrey Simon has called "the terrorist trap," that web of psychological, political, and social entanglement in the "dramas of international violence" that will persist and worsen unless Americans learn to address the problem of terror comprehensively and democratically in its many dimensions.[11] The nation's profile of terror is a dangerous caricature of the enemy, a crude portrait of absolute evil that only confounds the quest for peace and security in a global village where diversity resists conformity, tribalism confronts empire, and, in Benjamin Barber's phrase, "Jihad vs. McWorld."[12] Fighting terror in this way is yet another self-perpetuating exercise in republican fear of the distempered Other that would suppress the nation's democratic impulse rather than deploy it vigorously to meet the challenge at hand.[13]

Profiling Terrorism

Profiling is a dangerous practice, for as Friedrich Nietzsche observed, language is necessarily an exercise in interpretation, and "interpretation itself is a form of the will to power" that leads all too easily to caricature and the scapegoat—that dark alley where words dilute, depersonalize, and brutalize. "Every society," Nietzsche continues, "has the tendency to reduce its opponents to caricatures" so that "the 'good man' sees himself as if surrounded by evil."[14] We know from hard experience that racial profiling is more than just an abstract philosophical problem, but profiling terrorists quickly became a widely, if somewhat reluctantly, endorsed practice by Americans—including even victims of racial profiling—out of concern for their safety following the devastation of 9/11. Profiling, in fact, is a microcosm of the problem of terrorism in a pluralistic world, of the difficulty of living safely and not overreacting to Others in an interconnected global village where religious, cultural, and other differences directly confront and threaten one another.[15] And if profiling itself is a mirror of terrorism, we must become especially alert to the distortions in the image of the enemy that it necessarily reflects, for every perspective on reality, as Kenneth Burke underscores, is a terministic screen that simultaneously enables and disables our collective action, a set of blinders that both directs and misdirects our attention, equipment for living together that easily degenerates into a trained incapacity and an appetite for victimage.[16]

Profiling in one form or another is as inevitable as it is dangerous. We are language-using and language-misusing beings destined to interpret and reinterpret our world through the fog of symbols and with an eye toward adapting in the best way possible to ever-changing circumstances. To persevere, we must remain to some degree in a state of rhetorical becoming, forever skeptical of representations of evil, so that we might act with maximum consciousness and with the least possible harm to ourselves and others. As Nietzsche noted, language is inherently rhetorical in its articulation of perspective and motive.[17] All we can hope to do is to hold our limited perspectives accountable to one another, to retain an agonistic edge, especially where the presence of one narrow point of view or profile threatens to overtake our collective conscience and tyrannize our political consciousness. Thus, we should stand ever ready to critique the language that constitutes extreme attitudes of Othering and, in the immediate case, to scrutinize the prevailing profile of terror.

None of this denies the fact of terrorism or questions the imperative of responding effectively to the reality of violence perpetrated against civilians, which is the modus operandi of terror used as a weapon of political influence and change.[18] Terrorism is not something entirely new to Americans. The United States, its property, and its citizens became a primary target of international terrorism overseas well before the more recent strikes against the home territory, strikes that galvanized the nation and focused its attention on "doing something" to avert disaster.[19] The problem is how best to interpret the continuing fact of terrorism and thus what general attitude to assume in formulating specific responses. Declaring a war on international terrorism and totalizing the divide between good and evil may well be the worst attitude for meeting such a challenge. Yet, that is exactly the posture President George W. Bush took with the overwhelming support of the American public, perhaps because the options seemed so limited to them.

The president's profile of terrorism, it goes almost without saying, was the single most influential interpretation of the danger at hand. It was his role and the responsibility of his office to shape public opinion, to put events in perspective, and to set the nation on a sensible course of action. "Terrorism is a complex and frightening experience for the general public," Simon notes, "and it becomes natural to look toward Washington for guidance and reassurance." The president's words were magnified by the exigency of the moment and the prominence of his position of leadership. He could either fuel the crisis in "a highly charged emotional and political atmosphere" or help defuse it in order to avoid falling prey to the terrorist trap. He could raise unrealistic expectations, which was the easiest course to follow in the short run, or he could undertake the more difficult task of guiding the nation steadily in the service of long-term interests. The latter approach required a balanced and more complex perspective on terrorism; the easier and more dangerous course was to declare a war that promised to defeat international terrorism even though realistically "terrorism is an endless conflict."[20] Terrorism, as Walter Laqueur insists, is relatively cheap to carry out and too expensive in every way to combat for long in all-out war. It "will be with us for as long as anyone can envision."[21]

Unfortunately, the president chose to view terrorism through the prism of war. He remained consistent from September 11 forward in his condemnation of terrorists as agents of evil and foes of freedom and stayed on message to the point of sheer redundancy bolstered by celebrity spectacles, solemn memorials, and patriotic witnessing at major sporting events and other public occasions, including the high-profile anniversary ceremonies a year after the terrorist attacks on the World Trade Center and the Pentagon and a prime-time victory flight to the deck of the aircraft carrier *Abraham Lincoln* after the fall of Iraq. The primary burdens of citizenship in this war against terrorism were to wave the flag and exercise the courage to consume. The patriot knew, according to this logic, that freedom must be sacrificed in some undefined measure and for an indefinite period of time in order to defend against the enemies of freedom and civilization.

The opening lines of Bush's first State of the Union address pushed his favorite theme of war, patriotism, and consumerism in the defense of freedom and civilization by declaring "our nation is at war, our economy is in recession, and the civilized world faces unprecedented dangers."[22] Since the "shock and suffering" of four months earlier, he continued, "our nation has comforted the victims, begun to rebuild New York and the Pentagon, rallied a great coalition, captured, arrested, and rid the world of thousands of terrorists, destroyed Afghanistan's terrorist training camps, saved a people from starvation, and freed a country from brutal oppression." The terrorists who survived our bombing campaign in Afghanistan were now either occupying cells at Guantánamo Bay or running for their lives. The women of Afghanistan were free, no longer "captives in their own homes." America was "winning the war on terror" against a hateful and mad enemy that "laugh[ed] about the loss of innocent life" while plotting to destroy American nuclear plants and poison public water supplies. The president's aim was to "eliminate" these "terrorist parasites" worldwide and to prevent the "axis of evil" regimes in Iraq, Iran, and North Korea from threatening the United States, its friends, and allies with weapons of mass destruction. The war would continue indefinitely until an evil enemy that embraces "tyranny and death" is defeated by those who "choose freedom and the dignity of every life."

Not only did the president's State of the Union address establish a focus of evil, but it also reduced all other political questions to this singular focus as extensions of the war on terror that, he stressed, "is well begun, but it is only begun." Just as September 11 had brought about the unity and resolve of America and Congress, "this same spirit [would be] directed toward addressing problems here at home." Not only did the president propose the largest increase in military spending in two decades as the price of freedom and security, but he also requested new funding for homeland security to protect against bioterrorism, provide for emergency response, fund airport and border security, and enhance intelligence gathering. Research on bioterrorism would yield knowledge to "improve public health." Training and equipping "heroic police and firefighters" would mean "safer neighborhoods." Stricter border enforcement would "help combat illegal drugs." And better intelligence meant depending "on the eyes and ears of alert citizens."

Moreover, to revitalize the economy, the president's budget, or what he referred to as his "economic security plan," would promote good jobs, good schools, and reliable and affordable energy production along with expanded trade, new world markets, and tax relief that would "grow the economy by encouraging investment in factories and equipment." "Health security" and "retirement security" were further measures of the nation's "true character" in this "time of testing," in this time for "courage and compassion, strength and resolve." Each American patriot was called upon symbolically to dedicate four thousand hours to public service over the rest of his or her lifetime, thus signaling that our enemies who believed us to be weak, divided, and materialistic "were as wrong as they are evil."

Although the language of evil was not entirely wrong for characterizing heinous crimes against humanity, it was not the most serviceable term for guiding the nation's thinking about how best to address the continuing problem of terror. Rather than bringing Americans together as a diverse and democratic people committed to respecting pluralism at home and abroad, the rhetoric of evil constituted them negatively through a ritual of victimization. By premising the defense of freedom on a caricature of terrorists as the personification of evil, this rhetorical practice constructed, celebrated, and witnessed patriotism as a public exercise in extreme Othering, thus undermining the nation's own democratic values and its capacity for coping with the condition of diversity except by the futility of coercion and domination. The administration's problematic profile of evil promoted the rhetoric of the scapegoat as an exercise in blaming rather than problem solving, a way of asserting America's innocence and legitimizing a strong desire for righteous revenge instead of looking for ways to curtail the cycle of violence. Declaring total war on absolute evil escalated the level of violence and played directly into the likely designs of at least some terrorists. That, in short, was the problem with the perspective the president articulated for fighting terror.

A longer explanation of the limitations of the president's narrow perspective, especially for promoting peace and fostering democracy, requires us to place the present crisis in a wider frame, one that expands the definition of terrorism, complicates the question of culpability, and redirects the impulse to war. This is a task of the kind indicated in the hypothetical dialogue composed by Kenneth Burke between Satan and the Lord. Titled "Prologue in Heaven," Burke's dialogue is a "Parable of Purpose" about the subject of humans as the "symbol-using animal"—those "talking animals" who "derive purposes from their physical nature" but also invent purposes with "the resources of language" from which their quandaries arise and by which they are goaded "to further questioning" because language makes questioning easy. "Given language, you can never be sure where quest ends and question begins." Satan is portrayed in this dialogue as "an agile youth," a robust figure wearing a "fool's cap," an "over-hasty, mercurial" fellow seated "at The Lord's right hand" and quick with easy answers to difficult questions. Our two speakers are on "friendly terms," and the Lord is "affectionately amused by his young companion."

The immediate relevance of this celestial conversation to those of us here on earth is that "the complications [of our world] will be unending." Each time Satan, as the Lord's eager interlocutor and interpreter, confidently pronounces the meaning of the human condition, he is told by the Lord that, although he is right in a limited sense, the human condition is "more complicated than that," it is just "not quite that," and he needs to adopt a wider frame of reference because "there can be no perfection but here in heaven." Certainly no perfection exists down there on earth. "Where the Earth-People are concerned," says the Lord, "any terminology is suspect to the extent that it does not allow for the progressive criticism of itself."[23]

The Lord's advice to the Devil is all the more applicable to human beings. Mere mortals are but talking animals that must keep questioning and criticizing easy answers to complicated issues, remaining in a state of rhetorical becoming so that they might invent the most serviceable attitudes possible to govern their everyday lives and relations toward Others. This is a crucial lesson to remember when a powerful nation thinks it has gotten the exact answer to something as complicated as terrorism and particularly when it is convinced that it can solve the problem simply and unilaterally by eliminating evil itself. It is the lesson Burke teaches as a comic corrective to humanity's tragic inclinations, the lesson of practical humility, of casuistically stretching favored frames of acceptance so that they take into account greater degrees of complexity in order to protect against the pitfall of oversimplification. Probing the incongruities of a trite and tired perspective is the best antidote for hubris and the first line of defense against radicalism and escalating cycles of violence. In particular, the meaning of terror, the question of culpability, and the impropriety of all-out war are all key complications that are badly underrepresented or missing in the president's profile of evil incarnate.

First, there is the question of whether terrorism is a *crime* against humanity or, as the president insisted, an act of *war* on freedom. In the spirit of Kenneth Burke's preference for the more complicated "both/and" answer over the less-serviceable "either/or" dichotomy, a good answer to this question would acknowledge that terrorism is both a different kind of war and a unique form of crime. It is not exactly war or crime but instead a hybrid of both that must be understood distinctly from its two most likely counterparts. Terrorism on its own terms is a politically motivated and systematic act of violence against civilians. As Bruce Hoffman explains, it "is fundamentally and inherently political. It is also ineluctably about power: the pursuit of power, the acquisition of power, and the use of power to achieve political change. Terrorism is thus violence—or, equally important, the threat of violence—used and directed in pursuit of, or in service of, a political aim. . . . It is a planned, calculated, and indeed systematic act."[24] And its principal target is noncombatants. In Caleb Carr's words, terrorism is the "modern permutation" of "warfare deliberately waged against civilians with the purpose of destroying their will to support either leaders or policies that the agents of such violence find objectionable."[25] To the extent it is a crime, terrorism is a politically motivated crime rather than an exercise in personal gain; to the extent it is warfare, terrorism victimizes defenseless civilians primarily and on purpose rather than directly attacking armed, and therefore far more dangerous, military combatants. Thus, as Philip Heymann concludes, terrorist "assault[s] on civilians to advance political purposes" are "both crimes and forms of warfare."[26] Or, seen from the reverse angle, such politically motivated assaults on civilians are acts neither of war nor crime in the conventional sense of either term.

Consistent with this basic definition and as a clarifying extension thereof, we might now ask two related questions: Who are the perpetrators of such heinous tactics? And what motivates the use of violence against civilians? Answers to these questions help widen the circumference of the problem at hand, complicate the nation's working image of terrorists, and reassess the plausibility of eradicating terrorism.

The most typical terrorist tactics include hijacking, kidnapping, and hostage taking; various forms of bombing (including car bombing, aerial attack, midair, and suicide bombing); arson; murder and assassination; armed assault and missile attack; contamination of consumer products; and increasingly the threat of chemical, biological, and nuclear weapons of mass destruction.[27] On the lighter side, and in the spirit of instructive comic relief, this list might remind some of a scene in Mel Brooks's lunatic film *Blazing Saddles,* where arch villain and state attorney general Harvey Korman is about to recruit "an army of the worst dregs ever to spoil the face of the West" for the dastardly purpose of terrorizing the simple and pacific, although racist, people of Rock Ridge in the higher cause of railroad expansion and personal gain. In a crescendo of gleeful, parodic panegyric, Korman instructs his hapless sidekick and gofer Slim Pickens "to round up every vicious killer and gunslinger in the West." Specifically, he exclaims, "I want rustlers, cutthroats, murderers, bounty hunters, desperados, mugs, pugs, thugs, nitwits, halfwits, dimwits, vipers, snipers, conmen, Indian agents, Mexican bandits, muggers, burglars, bushwhackers . . . horse thieves . . . train robbers, bank robbers . . . and Methodists." An enthusiastic Pickens even manages to add Hell's Angels, Nazi storm troopers, and Ku Klux Klansmen to Korman's long list of assembled thugs boasting impressive credentials in murder, arson, armed robbery, and mayhem.

As parody, such comic stereotypes reveal the incongruities in everyday distinctions between good and bad characters, but taken literally, especially in the context of terrorism, these same caricatures lack the necessary texture of life; all shades of grey are lost and ironies of division missed to America's own detriment. Actual agents of mayhem are not simply or exclusively located on the dark side of inhumanity and outside the boundaries of enlightened civilization. They are not always foreigners or even necessarily strangers, and it is dangerously misleading to think of them simply or singularly as sick, irrational madmen who lack roots, rationale, motivation, and strategic objectives.[28]

As a resident of rural Indiana, for example, I am particularly mindful of the virulent history of the Ku Klux Klan in my state (and throughout America) and the more recent activities of the Indiana Militia, which has been described as a "particularly militant anti-gun-control organization" whose "members proudly proclaim," in an ironic twist of enemy imagery, "that they are 'sick and tired of being raped and pillaged by the bunch of thieves that run the federal government.'"[29] As Americans generally learned after the intense publicity surrounding Timothy McVeigh's infamous bombing of the Alfred P. Murrah Federal Building in Oklahoma City on April 19, 1995, the militia movement was spread all over the United States. These militias consist of individuals who "consider themselves 'minutemen': ordinary citizens and patriots ready to take up arms at a moment's notice to defend their inalienable rights, self-styled heirs of the tradition of the American Revolution."[30] The day that 168 men, women, and children died in Oklahoma City at the hands of Christian patriots attempting to start a new revolutionary war was chosen to coincide with Patriots Day in New England— the anniversary of the beginning of the American Revolution in 1775—and, more recently, the day in 1993 on which the Branch Davidian compound burned to the ground in Waco, Texas.[31]

Terror, like politics, is local and personal, not something remote, not something safely removed from our everyday lives or perpetrated by a subspecies entirely alien or unknown to us. As a member of the faculty of Indiana University, I learned how close to home terror can strike when Benjamin Smith, a student who had attended both Indiana University and the University of Illinois and was a member of a white supremacist church, chose Independence Day 1999 to begin a racially motivated shooting spree that killed an African American basketball coach at Northwestern University in Evanston, Illinois, and a Korean graduate student at my university in Bloomington, also seriously wounding six Orthodox Jews, a Taiwanese student, and two other African Americans. According to Smith's girlfriend, he wanted to protect the freedom of white Americans "from the increasing pluralism of American society."[32] As a white American, I do not feel any safer for his efforts, nor do I think freedom needs protection from pluralism, but I cannot just dismiss his behavior as alien to American political culture and continue to insist on the innocence of American experience. Benjamin Smith is a product of that culture and that experience and a disturbing symbol of the nation the United States might all too easily become in a global crusade against evil Others.

Domestic terrorists abound, whether they are militiamen like Timothy McVeigh who truck-bomb federal buildings, white supremacists like Benjamin Smith who randomly murder racial minorities, or antiabortion militants like Eric Rudolph who set off a bomb in Atlanta, Georgia, at the 1996 Summer Olympics and the Reverend Paul Hill who killed Dr. John Britton on July 29, 1994, for performing abortions at a clinic in Pensacola, Florida. The actions of homegrown terrorists are disturbingly similar to those of foreign or international terrorists who blew up Pan American Flight 103 over Lockerbie, Scotland, in 1988, truck-bombed U.S. embassies in Kenya and Tanzania in August 1998, van-bombed the World Trade Center in 1993, and then used commercial aircraft to destroy it eight and a half years later, killing thousands of unsuspecting civilians. Thus, we should not be overly surprised to learn that right-wing hate groups in the United States celebrated the terrorist attacks of September 11 with expressions of glee that a revolution was finally under way. "WONDERFUL NEWS BROTHERS!!" exclaimed Hardy Lloyd, Pittsburgh coordinator of the racist, anti-Semitic World Church of the Creator. "Hallelu-Yahweh!" exulted "Pastor" August B. Kries III of the Sheriff's Posse Comitatus. "May the WAR be started! Death to His enemies, may the World Trade Center BURN TO THE GROUND! . . . We blame no others than ourselves for our problems due to the fact that we allow . . . Satan's children, called jews [sic] today, to have dominion over our lives."[33]

Yet, religiously motivated terrorists foreign to the U.S., including suicide bombers and those dangerously inclined toward using heinous weapons of mass destruction, are most often highly intelligent and well-educated operatives, not despairing, impoverished, ignorant, irrational, and homicidal misfits. They include "bright scientists skilled in the modern technologies of the computer, telecommunications equipment, information databases, and financial networks" and are increasingly recruited "from fields such as communications, computer programming, engineering, finance, and the sciences."[34] A surprising number of Al Qaeda captives in U.S. custody who have been interrogated at Guantánamo Bay came from high-status families and held graduate degrees. Recruits are selected to be "intelligent, psychologically balanced and socially poised. Candidates who mostly want virgins in paradise or money for their families are weeded out. Those selected show patience and the ability to plan and execute in subtle, quiet ways that don't draw attention." They typically have good self-esteem, often hold respectable jobs, and generally invoke religion as their primary value. Multiple studies in 2001 and 2002 alone showed that terrorists and their supporters are "rarely ignorant or impoverished" nor "crazed, cowardly, apathetic or asocial." One poll of Palestinian adults even found that individuals with twelve years or more of education were more supportive of suicide attackers than were people who were illiterate. Multiple polls of the Muslim world also show that Arab attitudes are strongly in favor of democracy, personal liberty, and education. U.S. actions are what they oppose, not America's form of government or freedom. When the United States began to build up its military forces to invade Iraq, Al Qaeda recruitment actually increased in dozens of countries, and the number of volunteers mushroomed. U.S. military strength has not dissuaded these highly motivated, purposeful, and intelligent adversaries from their terrorist ways.[35]

Indeed, their terrorist acts are crimes against humanity, writes Phil Scranton, "derived from a reasoned hatred, a distorted fundamentalism that transformed belief, intellect and compassion into a mutant, predatory 'final solution' politics." Moreover, he insists, "to portray such men as psychopathic killers, whose 'lust for blood' emanates from individual or cultural pathology, diminishes the historical, political and economic contexts which fed and nurtured their absolute moral purpose." On both sides of the divide, perpetrators of terror and counterterror draw upon a familiar vocabulary to reduce one another to demons that savagely massacre innocent people and thereby threaten to destroy all of civilization. Each side marks the Other for eradication as subhuman, barbarian, insane, and wicked outlaws. This is a "dangerous construction," Scranton concludes, which invariably leads to "an abandonment of the rule of law and established rules of engagement. If the 'enemy' is beneath contempt, the war against it can be unconditional."[36]

Unfortunately, terrorist and counterterrorist acts, like the demonizing language to which they respond in common, are not completely unlike one another. The U.S. military's supposed "precision" missile and bombing strikes against Iraq during the Desert Storm conflict of 1991 reportedly killed more than 35,000 Iraqi civilians when only 370 Allied soldiers died in combat, and most of those soldiers were victims of friendly fire.[37] The Pentagon did not even attempt to count the number of civilians in Afghanistan killed by the bombing campaign against the Taliban and Al Qaeda forces, a number that may have exceeded three thousand, although America's high-altitude weapons this time around were allegedly even more precise than the precision weapons used so confidently a decade earlier in Desert Storm. It is difficult to ignore the disturbing parallel between the enemy's terror and America's counterterror when the world's richest and strongest nation pulverizes one of the world's poorest countries without even bothering to count civilian casualties. As Caleb Carr warns, "Warfare against civilians" must "never be answered in kind," for it is a "failed tactic" that brings about "retaliation in kind" and "perpetuates a cycle of revenge and outrage that can go on for generations," planting "the seeds of our own eventual downfall"; "a nation must never think that it can use . . . the agents of terror when convenient and then be rid of them when they are no longer needed."[38]

Performance Violence and the Terrorist Trap

Given this counterproductive cycle of terror and counterterror, why are such tactics ever used? What so strongly motivates the political use of violence against civilians? What are the roots of terrorism? What makes them grow ever deeper? And how have we become so thoroughly entangled in them?

Terrorism is a problem, as Walter Laqueur notes, that "has rarely been absent from history" and a threat, as Philip Heymann observes, that "cannot be completely eliminated."[39] Its sources are intensely complex in their political, economic, social, cultural, and religious dimensions of grievance, and they will never be fully resolved, for ethnic conflict, nationalism, imperialism, revolutionary ideology, economic exploitation, poverty, religious fervor, and political alienation are not finite problems, especially as they reassert themselves against the continuing presence of empire in the post–cold war "power vacuums left by the collapse of the old order" of the U.S.-Soviet rivalry.[40] One characteristic is constant, however: whether the source of violence is cultural, ideological, religious, economic, state terrorism, or some combination of these, the "us-them" dichotomy is "paramount in the thinking of terrorists" and counterterrorists.[41] Herein lies the key to the terrorist trap and the problem of escalating violence insofar as it is within America's power to widen its circumference of understanding and develop a more serviceable attitude toward the problem at hand.

In its most extreme form, the form it has taken in defending Western civilization against Islamic revolution (and vice versa), the dichotomization of "us versus them" in a dramatization of "good versus evil" is a call to cosmic war. This is no ordinary political strategy or statement but instead a public performance of violence that serves as a symbolic assertion of empowerment. It is what Mark Juergensmeyer calls "performance violence," which must be understood and analyzed as symbol, ritual, and drama. "In speaking of terrorism as 'performance,'" he emphasizes, we are "not suggesting that such acts are undertaken lightly or capriciously. Rather, like religious ritual or street theater, they are dramas designed to have an impact on the several audiences that they affect." It is a drama that promotes "satanization" of the enemy, a ritual that transforms death into salvation, a symbolization of cosmic struggle that prolongs the battle endlessly, and a legitimization of unlimited escalations of violence to the point of utter extermination of the evil Other.[42] And it is an attitude assumed by all the parties to terrorism—domestic, international, and state sponsors of violence against civilians to achieve political aims. Each side enacts its own performance violence in response to the Other's enactments, reinforcing one another in an escalating dance of death.

Not only does this reciprocal satanization of enemies by both sides mark everyone as legitimate targets of escalating violence—because even civilians are considered to be consenting and contributing members of one evil order or the other—but it also renders Americans all the more prone to the myopia of empire, less capable of self-critique, and thus increasingly vulnerable to destruction by instruments of our own making. By ritualizing the "us-them" divide, Americans become unwitting agents of their enemy's designs. Osama bin Laden's jihad is an immediate case in point.

In his fatwa of February 23, 1996, bin Laden declared war against Americans for occupying Muslim holy lands and because of America's "barbaric treatment of Muslim people during its [first] war against Saddam Hussein," citing in particular the killing of thousands of innocent civilians by U.S. bombs. Later, in an interview with ABC News in 1998, he referenced the atomic bombings of Hiroshima and Nagasaki as further evidence of U.S. terror and evil. Thus, "every American man, woman, and child" was deemed a legitimate target of Al Qaeda's righteous warriors.[43]

The spiral of reciprocal violence is apparent here. Add yet another twist, and one can see the makings of an even greater blunder by the United States when it took bin Laden too literally and reacted too predictably. That is, as Michael Scott Doran argues, bin Laden had no expectation or intention of defeating the United States, per se, but was baiting the United States, banking on a predictable reaction that would further his primary goal of fomenting an Islamic revolution within the Muslim world.

This was an exercise in performance violence, a piece of political theater of the kind David Fromkin suggests is "aimed at creating fear in order that the fear, in turn, will lead somebody else—not the terrorist—to embark on some different program of action that will accomplish whatever it is that the terrorist really desires." In this case, Doran believes, "Osama bin Laden sought—and has received—an international military crackdown, one he wants to exploit for his particular brand of revolution." In his script, "America, cast as the villain, is supposed to use its military might like a cartoon character trying to kill a fly with a shotgun," and the Islamic community "will find it shocking how Americans nonchalantly cause Muslims to suffer and die." Their ensuing outrage will advance the cause of Islamic revolution against secular governments in Arab countries and especially Saudi Arabia and thus embroil the United States in an "intra-Muslim ideological battle."[44] Just as Al Qaeda terrorists used U.S. training facilities to learn how to fly American civilian aircraft into America's own buildings that then collapsed on themselves to kill so many civilians, bin Laden set a trap in which the United States was to use its own military might inadvertently to help bring down more secular Arab regimes in the Middle East—regimes that were neither paragons of liberal democracy themselves nor invulnerable bulwarks of stability against revolutionary forces.

How does the United States begin to disentangle itself from this self-perpetuating, self-defeating, and dangerously escalating cycle of performance violence? Given that terrorism thrives on overreaction, it is imperative that America respond wisely according to democratic principles, for terrorists gain a victory when "we begin to live our lives in constant fear . . . and take measures that erode our basic democratic values."[45] The aim has to be one of protecting life while maintaining "the liberties necessary to a vibrant democracy" and the civic health of a diverse nation.[46] An attitude of war all too easily trumps a healthy regard for civil liberties and human rights, and an overemphasis on the rhetoric of "us versus them," reinforced by sweeping condemnations of terrorism as evil incarnate, achieves little of value even as it works against the democratic value of accommodating pluralism.[47] Americans have to recognize that war in general and killing an Osama bin Laden in particular does not make terrorism disappear and that it may very well even fan the flames of global terrorism.[48] Already, as Michael Doran has observed, "many Muslims who do not belong to bin Laden's terrorist network consider the United States to be on a moral par with Genghis Khan."[49]

Accordingly, emphasis must shift from escalating the violence to encouraging a contest of ideas because, in the words of Samuel Berger and Mona Sutphen, pluralism is an enemy of extremism.[50] Shedding the vestiges of a cold war mentality and the habits of unilateralism would help to relax the "suffocating embrace" of empire and to rely more heavily on diplomacy and leadership by example than military force and economic bullying.[51] Achieving a peaceful resolution of the Israeli-Palestinian conflict, for example, would amount to an affirmation of pluralism, a blow to Al Qaeda's interests and objectives, and an advance toward identifying a significant number of Muslims and their interests with those of the United States.[52]

Too much emphasis on the methods of war ignores the complexities of the threat in its multiple dimensions and gets the United States all the more deeply entangled in the terrorist trap of escalating performance violence for dubious political purposes. The particular policies America might adopt to reduce its overreliance on military measures and to increase its emphasis on law enforcement, intelligence gathering, diplomacy, multilateralism, and economic assistance as principal means of countering terrorism must be crafted in a context of renewed respect for pluralism and emphasis on democratic principles at home and abroad so that patriotism and national unity are not defined narrowly in opposition to an evil Other.[53] Adopting a wider and subtler perspective over the method of caricature is the most realistic antidote to the hubris of empire and the best attitude for responding wisely to present exigencies. Terrorism is a heinous but maddening act. Exterminating every vicious killer in an upward spiral of performance violence is an impossible mission even as it undermines the very quest for freedom and democracy.

Addressing Terror Democratically

If a more comprehensive view of the realities of terrorism is adopted, rather than continuing to fixate piously on a vain and doomed attempt to eradicate evil, how might the United States respond differently in order to decrease the otherwise escalating cycle of performance violence against civilians? That is, what are the implications of a revised attitude toward terror, an attitude that takes into account the complexities of its causes and the limitations of military and other methods of counterterror on which Americans have become so overly dependent within the restricted framework of a war on terrorism? What better options exist, *if* one thinks outside the limits of the present profile of terrorism and corresponding military mindset? *If* Americans recognize their own complicity in the problem? *If* they acknowledge that empire—their considerable economic, cultural, and military presence and influence throughout the world—is a continuing reality and a compelling reason to enact democratic values instead of fearing democracy itself, succumbing to the arrogance of power, or wishing away the responsibility of exercising constructive leadership? And *if* they accept the challenge and demonstrate the courage to practice democracy in a pluralistic world here and now, rather than restrain, defer, and suspend it until a future time in a hypothetical world where it supposedly will become safe to practice after human diversity and divisions have somehow disappeared? What, then, is the wider range of options for coping with terrorism sensibly as a strong and democratic people residing necessarily in a deeply conflicted world—a people who understand that diversity is the condition and the challenge of democracy, not its risk and ruin? Beyond the prevailing caricature of terrorists and terrorism, how might Americans begin to address this problem at home and abroad more democratically and less coercively?

Modifying unrealistic expectations is the first crucial step toward developing an effective response to terror. Thinking in terms of a "war" against terror is a recipe for demoralization and self-defeat. In the words of Paul Pillar, a former deputy chief of the Counterterrorist Center of the CIA and executive assistant to the CIA director, "If there is a 'war' against terrorism, it is a war that cannot be won. Counterterrorism, even though it shares some attributes with warfare," he continues, "is not accurately represented by the metaphor of a war." It has no fixed enemies, no clear beginning, nor any prospect of closure, final victory, or internal collapse of the adversary. It is more like a continuous public health campaign than a war, where threats "come in many different forms, some more virulent than others. Some of the threats are waxing; some are waning. Some are old; others are very new." Just as progress is made against one disease, a different strain or new type of disease appears on the scene. Disease itself is never conquered; we will never live in a disease-free world. Likewise, terrorism as a whole "*cannot be 'defeated'— only reduced, attenuated, and to some degree controlled.*" To hope for more is to set unrealistic expectations that can only damage public morale with each new terrorist attack. Rather than winning a war, Pillar argues, the standard for counterterrorist policy should be to save lives without compromising national interests, compromises that range from violating civil liberties and human rights to reinforcing Islamic distrust of the United States and rankling allies. Without ever accepting terrorism's legitimacy, we must learn to expect that it will continue to be a part of our lives.[54] Moreover, Laqueur emphasizes, "there is not one terrorism but a variety of terrorisms and what is true of one does not necessarily apply to others."[55]

Accordingly, Americans should expect policies that are flexible, adaptive, multifaceted, and responsive to a wide range of immediate, emerging, and long-term terrorist threats, that emphasize a combination of diplomacy, international cooperation, intelligence gathering, economic assistance, police work, and criminal prosecution over a preponderance of military means, and that eschew the temptation of national leaders "to use emotional or simplistic themes that, although effective at drumming up [public] support in the short term, may reduce the political room for maneuver when it comes to the more complex and delicate issues in counterterrorism."[56] Just as the world does not reduce to a simple dichotomy between good and evil, an effective response to terror cannot be premised on "absolute solutions and a rejection of accommodation, [compromise], and finesse."[57] Nor can we reasonably judge any serviceable policy by the explicit or implicit criterion of eradicating the threat.

Not even military action can hope to defeat terror completely or permanently; in fact, used too vigorously, it can backfire and escalate the reign of terror. Its role, therefore, must be very carefully calibrated and its use severely restricted and closely coordinated with more progressive instruments for managing terrorism. Even when the military option is taken to rescue hostages, success is difficult to achieve, and luck (or the lack thereof) is a major factor in the eventual outcome, as elite Israeli special forces have learned from the bitter experience of failure. In addition, as a means of retaliation, military force is motivated more by a desire to "do something" dramatic than by faith in its ability to prevent further attacks. Such incursions serve mostly to bolster an administration's popularity and to satisfy momentarily a blinding thirst for revenge.

Although a military strike may send a message of national resolve and may temporarily impede some terrorist activity, it degrades terrorist capabilities minimally, for terrorists typically do not present easy, fixed, concentrated, or substantial military targets. *Our* military attacks are *their* rationalization for retaliation and can even serve their larger purpose—as in the case of Osama bin Laden's desire to foment an Islamic revolution within the Muslim world by goading the United States into a military crusade against Al Qaeda and Taliban forces. In the court of world opinion, a large or sustained exercise of military might by the United States against terrorist targets all too easily crosses the threshold from perceptions of self-defense to the unsavory spectacle of bullying behavior.[58] Little can be achieved, and a great deal of harm is likely to result from relying on the armed forces for protection against this kind of threat.

Israel's reaction to Palestinian terrorism is a dramatic case in point. Even with the benefit of overwhelming military superiority, the advantage of occupation, and the devastating impact of point-blank attacks on enemy strongholds, terror survives and even thrives. Nor can one explain away the inevitable failure of the April 2002 Israeli military escalation by saying it would have succeeded except for outside interference that momentarily blunted the West Bank invasion. Not only is there a long and failed history of Israeli attempts to eradicate Palestinian terrorism by military means of counterterror, but also outside interference from Arab nations as well as Western powers is a reality of inherently conflicted international interests and pressures with which any state, including Israel, must contend and from which it cannot realistically expect immunity. Accordingly, as U.S. Secretary of State Colin Powell prepared on April 11 to travel to Israel on a peace-seeking mission, he "challenged the idea that strong Israeli military action on the West Bank could enhance security from terror." Because of the depths of Palestinian anger and frustration, he said, "there will still be people who are willing to resort to violence and terror, people who are willing to use suicide bombs and other kinds of bombs," no matter how much counterforce is applied.[59] For the United States there was the double embarrassment of countermanding a client state such as Israel even as Prime Minister Ariel Sharon justified the escalation of military strikes against Palestinians by quoting from President Bush's own call to arms against global terrorism, including the president's call to destroy terrorism's very infrastructure. Not only has the United States itself resorted to the perilous course of military assault on an illusive enemy, but also it has inadvertently reinforced the most counterproductive inclinations of frustrated and beleaguered Israelis and Palestinians.

Even Caleb Carr, who harbors some faith in military force as a limited instrument of counterterrorism, cautions against the temptation of the traditional American style of warfare that relies "on overwhelming force and the debilitating power of attrition to reach its military goals." Such military tactics of total war, he argues, including long-range destruction and "particularly bombing campaigns" that necessarily result in substantial "collateral damage" (no matter what the expressed or actual intentions or even official claims to the contrary), must be abandoned in favor of more precise, selective, and limited methods that avoid civilian causalities and reduce the loss of America's moral authority. Even then, such strictly limited and discriminating tactical operations are self-defeating instruments of counterterrorism to the extent that they function as "warfare against civilians, whether in-spired by hatred, revenge, greed, or political and psychological insecurity."[60]

Accordingly, skepticism should be the first response and sustained reac-tion to the military option. But what other options exist? And what are *their* limitations? No one of them, we should forever remind ourselves, is a silver bullet, nor do all of them in concert amount to a final solution. Diplomacy, for instance, is a necessary medium for enlisting cooperation from other gov-ernments and coordinating counterterrorist policies and practices, such as gathering and sharing intelligence, negotiating treaties of extradition and sanctions against state sponsors of terrorism, reinforcing international norms against terrorism, and so on. Law enforcement is another key component of any comprehensive strategy for apprehending and prosecuting some terror-ists, disrupting the free movement of others, and perhaps even deterring rela-tively few. Yet, the arrest of one may prompt retaliation from others, even in those rare cases where leaders rather than low-level operatives are appre-hended. Such rare cases are usually difficult to prosecute successfully be-cause of appropriately high standards of evidence. Moreover, a decision to ar-rest a suspected terrorist must be balanced against the possibility of losing an unwitting source of counterterrorism intelligence. Disrupting terrorists' fi-nances is yet another partial tool for managing the threat. Freezing assets and blocking material support causes some damage that complicates terrorist operations, but the fact remains that terrorism is cheap, and the money trail is very hard to follow because much of it moves outside the formal bank-ing system or via offshore banks that make a business of confidentiality. Fi-nally, although intelligence gathering is crucial to monitoring terrorist ac-tivity, forewarning targets of attack, and even foiling some of the violence, agents cannot easily infiltrate decentralized terrorist cells or get close to tight-knit, highly motivated, and fiercely loyal members of inner circles. Be-sides the nearly impossible task of infiltrating terrorist organizations and col-lecting good information, analyzing the massive amounts of intelligence data accumulated from other sources, such as electronic surveillance, is equally challenging.[61]

Given the inherent advantage of terrorists over any and all countermeasures at America's disposal, from military assaults to diplomacy, law enforcement, disrupting finances, and gathering intelligence, how might a democratic people best address the root causes of the problem, short of any expectation of eliminating terrorism altogether but in the reasonable hope of reducing its intensity and lessening its incentives? The interconnected origins of terrorism and accompanying rituals of victimization include ideological, religious, ethnic, economic, and other profound sources of competing hierarchies, frustrated aspirations, divisive differences, and perceived injustices. Just as terror is itself a symbolic act, a dramatic performance of escalating violence against civilians that is intended as a deadly message for targeted audiences, the manner of addressing terror is also a symbolic act that can either exacerbate or ameliorate the human divide.

In the short run, the United States must do what it can to defend against imminent threats and attacks without anticipating complete success or resorting to counterproductive measures and methods incompatible with its aims and values. For the long haul, though, the greatest challenge is to engage a deeply conflicted world democratically. Coping democratically with underlying sources of recurrent terror means recognizing that (1) conflict and division are inherent to the human condition, (2) a positive conception of peace (as contrasted with negatively defining peace as the absence of war—or, in this case, the eradication of terrorism) involves continuously bridging differences instead of attempting to eliminate or suppress them, and (3) America's material strength is matched by the potential of its political culture to acknowledge, deliberate, and constructively respond to the competing interests of domestic and foreign Others.

Using the nation's considerable strength aptly and confidently to engage deep divisions democratically is no small challenge to be undertaken lightly or dismissed unrealistically. It is the best means of determining, for example, where and how distributive injustices can and should be eased in order to reduce economic desperation as a motive for tolerating terrorism. And it is a process that potentially promotes hope instead of alienation by inviting wide and diverse participation—including the participation of those who are immediately impacted by the outcome of problem-solving deliberations over conflicted interests and issues, even though extremists themselves are resistant to democratic means. A world completely free of terrorism, like a world free of crime, disease, or conflict and competition, is inconceivable. Some combination of "paranoia, fanaticism, and extremist political (or religious) doctrine" will stir terrorists to deadly action regardless of the state of political, social, and economic conditions in the world.[62] The only realistic alternative is to translate agonistic propensities and divisive circumstances into a productive political process for the populace at large—a political process guided by democratic values and employing democratic procedures.

There is a danger of being misunderstood when I say that the United

States should promote democracy or more specifically when I call for engaging the world's deep divisions democratically. This is not the same as Woodrow Wilson's World War I call to make the world safe for democracy, nor is it an endorsement of the post–cold war policy of democratizing nations throughout the world on the dubious premise that democracies, or at least stable democracies, do not fight one another. Both of these conventional interpretations amount to defending or imposing on others one's own political system, i.e., advancing narrow national interests under the universal flag of democracy. They also imply that democracy is weak, vulnerable, and fragile, that it must be protected, even curtailed or suspended, when the nation is under attack, and that it should be deferred or delegated until divisive circumstances subside and a supportive, sophisticated political culture with a reliably informed, intelligent, and rational citizenry finally emerges globally. These are the traditional attitudes toward democracy that have diminished the democratic experience throughout American history, that make democracy something to protect more than to practice, something to fear rather than something safe and secure, something to contain and control rather than a guide to political action, something to rationalize and mask a policy of empire rather than to motivate and define constructive participation in world affairs.

Instead of reducing democracy to an endangered (and dangerous) object of protection and containment and thus to an all too readily available justification for war and domination, and rather than persisting in the futility of attempting to impose America's will on a recalcitrant world, a better option is to explore the untapped potential of democratic persuasion for addressing present exigencies more thoroughly and effectively. This is not the same as making a simple choice between persuasion and coercion, democratic practice and military force, isolationism and internationalism, idealism and realism, or any other false dichotomy or phony dilemma. Instead, it amounts to a shift of emphasis. America's potential for constructive leadership and responsible citizenship is not limited to its economic strength and military might. Moreover, any expectation of directing world affairs as a right and responsibility of superpower status is a recipe for more terrorist blowback. Exercising U.S. power without translating democratic values into actual practice forfeits America's best chance to mitigate the underlying causes of support for terrorism in a global information age that makes imperative the accommodation of competing interests and perspectives. Pluralism on a global scale is the reality with which America must learn to cope constructively. Accordingly, the next frontier for Americans boldly to explore is the uncharted territory of democratic persuasion where they may seek to increase their security in a profoundly conflicted world by articulating common ground on which to contest differences that otherwise intensify the motives for violence.

To chart this democratic frontier will require the same fortitude of purpose, strength of faith, courage, and ingenuity, the same desire for adventure, and the same aptitude for experimentation that has characterized Americans throughout a remarkable history of extraordinary achievement. Moreover, responding to the present exigency of global alienation and politically motivated violence against civilians by exploring the full potentiality of the nation's democratic temperament conforms to a general historical trajectory of increasingly democratizing U.S. political culture by extending the vote to previously disenfranchised groups and creating new opportunities for greater public participation. The remaining democratic deficit, as political philosopher Chantal Mouffe argues, prevents a people from addressing adequately the global challenge of pervasive pluralism and thus from reducing the temptation to violence and victimization.[63] The question to consider now is how to engage a deeply conflicted world democratically, not whether to wait until some mythical time when the human divide is somehow abolished by the righteous force of arms. The piece of the puzzle still missing from such a strategy for easing the rule of terror is an understanding of the ways of transforming violence into rhetorical agonistics and thus enemies into adversaries.

Rather than waging peace in this way, however, the Bush administration opted again for an exercise in unmitigated empire when it determined to extend the terror war by forcefully overthrowing the government of Iraq, a decision that Jonathan Schell aptly characterizes as marking "a culmination in the rise within the United States of an immense concentration of unaccountable power that poses the greatest threat to the American constitutional system since the Watergate crisis." It is a transformation of power of Augustan proportions in the U.S. presidency that "threatens to push the world into a new era of rivalry, confrontation and war," with the awesome power of an unchallenged military machine at the administration's disposal, without opposition from a Congress that has abdicated its constitutional authority to deliberate and declare war, influenced by "corporate money that inundates the political realm," and committed to a strategy of deep secrecy and restricted civil liberties at home. Popular support of such a regime, Schell observes, is rooted in "fear that has been manipulated to extend far beyond its proper objects" with the "overriding goal" of accumulating "ever more power, whose supreme expression is its naked ambition to establish hegemony over the earth." Even when the world rebelled, the Bush administration persisted in another act of "regime change" consistent with its "radical new policy of dominance asserted through the unilateral, pre-emptive use of force."[64]

By what rhetorical means might America's political culture right itself before even more damage is done to the cause of freedom, democracy, and peace? This is the question to which we now turn directly.

5
Idiom of Democracy

An issue raised in our earlier critique of traditional republican demophobia, as reconstituted in contemporary notions of deliberative democracy and democratic peace, is especially salient to the so-called war on terror. How, we may now ask in the particular instance of terrorism, might liberal values be realigned to support rather than restrict democratic practice? Can a democratic attitude be articulated so that it is faithful to liberal values but also accommodating to diversity without vilifying foreign Others or policing self-serving universals? The Bush administration's reaction to the terrorist attacks of September 11, 2001, brought these questions into urgent focus by relegating liberty and democracy to the low status of war objectives. By the president's reckoning, liberty was to be restricted and democracy restrained indefinitely while freedom remained under attack from ubiquitous evildoers.[1]

This is a common way of justifying war and curtailing public deliberation that, although deeply rooted in cultural convention, leaves a residue of unresolved friction. The administration's call to arms necessarily was conflicted in some degree because of opposed or misaligned valences among its own rhetorical constituents. A war that supposedly aimed to preserve freedom and civilization, for instance, undercut the same liberal values it purported to defend. Such friction destabilized the rationale for a protracted war marginally but just enough to put back into play the possibility of elevating democracy itself and achieving in turn a better purchase on the deeper challenge of terror.

The chance of widening this rhetorical crack in the administration's conflicted rationale for war hinges on still another consideration. Engaging terrorism's complexity, instead of just vilifying an enemy and escalating the violence, requires shifting from an anemic representation of democracy to the more democratically robust perspective of agonistic pluralism.[2] Although the idea of embracing agonistic democracy as a means of attenuating antagonism and accommodating liberal values currently exists only on the horizon of America's political imagination, the incentive to explore that frontier could very well increase as the tensions internal to an illiberal war are intensified.

Meanwhile, understood as an exigency for war, terror has closed democracy's unexplored frontier and spawned a prolonged military campaign to defeat the dark forces of evil—demonic forces that otherwise would prevent the civilizing influence of democratic enlightenment. From this narrow perspective, democracy is a legitimizing symbol for conquering by military force a wilderness of intimidation and oppression, not a frontier itself to explore. Such a war of terror channels the dissonance of democratic pretense into an attitude of extreme Othering. Diverting rather than defaulting to this ritual of victimization is the challenge at hand if the nation would face more squarely the presence of global pluralism. By engaging diversity agonistically, so that divisions are bridged enough to moderate rather than exacerbate destructive antagonism, a revitalized democratic culture could focus not just on defeating the means of terrorism but also on taking into account terrorism's underlying causes and conditions, what George Lakoff calls conflicting worldviews and "cultures of despair."[3]

As a case in point, George W. Bush's presidential speeches on terrorism direct the dissonance of suppressed political values into a singular focus on destroying the means of terrorism. Placed under the sign of a war on evil incarnate, democracy is closed off to full expression let alone further exploration, and vilification supplants deliberation. Yet, Bush's speeches also demonstrate a limited capacity to restrain less-warlike motives. One can even extract from his discourse the rudiments of a strategy for reframing the nation's perspective on terrorism. To this extent, at least, the administration's case for absolute war contributes to its own potential deconstruction. My aim, therefore, is to show where this occurs and how, although inadvertently, it invites a stronger expression of democratic culture.

Reframing Terrorism

The president's profile of terrorism and the threat it poses to national security was articulated in direct response to the infamous attacks on the World

Trade Center and the Pentagon. The dramatic fall of the twin towers before millions of bewildered viewers crystallized an image of menace in a metonymic moment of unanticipated conflagration. This horrific image engaged a number of visual metaphors, Lakoff explains, including the sense of an airplane as projectile striking someone's head and the tower falling like a mortally wounded body. Television viewers might feel the menacing approach of the plane and sense the building toppling as if being shot dead themselves. And when the two tallest buildings in the middle of Manhattan suddenly crumbled, the world witnessed the abrupt disintegration of a symbol of American power. If control is represented by being placed high up and on top of things, loss of power is suggested by toppling the great city's highest skyscrapers. Destroying "the temple of capitalist commerce" was tantamount to shaking the very foundation of society. All that remained, in Lakoff's view, was a "charred and smoking . . . image of hell" in which the city's now unbalanced skyline signaled the nation's sinking prospects.

Framing this dreadful image proved difficult from the very beginning. On the first day, the president spoke of "a national tragedy" and a crime of "mass murder," promising "a full-scale investigation to hunt down and to find those folks who committed this act." He would direct the "full resources" of "law enforcement" to "find those responsible and to bring them to justice." This was a crime of huge proportion. But by the end of the day, Bush was already speaking of seeing "evil," standing down "enemies," and winning a "war" against terrorism.[4] A terrible crime was rapidly becoming a full-scale act of war. "War has been declared on us," Bush proclaimed.[5]

Just as the metaphor of crime seemed inadequate to express the immensity of the terrorist outrage, the image of war also proved difficult to resolve. There was no enemy army in sight or even a clear measure of victory. Targeting Al Qaeda fighters and Taliban forces in Afghanistan, it would seem, was an initial attempt, consistent with the logic of the metaphor of war, to meet the expectation of fighting an actual army. Identifying an axis of evil and planning an invasion of Iraq to effect a "regime change" served the same purpose. Despite such efforts, the administration was still saddled, in Bush's own words, with "a new kind of war"—"a different kind of conflict against a different kind of enemy . . . a conflict without battlefields or beachheads, a conflict with opponents who believe they are invisible."[6]

Because the vehicle of war did not fit especially well the tenor of terrorism, other metaphors quickly appeared in administration statements to manage this potentially deconstructive internal friction by directing it outwardly toward an enemy of "cowards," "rodents," "swamp" creatures, "snakes," and other lowlife forms.[7] Dehumanizing and decivilizing terms of vilification focused the nation's attention on an image of evil in order to distract the public from the inadequacies of declaring the events of 9/11 an act of war. Americans were prodded linguistically into performing a patriotic ritual of victimization in order to affirm the nation's inherent goodness and prove its moral strength by standing up to and triumphing over evil. Thus, "whipping terrorism," the president announced, had become "the focus of my administration."[8] This "unconventional war" was America's "fight against evil" to "save civilization, itself."[9]

The distraction of the administration's unrelenting discourse of vilification and victimization served not only to intensify an already traumatized nation's appetite for retribution but also to exacerbate the causes of terrorism by focusing exclusively on eliminating its most immediate means and agents. "The focus right now is on Osama bin Laden, no question about it," the president declared less than a week after the attacks on New York and Washington, D.C. "I want him," as "an old poster out West" said, "Dead or Alive." This was going to be a long war that would require the American people "to be more patient than ever" (an implicit recognition of the dissonance created by the ill-fitting metaphor of war) because there are also "other terrorists in the world . . . who hate freedom," and "it's going to require a new thought process" to "get them running . . . and to hunt them down."[10] When Osama bin Laden disappeared from sight and could not be found after a massive U.S. military assault on Afghanistan, the president began to shift focus in this war "to defend freedom against ruthless enemies" onto the target of "outlaw regimes" who possess "weapons of mass destruction." The "dark threat" to freedom now consisted of "mad terrorists and tyrants," not the least of which was Saddam Hussein, the evil dictator of Baghdad whom Bush branded "an enemy until proven otherwise."[11] This was now the threat to which the United States would "respond decisively," the president proclaimed, for "poverty doesn't create terror . . . terror takes root in failing nations that cannot police themselves."[12] Terrorist leaders and countries harboring them, the training facilities, weapons, and financial resources of terrorists—but not the social and political conditions underlying cultures of despair—fell within the president's framework of Operation Enduring Freedom to save civilization.[13]

Yet, as Lakoff argues, this singular focus on the "enabling cause" of an evil enemy, which precludes taking primary causes seriously, re-creates the very conditions in which "terrorists will continue to be spawned." A policy of just war on terror is America's own contribution to terror that swells rather than shrinks the breeding grounds of terror. The radical worldviews of terrorist operatives will be positively influenced, if at all, by "moderate and liberal Muslims—clerics, teachers, elders, respected community members," an "organized, moderate, nonviolent Islam" motivated by the West's serious efforts "to address the social and political conditions that lead to despair." Military methods cannot change radical minds, except to make them more radical. What is needed, then, is a way to "reframe" public discourse so that it no longer is rendered "hypocritical" by violating the government's "own stated ideals" of promoting freedom, pluralism, democracy, justice, and prosperity.[14]

Holding fast to an ill-fated war on evil at the level of official policy increases the likelihood of what was initially a marginalized perception of hypocrisy developing into a wider desire for change and greater receptivity to reframing the discourse of terror. Should an intersection of world and American public opinion occur along these lines, the stakes would be raised even higher. As one American professor reported, although he wanted to understand the U.S. military operation in Afghanistan as fundamentally one of "liberation," his international students perceived it as "superpower bullying." Students "moved by values of human rights and democracy" had "become convinced that the existence of these rights in America is predicated on their repression elsewhere."[15]

Herein lay the tension tenuously contained by the administration's troubled rationale for war and the corresponding possibility of reframing the challenge of terrorism to conform more closely to the nation's political values and to reduce more effectively the threat to national security. But a mere glimpse of these fissures does not reveal so well the possibility of reconfiguring the prevailing public discourse of terror as a more sustained mapping of rhetorical fault lines can. How is it that the president's attempt to co-opt universal values on behalf of war comes up short of satisfying the very cultural expectations it activates? And where can these potentially deconstructing points of fissure be located in his speeches? Answers to these questions help to specify a strategy, or at least to sketch the outline of a strategy, for revising a badly flawed perspective that distorts America's response to terrorism.

A Paradoxical Defense of Freedom

The war on terrorism, the president insisted, was first and foremost a defense of freedom from terrorist evildoers. "They have attacked America," he proclaimed at the National Cathedral, "because we are freedom's home and defender."[16] The collapse of the Twin Towers shook freedom's foundation and exposed its vulnerability to the dark forces of savagery. As freedom plummeted toward the hellish abyss of chaos, only the heroism of a wounded but determined and united nation could forestall its ultimate demise. "These acts shattered steel," Bush assured Americans, "but they cannot dent the steel of American resolve. America was targeted for attack because we're the brightest beacon for freedom and opportunity in the world. And no one will keep that light from shining."[17]

But "night fell" on "a world where freedom itself is under attack," the president acknowledged while proclaiming that "freedom and fear are at war. The advance of human freedom—the great achievement of our time, and the great hope of every time—now depends on us."[18] Out of the destruction of September 11, America was "building a House of Freedom."[19] As a people "awakened to danger," fighting to protect freedom and to preserve civilization from "a nightmare world where every city is a potential killing field," Americans would "write the story of our times, a story of courage defeating cruelty and light overcoming darkness."[20]

Freedom's fight, in the president's summarizing words, was the "great divide in our time . . . between civilization and barbarism."[21] The presidential tapestry of symbolism, which portrayed the meaning and urgency of this momentous battle, was woven in light and dark strands starkly contrasting courage and cowardice, crime and punishment, morality and evil, liberty and slavery, and savagery and civilization in an epic test of America's strength and determination to transform a tormented world. This narrative of light overcoming darkness was haunted by the visual metonym of Twin Towers falling and a sudden descent of American power, leaving freedom vulnerable to the ravages of terrorism and tyranny. The essence of Bush's call to arms, in response to this defining image of falling from power, was to pit freedom against fear so that securing freedom was tantamount to conquering fear. Yet, as Benjamin Barber observes, "fear's empire leaves no room for democracy."[22]

The ambiguity of Bush's basic rhetorical formulation was fraught with conflicted motivation. Would the president have Americans overcome a fear of or for freedom? Did a defense of freedom amount to advancing or containing it? Was freedom secured by practicing or curtailing it? Did the bright beacon of freedom represent a way of life or signal distress? Was freedom really the greatest achievement of our time or merely a hope for some future age? Though Bush may have wished to avoid confronting so blunt a choice as this, the symbolic framework in which he operated exacted a sacrifice of freedom as the price of preserving its promise in a violently transformed world.

In using law as a weapon to defeat terrorism, civil rights would be sacrificed. In fighting repressive regimes, freedom of speech would be curtailed. To uncover hidden terrorist cells, citizens were to spy on one another. To increase airport security, agents would resort to racial profiling. To "tighten the noose" on terrorism, the administration would undertake "preemptive" military action. To bring terrorists to justice, citizens' privacy rights would be breached and legal representation denied. To kill terrorists, civilians were reduced to "collateral" damage. To act patriotic was to silence political dissent.[23] "In our desperation to feel safe," wrote Nancy Chang, "we are sacrificing the core democratic values that have guided this nation since its founding without first examining whether we are, in fact, any safer as a result."[24] Or, as Howard Zinn put the matter in his foreword to Chang's book, "The juggernaut of war crushes democracy, just when the nation claims it is fighting for democracy."[25]

The political consequence of forcing such an unhappy choice upon the nation was to widen the gap between American values and the very policy that became the focus of Bush's presidency. Accordingly, the president's attempt to reduce that gap deployed a trope of transformation of the type that commonly provides, as Kenneth Burke has observed, the rhetorical ground for strategically making such troubled choices. As Burke explains, to transcend a conflicted choice, one might turn to "imagery of the Upward Way and Downward Way, or of the Crossing and Return, or of Exile and Homecoming . . . etc., where the pairs are not merely to be placed statically against each other, but in given poetic contexts usually represent a development *from* one order of motives *to* another." Through these kinds of images and others such as life and death, rhetors attempt to articulate a principle of transformation that transcends an otherwise divided symbolic terrain.[26]

Any such transcendence is necessarily rhetorical in that it favors some options over others according to their relative placement on whatever hierarchy of motives is privileged in a given strategy of transformation. Being subsumed symbolically under a single principle does not make every choice equally desirable. Bush's trope of transformation was no exception to this rule of strategic transcendence, for he would make the sheer promise of transforming the world reason enough to restrain freedom while bolstering the nation's defenses against terrorism. The images through which this presidential discourse articulated its strategic theme of transformation included a recurring set of contrasts to replace darkness with light, crime with punishment, evil with morality, weakness with strength, cowardice with courage, savagery with civilization, and tyranny with freedom. All of these images of contrast and replacement culminated in the obligatory annihilation of terrorism to prepare the way for a better world. By facing fear bravely in a test of strength and endurance, America would vanquish the tyranny of evil and transform the darkness of savagery into the light of civilization. The death of terrorism heralded the beginning of world peace and a renewal of freedom.

In the president's words, "I see a peaceful world beyond the war on terror."[27] The United States, he insisted, "will defend the peace that makes all progress possible"[28] and will "fight tyranny and evil" to build a "house of freedom,"[29] for so long as terrorism exists, "freedom is at risk."[30] By this logic of transformation, freedom was valorized but also subordinated to war as the kind of progress that only victory made possible. Defending freedom meant protecting it more than practicing it. That is, until terrorism's demise, a full expression of freedom would be dangerously premature. As Attorney General John Ashcroft told the Senate Judiciary Committee, "To those who scare peace-loving people with phantoms of lost liberty, my message is this: your tactics only aid terrorists." In his view, criticizing the administration's methods of fighting terrorism amounted to providing "ammunition to America's enemies."[31]

The strategic ambiguity built into this troublesome logic of transformation yielded a tenuous transcendence at best. Even as it suggested a rationale for curtailing certain liberties until some future time of peace and safety, it necessarily reaffirmed the nation's commitment to freedom during the present struggle. Terrorists hate America, Bush insisted, because they hate "a democratically elected government. . . . They hate our freedoms—our freedom of religion, our freedom of speech, our freedom to vote and assemble and disagree with each other."[32]

Attempts to achieve at least a sufficiency of transcendence, by displacing the tension of Bush's conflicted stance on freedom, were premised on the existence of a great divide. There was "no neutral ground" between "barbaric criminals" who "burrow deeper into caves" (hiding even "in the shadows within our own society") and the defenders of freedom who would "drive them out and bring them to justice."[33] There was no place for "negotiation or discussion." Every nation had "a decision to make. Either you are with us, or you are with the terrorists."[34] This was the "great divide in our time" between "civilization and barbarism," the "dividing line in our lives and in the life of our nation" for choosing "lawful change over chaotic violence." In the president's ominous words, the "vast majority of countries are now on the same side of a moral and ideological divide," but "staring across this divide are bands of murderers, supported by outlaw regimes. They are a movement defined by their hatreds. They hate progress, and freedom, and choice, and culture, and music, and laughter, and women, and Christians, and Jews, and all Muslims who reject their distorted doctrines."[35]

The image of this total divide was maintained in the president's war discourse by rigid contrasts that left no middle or neutral ground but also provided no sanctuary for those who would actually exercise their freedom to dissent and to critique the administration's policies. Patriotism was reduced to inflexible conformity without a sense of irony in this "fight of all who believe in progress and pluralism, tolerance and freedom."[36]

The rigidity of these oppositions was antithetical to the very idea of freedom with its implications of movement, latitude, choice, openness, independence, freethinking, and creativity. Yet, in his State of the Union address, the president tightened the discipline of these strict oppositions even more by extending the totalizing logic of a war on terrorism to the full range of political issues. Freedom's fight now encompassed "economic security." As he put the matter: "Once we have funded our national security and our homeland security, the final great priority of my budget is economic security for the American people. . . . We have clear priorities and we must act at home with the same purpose and resolve we have shown overseas: We'll prevail in the war, and we will defeat this recession." By a similar extension of patriotic language and logic, Bush placed his partisan views about "health security" and "retirement security" under the universal rubric of national security. Even his favorite themes of volunteerism and compassionate conservatism were translated into the selfless patriotism of a "USA Freedom Corps" that would enlist citizens to provide for "homeland security" while "rebuilding our communities and extending American compassion throughout the world."[37]

Freedom was now so thoroughly disciplined and transformed into a symbol of political conformity that it had become its own antonym in the president's lexicon of war, strategically subordinated to the higher aim of eradicating evil and closely contained by a rhetoric of vilification in which there was no neutral ground but only a nonnegotiable, black-and-white divide between Us and Them. Yet, this was a compensatory rhetoric. Although powerfully intimidating under the circumstances, it was indicative nevertheless of unresolved tensions in a discourse that simultaneously hailed and discounted deeply felt values such as liberty, democracy, tolerance, diversity, and deliberation.

Such a palpable contradiction could never entirely disappear from Bush's text nor remain completely hidden under even a thick discursive layer of victimization and vilification. Whenever he spoke, the contradiction was present, at least implicitly but often overtly in the paradoxical voice of intolerance about tolerance, inflexibility over freedom, or some other self-negating expression. With typical insensitivity to an underlying spirit of pluralism and democracy, for example, Bush decreed that "America will always stand firm for the non-negotiable demands of human dignity: the rule of law; limits on the power of the state; respect for women; private property; free speech; equal justice; and religious tolerance."[38] Actually exercising free speech, however, to question the wisdom of absolutes and nonnegotiable demands in political affairs or to criticize the administration's encroachments on civil rights was downright unpatriotic—a crossing of the great divide to give aid and comfort to the enemy, as the attorney general put the matter so bluntly and infamously, by scaring "peace-loving people with phantoms of lost liberty."

It should come as little surprise, therefore, that such a conflicted discourse on freedom quickly drew fire not just from the left but from the center and right of the political spectrum as well. In the case of Yaser Esam Hamdi, a young man born in the United States and captured in Afghanistan, federal district court judge Robert G. Doumar challenged the administration's determination to imprison war captives indefinitely without formal charges or benefit of legal counsel. "So, the Constitution doesn't apply to Mr. Hamdi?" he asked rhetorically. "Isn't that what we're fighting for?"[39]

John Ashcroft's exceptional zeal in fighting terrorism even upset his most conservative supporters, including religious conservatives who complained that Bush's attorney general overstated the evidence of terrorist threats to bolster the power of big government. Paul Weyrich, president of the Free Congress Foundation, complained that "what was passed in the wake of 9-11 were things that had little to do with catching terrorists but a lot to do with increasing the strength of government to infiltrate and spy on conservative organizations."[40] Labeling the administration's Terrorism Information and Prevention System, or TIPS, "this most un-American of programs," a *New York Times* editorial complained that "the Bush administration's post-Sept. 11 anti-terrorism tactics—secret detentions of suspects, denial of the right to trial and now citizen spying—have in common a lack of faith in democratic institutions and a free society."[41] Criticism of this "snitch system" came not only from liberals in the U.S. Senate such as Patrick Leahy and Ted Kennedy but also from conservative Republicans in the House such as Dick Armey and Bob Barr. As Senator Jeff Sessions, Republican from Alabama, observed, "We get complaints from left and right."[42]

Despite such clear manifestations of broadly felt dissonance produced by the Bush administration's paradoxical defense of freedom, the problem still remains of how to channel such political dissatisfaction toward a better response to terrorism. How might a positive shift of perspective come about? Can a revised perspective arise out of the readily apparent incongruities so tenuously transcended by a rhetorical strategy of victimization? Might freedom exercised boldly and democratically, rather than tentatively and timidly, conform better to American values without succumbing to terrorism? With what symbolic resource might the nation turn its attention toward the underlying, rather than just the immediate, causes of terrorism? *Democracy*, I want to suggest, is such a resource, a term on which we might well focus efforts to convert the dissonance of antagonism into an incentive for agonistic politics. Yet, the rhetoric of evil persists as a strong distraction from taking democracy so seriously and as a continuing incentive for perpetuating the state of war.

The Rhetoric of Evil and the Presumption of War

Indeed, it was difficult after the horrific events of 9/11 to advance a constructive critique of the Bush administration's hyperbolic war rhetoric against the evil enemies of freedom and civilization. From Al Qaeda and the Taliban of Afghanistan to the "axis of evil" in Iraq, North Korea, Iran, and beyond, a dark and daunting image of international terrorism haunted America's post–cold war sensibilities. The specter of mass destruction—a kind of democratic hell of egalitarian violence—signified terrorism's global reach, insinuated its cultural ubiquity, and ensured its political utility. Thus, even the conventional prerequisite of a clear and imminent threat to national security was dismissed by the White House as irrelevant to justifying preemptive attacks on "terrorists and tyrants."[43]

Even as the perceived exigency of terrorism emboldened proponents of preemptive war to push the envelope of righteous coercion, the ensuing controversy over invading Iraq worked the ironic and perhaps inadvertent and unnoticed side effect of further reifying a deeply problematic representation of terrorism itself. Opponents of preemptive war characterized attacks on

Saddam Hussein as a diversion from the real "war" on terrorism, as if a so-called war on terrorism could be a solution or even an alternative to terror instead of a perpetuation and escalation thereof. Rather than unmasking an egregious caricature of terrorism, the ostensible "diversion" of Iraq helped transform a problematic but strategic profile of evil incarnate into an Orwellian presumption of perpetual (or at least protracted) war. This reinforced and self-sustaining pretext for perpetrating violence against civilians for political purposes in the name of a higher cause was terror, per se, redux and reduplicated by the United States and its willing allies.

Accordingly, it behooves us, given the deteriorated state of political discourse, to scrutinize the rhetoric of the evil enemy for its deleterious effect on democratic values and aspirations. Terror trumps democracy in the prevailing hierarchy of political aims and measures when demagogues play the rhetorical card of evil. Antagonism and coercion triumph over what Chantal Mouffe and other political theorists recognize as the democratic discourse of agonistic pluralism, that complex ensemble of practices that resists transforming adversaries into enemies.[44] A robust democracy operates in a fluid context of difference, division, and struggle between and among opponents noisily engaging one another to establish a modicum of identification and to achieve moments of assent rather than in a solid state of political quiescence and monolithic dogma that silences dissent and slays alien Others as the enemies of universal truths and univocal values.

By this criterion—that is, by the rule of democracy according to which agonistic Others robustly engage one another as adversaries rather than sheer enemies—a call to kill for democracy, or in the name of democracy, or to defend and extend democracy is a cloaked inducement to slay the soul of democracy. Just as it is audaciously oxymoronic to ask a people to sacrifice their freedoms (or some unspecified and vague degree of freedom) in a struggle to protect Lady Liberty from the ravages of terror, it is tragically ironic to conjure up a rhetorical spell against democracy's evil enemies as an excuse for abating, abandoning, or indefinitely suspending the actual practice of democracy. To the extent there is always an enemy lurking about, or at least a rhetorical incentive to construct such an enemy, there can never be a sufficiently secure time for democratic adversaries to engage and persuade one another.[45] Tangible democracy, then, must forever await history's mythical end, that fabled and enchanted state of human affairs in which diversity, error, and evil no longer exist, truth and beauty prevail, and, paradoxically, democracy is no longer deferred but instead rendered irrelevant.

Rather than allying us with democracy, the rhetoric of evil makes us complicit with terror, for terror is constituted in and sustained by a discourse of evil, especially in an era of what Robin Wright calls "sacred rage," Mark Juergensmeyer refers to as "religious violence," Rahul Mahajan identifies as America's "new crusade," and George W. Bush has rendered in apocalyptic overtones as America's "calling, as a blessed country," to protect and preserve "God's gift to humanity" from the "designs of evil men" who threaten to destroy freedom, liberty, and civilization with weapons of mass destruction.[46] "The president's faith in faith [was] readily apparent," writes Laurie Goodstein, "in his determination to vanquish Saddam Hussein."[47] He sees himself as "an instrument of Providence," observes David Gergen from the vantage point of a political veteran who served Presidents Nixon, Ford, Reagan, and Clinton.[48] Such religious language and attitudes are dangerously divisive, warns Elaine Pagels, a professor of religion at Princeton University: "If there is an axis of evil, that obviously places [President Bush] in the axis of good, and also means that anyone who disagrees with the policies he is advocating is placed on the other side."[49]

Terrorism in our time operates under a rhetorical spell of sacred duties and diabolical enemies. One side's devil is the other side's saving grace in these dueling discourses of good and evil. On both sides of the divide, the dialectic of rival religious visions transforms the act of killing civilians, destroying life-sustaining infrastructures, or both into a necessary and legitimate consequence of exercising righteous force over a demonic antagonist.[50]

In this way, the rhetoric of evil masks the politics of terror, a politics of coercion represented as a sacred mission, a secular politics of perpetrating physical assaults on civilians to advance political purposes in the name of a higher order.[51] The mask of evil makes it difficult for either partner in this escalating dance of death to detect the disturbing parallel between terror and counterterror. Thus, for instance, the Bush administration identifies terrorism as America's enemy, even defining it as "premeditated, politically motivated violence perpetrated against innocents," and then baldly warns that preemptive strikes taken by the United States to prevent the hostile acts of its adversaries should not be used by the "enemies of civilization" as a "pretext for aggression."[52] One side's terror and aggression is the other side's protective reaction.

To speak of evil, then, or of vanquishing evil enemies, is to step into a circle of reciprocal violence that supplants diplomacy and democracy with the method of terror. Within the narrow confines of this moralistic circle, war gains a presumption that frames, constrains, and distorts efforts to debate its wisdom, necessity, prudence, ethics, or consequences in any given case. Instead of war being conceived as the last resort of a beleaguered people reluctantly defending themselves against an overt act of aggression or even a clear and imminent threat to their national security, war considered in the context of terrorism presumes a preexisting state of danger sufficient to warrant preemption as a routine instrument for managing foreign affairs.

As recently as September 20, 2002, the Bush administration promulgated an official doctrine of preemptive war as basic to its national security strategy. Citing the president's speech at the National Cathedral just three days after 9/11, in which Bush vowed to "rid the world of evil," the published text of the administration's statement of national security strategy next observed that "the struggle against global terrorism is different from any other war in our history. It will be fought on many fronts against a particularly elusive enemy over an extended period of time." Accordingly, the United States would "not hesitate to act alone, if necessary, to exercise our right of self-defense by acting preemptively against such terrorists." And again, "We cannot let our enemies strike first" because "in an age where the enemies of civilization openly and actively seek the world's most destructive technologies, the United States cannot remain idle while dangers gather."[53] It took only a little over two weeks, in a televised speech from Cincinnati, Ohio, on October 7, for Mr. Bush to apply his new doctrine of preemption to Saddam Hussein's Iraq. "Understanding the threats of our time," he insisted, "knowing the designs and deception of the Iraqi regime, we have every reason to assume the worst, and we have an urgent duty to prevent the worst from occurring."[54]

Indeed, the ensuing debate over invading Iraq illustrates how the rhetoric of evil closes the circle of deliberation tightly around a presumption of war and leaves opponents little room to maneuver. Mr. Bush dramatically narrowed the circumference of debate in his State of the Union address on January 28, 2003, relying on the theme of evil to lower the threshold of war. His words are worth quoting at length to demonstrate the crux of his case:

Some have said we must not act until the threat is imminent. Since when have terrorists and tyrants announced their intentions, politely putting us on notice before they strike? If this threat is permitted to fully and suddenly emerge, all actions, all words, and all recriminations would come too late. Trusting in the sanity and restraint of Saddam Hussein is not a strategy, and it is not an option.

This dictator, who is assembling the world's most dangerous weapons, has already used them on whole villages leaving thousands of his own citizens dead, blind, or disfigured. Iraqi refugees tell us how forced confessions are obtained by torturing children while their parents are made to watch. International human rights groups have catalogued other methods used in the torture chambers of Iraq: electric shock, burning with hot irons, dripping acid on the skin, mutilation with electric drills, cutting out tongues, and rape.

If this is not evil, then evil has no meaning. And tonight I have a message for the brave and oppressed people of Iraq: Your enemy is not surrounding your country; your enemy is ruling your country. And the day he and his regime are removed from power will be the day of your liberation.

The world has waited 12 years for Iraq to disarm. America will not accept a serious and mounting threat to our country, our friends, and our allies. The United States will ask the UN Security Council to convene on February 5th to consider the facts of Iraq's ongoing defiance of the world. Secretary of State Powell will present information and intelligence about Iraq's illegal weapons programs; its attempts to hide those weapons from inspectors; and its links to terrorist groups. We will consult, but let there be no misunderstanding: If Saddam Hussein does not fully disarm, for the safety of our people, and for the peace of the world, we will lead a coalition to disarm him.

Powell's subsequent speech to the UN Security Council on February 5 was long on disputed details and short on basic themes. The few themes he emphasized echoed the crux of the administration's case for preemptive war, i.e., (1) the "burden on Iraq to comply [with UN Security Council Resolution 1441] and disarm" has not been met; (2) there is a "sinister nexus between Iraq and the Al Qaida terrorist network"; and (3) "Leaving Saddam Hussein in possession of weapons of mass destruction for a few more months or years is not an option, not in a post–September 11th world."[55]

What was at stake here was further indicated by the immediate reactions to Powell's speech from the three permanent members of the UN Security

Council opposing a rush to war. First, the foreign minister from China, insisting that "it is the universal desire of the international community to see a political settlement to the issue of Iraq within the U.N. framework and [to] avoid any war," called for continuing the UN weapons inspections and for the United States to share its intelligence information with the UN weapons inspectors so they could make their inspections more effective.[56] Next, the Russian foreign minister cautioned the members of the Security Council to let experts analyze and assess the information presented in Powell's speech, but insisted that Powell's information "convincingly indicates the fact that the activities of the international inspectors in Iraq must be continued" and that "everything possible [should be done] to facilitate the inspection process, which has proven its effectiveness and makes it possible to implement the decisions of the Security Council through peaceful means."[57] Finally, France's foreign minister called on the Security Council to strengthen substantially the operational capacity of the inspections regime so that it could disarm Iraq without resorting to military intervention.[58]

None of the three foreign ministers was willing to accept on face value the interpretation of evidence presented by Powell, and all insisted that the UN weapons inspections could achieve the goal of disarmament given enough time and support. Collectively, they resisted the notion that the burden rested solely on Iraq to prove it possessed no weapons of mass destruction and insisted on making every effort to resolve the matter peacefully. On February 10, in fact, France and Russia joined with Germany to call for intensified weapons inspections as an alternative to war in Iraq, noting that their position "coincides with that of a large number of countries, within the Security Council in particular." French president Chirac added that in his view "there's no indisputable proof" of weapons of mass destruction in Iraq, thus shifting the burden of proof from Iraq solely, where the Bush administration insisted it belonged, to those advocating war.[59]

In short, absent the theme of evil, the case for preemptive war appeared weak. As a corollary, the UN Security Council would have eroded the standard of peace and lowered the symbolic threshold of war if it had sanctioned the Bush administration's call for preemption based on the premise of evil. A precedent would have been set in the UN of treating war as a routine instrument for managing international disputes. At issue, then, was the question of which perspective should guide the interpretation of evidence and assessment of threat, one that privileged war or one that presumed peace unless and until a high burden of proof was met to establish the existence of a clear and imminent threat—a substantial threat, moreover, that could not be otherwise contained or defused.

No one, of course, including permanent members of the Security Council, was immune to the economic influence and military might of the United States or impervious to the Bush administration exercising its will. Consent can be coerced in some uncertain degree and for a limited duration, and coerced consent can even be rationalized after the fact as a principled position reasonably grounded in supporting evidence and ratified by military victory. Power, that is, cannot be bracketed in any practical assessment of political persuasion. Yet it is also true that strategically framing a case for war in a manner that decreases its burden of proof makes the rationalization of power more difficult to resist and less costly to impose. Indeed, the rhetoric of evil frames such a case to constrain, contain, and displace opposing arguments within the narrow confines of its own presumption of chronic danger. Arguing inside this box put the opponents of war decidedly at a disadvantage, just as stepping over the line and outside the box undermined their credibility as members of a loyal opposition.

A disarticulation of opposing arguments, when they are construed within the prevailing framework of vanquishing evil, was evident (although not always obvious) in the fettered debate over preempting Saddam Hussein. Some of the principal objections to military invasion were, as already noted, that efforts should be redoubled to disarm Iraq through diplomacy and arms inspections and that no compelling proof of Iraq's possession of weapons of mass destruction existed. Other objections included reservations about the lack of strong evidence to establish any substantial link between Al Qaeda and Saddam Hussein; the belief that an already weakened Saddam Hussein could be contained by means short of war; a concern that war was likely to involve urban fighting with significant civilian and military casualties and that an invasion of Iraq might embolden Al Qaeda, exacerbate the problem of terrorism, further destabilize the Middle East, and bring renewed terrorist attacks on the United States and Europe; projections that war would be a costly misappropriation of funds badly needed for other purposes and that rebuilding Iraq would be a herculean task far exceeding American moral or material resolve; protestations that U.S. unilateralism and designs on Iraq's oil reserves stank of hubris and imperialism; and suggestions that preemption was a diversion from the war on terrorism, even a violation of the time-honored taboo against preventative warfare.

Collectively, these were not unsubstantial or inconsequential arguments. They were all too easily answered or dismissed, however, from the administration's perspective of eradicating evil. To presume the menace of evil was to suggest no compromise was warranted and no cost was too high in the service of ultimate good, especially when the presumption itself was bolstered by the authority of the presidency and the unchecked power of the United States; when Americans had become accustomed to fighting antiseptic wars with no apparent consequences to themselves and were encouraged to go about their daily lives, consuming as usual without the unpleasant distraction of attending to world affairs; and when the public was intermittently alarmed by the likes of a strategically timed "orange" alert in the United States and corresponding deployment of British troops to guard Heathrow Airport in London, both vaguely justified as "precautionary" measures but each clearly serving "to provoke a sense of gathering crisis."[60]

The audacity of such power to coerce and distract in the name of eradicating evil was such that it branded anybody who might demur as an irrelevant debating society in the case of the United Nations, as suffering a crisis of credibility in the case of dissent within the NATO alliance, as passé in the case of "old Europe," as shrinking in the heat of crisis or lacking the courage of leadership, and so on. The divide between right and wrong was rendered absolute with no shades of gray or any room for disagreement. Minimal evidence was required to affirm the existence of hidden diabolical weapons, a satanic dictator's conspiracy with terrorist organizations, and the futility of arms inspections relentlessly foiled by deceit and deception. How could anyone contain a diabolical dictator when evil knows no bounds? How could anyone expect to do the right thing on the cheap or without incurring a regrettable loss of life abroad and perhaps even at home? And how could anyone rightfully accuse America of imperialism when its humble mission was to bring the gift of democracy and the promise of prosperity to troubled lands? When evil stalked the civilized world, the preemption of tyrants and terrorists was a defense of freedom, not a distraction or a war of aggression. Trump, trump, and trump. Any argument one might advance on behalf of peace was tricked in the game of fighting evil, a game that made the United States complicit in the spiraling cycle of terror by legitimizing the preemptive killing of Iraqi civilians as the chosen means to political ends.

If the rhetoric of fighting an evil enemy, especially when reinforced by U.S. military might, economic clout, and presidential resolve, lowers the threshold of war, trumps arguments for pursuing peaceful resolutions, and masks America's complicity in the spiraling cycle of violence, what alternative to this tragic perspective might prove to be a more serviceable response to terrorism? How can the debate be reframed to privilege the presumption of peace consistent with democratic values, to shift the burden of proof back to the advocates of war, and to increase the force of arguments for diplomacy and against preemption? From what perspective might we gain a greater degree of appreciation for the complexities of the human condition, more tolerance of differences, and increased resistance to the legitimization of coerced consent? What conceptualization of the Other promotes the practice of democracy instead of playing the trump card of an evil enemy to diminish and indefinitely defer democracy in the name of defending it? How can the rhetoric of antagonism be transposed into the more constructive discourse of democratic agonistics?

Speaking in the Democratic Idiom

Here is where the exigency of terror engages democracy's rhetorical frontier. In the spirit of Giambattista Vico and Ernesto Grassi, exploring this frontier is an exercise in cultural production, the pursuit of *ingenium* within a *sensus communis* guided by metaphor as a medium of rhetorical invention.[61] Just as Lakoff equates metaphor with conceptual frames, Burke identifies metaphor with motivating perspectives. In Burke's tropology, an orientation is a reification and elaboration of a master metaphor. As the summarizing or culminating term of a given perspective, it subsumes a diversity of contributing terms. Each term contributing to the articulation of a perspective contains its own organizing principle or subperspective that is simultaneously adjectival and substantial and thus less than completely stable. This collection of incongruities and competing subperspectives is mustered more or less into a relatively coherent whole under the organizing principle of the literalized master metaphor. By observing how these terms interact with one another, both blending and clashing within a given framework of interpretation, we might locate where the potential for "perspective by incongruity" is greatest, that is, where a situation could be gauged differently by elevating a contributing term, or subperspective, to a more substantial position in a troubled hierarchy of motives.[62]

Indeed, the president's perspective on terrorism is troubled by a conflicted hierarchy of motivating terms. "War" is an awkward framing metaphor that does not quite fit the situation and thus requires qualification as a "different kind of war," an "unconventional war," and so on. To fight a so-called or pseudo war against "evil" adds yet another layer of difficulty because the presence of evil demands absolute condemnation and requires rigid, black-and-white contrasts to maintain the pretext of defending "freedom," itself a term for flexibility, movement, openness, independence, and the like. Attempting to identify such an inflexible perspective with civil liberties, justice, tolerance, pluralism, and other liberal values is fundamentally paradoxical. Surely, without the shock of collapsing towers as the visual metonym of conflagration, Bush's profile of terrorism would begin to deconstruct under the pressure of a master metaphor misaligned with its subordinate terms, especially when such a narrow profile frames the underlying causes of terror so completely out of consideration.

Among the terms contributing to Bush's problematic perspective, "democracy" is the least developed but most promising vehicle for redressing freedom's paradoxical relationship to war. In fact, "democracy" is a word nearly absent from the president's lexicon of war and thus somewhat easier to dislodge from associations with hatred and hostilities. Freedom and, to a lesser extent, liberty are his chosen symbols of national insecurity, and when democracy is mentioned, it functions primarily as a synonym for freedom and liberty. Whereas America and its European allies have "the democratic vision to protect our liberty," he once remarked, terrorists "hate democracy and tolerance and free expression."[63] As a seldom-used substitute for freedom (and liberty) in Bush's war rhetoric, democracy signifies the promise of freedom's fulfillment after victory rather than the practice of agonistic politics here and now.

Once, in a fleeting gesture, an apparent hint of agonistic democracy embellished Bush's speech on terrorism when he addressed the United Nations. "Every nation," he professed, "must have avenues for the peaceful expression of opinion and dissent. When these avenues are closed, the temptation to speak through violence grows."[64] Had the president pursued this theme further, he might have discovered an unexplored alternative to the politics of vilification and a more constructive means of addressing the deeper problem of terrorism. He might have discovered, in the realm of symbolic action where partisan rivalries need not necessarily escalate into deadly sacrifices, democracy's genius for managing divisive relations and reducing predispositions toward violence. But Bush's small gesture took him in a different direction, reducing democracy to a mere instrument for defusing and displacing a dissenting public's displeasure. In his view, democracy is little or nothing more than a system of tolerating expressions of disagreement by the public (and even the disagreement of elected officials) with decisions derived independently by the president acting in his capacity as supreme leader of the world's sole superpower. He makes no provision for the complexities of competing perspectives and constraints of democratic decision making.

From the standpoint of symbolic action, as conceptualized by Kenneth Burke, the drama of human relations and of political affairs in particular is decidedly agonistic, tending toward antagonistic. Burke's dramatistic perspective, which is his perspective on the role of perspective in matters of society and state, treats conflict as a given, a condition of hierarchy inherent to symbol-using and symbol-misusing beings that articulates the human divide within alternative frames of acceptance or rejection. "Out of such frames," he insists, "we derive our vocabularies for the charting of human motives. And implicit in our theory of motives is a program of action, since we form ourselves and judge others (collaborating with them or against them) in accordance with our attitudes." Polemical debunking, caricature, and burlesque leading to a narrow focus on evil and a corresponding appetite for war is the operative attitude within a frame of rejection. Alternatively, comic ambivalence and charity short of gullibility cultivates an appreciation for the "complexities of sociality" and "relieves the pressure towards opportunism by a broadening, or maturing, of sectarian thought." This wider frame of acceptance promotes an attitude of sufficient humility over extreme hubris, of acting with maximum awareness of social complexities and understanding of human limitations, of correcting for error rather than crusading against evil.[65]

Together, Kenneth Burke's dramatistic agonism and Chantal Mouffe's agonistic pluralism constitute a rhetorically robust formulation of what Benjamin Barber might well consider strong democracy. It is a formulation that serves liberal values rather than suppressing them, that channels partisanship constructively instead of condemning it, and that recognizes the power of perspective. It is a perspective that promotes understanding over vilification, that seeks compensatory points of identification and articulates shared symbolic space, and that operates on the frontier of managing "us/them" relations rather than eradicating evil enemies. Viewing antagonism from the perspective of agonistic pluralism transforms terrorism into a problem aggravated by the absence of strong democracy. It is the very reframing of the problem that Lakoff seeks in order to focus attention on the underlying sources of despair that are the breeding grounds of terrorism. Just as prosecuting a war of terror alienates the nation from liberal democracy, exploring democracy's rhetorical frontier would reconcile America's political values and the challenge of pluralism in a global information age.

In the simplest terms, what is being suggested here is that a basic shift of perspective, achieved by insisting on the primacy of democracy, would entail a wholly different order of priorities than the prevailing accent on evil. Rather than reducing democracy to a convenient excuse for war—trading on it as a legitimizing symbol, protecting it as an imperiled and vulnerable institution, restraining it as a risky practice in times of crisis, and promising it as the prize of victory—advocates of preemption should be held squarely accountable to meeting the standard of democracy and all that it involves. Similarly, those troubled by the prospect of war mutating into a routine instrument of statecraft and creating a post-9/11 dystopia of terror and counter-terror should rearticulate their arguments to feature democratic criteria, repositioning the most salient corollaries of a robustly democratic ethic at the forefront of political consciousness and with sufficient presence to displace otherwise disquieting images of evil. As Barber insists, "Preventative war and democracy are simply self-contradictory."[66]

Democracy, unlike a seamless political ideology of universal values, means, and ends, comprises a multifaceted and situation-specific cluster of simultaneously overlapping and conflicting terms such as liberty, equality, self-rule, rights, pluralism, elections, debate, protest, and the rule of law. As Michael Walzer avers, big ideologies do not provide sufficiently concrete and intimate knowledge of society and the world to prompt healthy criticism and promote democratic rule in which delimited perspectives are held accountable to one another and thus kept appropriately humble and suitably open to the force of evidence and the influence of deliberation.[67] At its best, democracy manages the human divide peacefully, channeling competing interests and differences among groups of engaged citizens into a continuous struggle for one another's qualified assent.

Persuasion is the paradigm of democratic communication in managing divisive relations. Within this paradigm, adversaries are addressed as rivals who, in Mouffe's words, "share a common symbolic space but . . . want to organize [it] in a different way," not as sheer enemies holding nothing in common.[68] Sheer enemies hold nothing in common, that is, except perhaps a shared propensity for engaging in rituals of victimization through which they transform one another into convenient scapegoats, thereby alleviating social guilt at each other's expense and without confronting their own culpability.[69] Sheer enemies speak of one another as evil; democratic adversaries speak of one another as wrong, mistaken, stupid, and even dangerously misguided. Thus, democracy is lost when the agonistic Other is rendered rhetorically into a diabolical enemy, and when democracy vanishes, so, too, the rule of law, liberty, respect for diversity, and accountability to the people wane.

Put another way, addressing one's adversary as wrong, even deadly wrong, rather than evil is requisite to achieving and featuring a democratic perspective. If sharing symbolic space while competing over its organization is the sine qua non of democracy among mortal beings, demonizing the Other is tantamount to throwing Satan out of heaven—a heaven, it should go without saying, that neither exists on earth nor warrants making a living hell of earth. Just as the rhetoric of evil promotes war, the rhetoric of identification, as Kenneth Burke calls it, enacts democracy and advances a positive conception of peace among consubstantial rivals. Peace in this sense is not merely the absence of war, which is a hopelessly negative notion of erasing the human divide and ending the struggle for advantage, but instead a positive strategy of crossing conceptual boundaries and articulating common ground in a continuing context of competition, conflict, and division. Indeed, Ernesto Laclau and Chantal Mouffe allow that "without conflict and division, a pluralist democratic politics would be impossible," for any democratically derived agreement is the result not of universal truth and reason but of a "hegemonic articulation" that is itself incomplete, impermanent, and contingent upon rearticulation.[70]

The sheer polemicist wages war, as Michel Foucault observes, when an opponent is confronted not as a partner in search of an understanding but as "an enemy who is wrong, who is harmful, and whose very existence constitutes a threat." Polemics, Foucault continues, abolishes the adversary "from any possible dialogue" and "establishes the other as an enemy . . . which one must fight until the moment this enemy is defeated and either surrenders or disappears." In this rigid and totalistic order of discourse, which gesticulates "anathemas, excommunications, condemnations, battles, victories, and defeats," the polemicist mimics war and annihilation, "putting forward as much of one's killer instinct as possible."[71]

Addressing adversaries in the democratic idiom of correcting error and holding competing perspectives accountable to one another, rather than in the polemical and coercive voice of vanquishing evil, makes them consubstantial rivals by virtue of acknowledging the existence of competing interpretations in the very act of engaging their inadequacies for coping with given situations. Attempting to fix necessarily flawed and overly efficient frameworks of interpretation by reintroducing complicating factors and shedding light on overlooked considerations constitutes what Kenneth Burke calls a project of "symbolic bridging and merging" in which tragically divisive frames of acceptance are subjected to comic correctives. In Burke's now somewhat outdated language, "Comedy deals with *man in society*, tragedy with the *cosmic man*." Comedy, in this sense, is the attitude of achieving "maximum consciousness," of employing a discourse of "perspective by incongruity" (i.e., of reconfiguring reified, rarified, and rigid linguistic categories) that enables "people to be *observers of themselves, while acting.*"[72]

In the realm of myth, which expresses the sacred, profane, and constitutive sensibilities of humanity, Burke's comic corrective is articulated variously in different cultures as the disruptive but renovating work of trickster figures that is critical to retaining the flexibility and viability of any worldview. One such mythical character, Old Man Coyote, reminds us that all cultural categories produce "dirt," which consists of the elements or associations left out, left over, purged, excreted, abstracted, or otherwise disposed of in the desire to achieve a more perfect order. The trickster performs a needed service by engaging in "dirt work," which muddies clear waters and confounds reified conceptions by crossing established or reified symbolic borders, stealing symbols back and forth, embodying ambiguity and ambivalence, speaking freely and tactlessly, and acting out. Coyote is the shaggy, shiftless cultural figure who transgresses pure archetypes through cleverness, humor, and deception and is symbolically killed for trespassing sacred borders but never actually dies. This amoral troublemaker is the trope of cultural fluidity and ambiguity, the life-sustaining blood that courses through the body culture and yields the saving grace of humility as an antidote to poisonous hubris and excessive fear of the Other. Coyote, that is, signifies rhetoric's potential contribution to democratic pluralism as a vehicle for exploring what awaits us on the "other" side of a troubled boundary. Tricksters, as Lewis Hyde explains, are the sources of mischief necessary to sustaining the worlds in which we live together. They are boundary crossers extraordinaire whose imaginative and disruptive behavior is required for the "origins, liveliness, and durability of cultures."[73]

Achieving a democratic perspective by addressing the Other agonistically, hence as a consubstantial rival, requires rhetorical flexibility unlike the rigid rhetoric of preempting evil. The comic corrective of the democratic idiom is enacted by seeing things for what they are not, both by pointing out similarities where others see only differences and by underscoring differ- ences when others treat mere similarities as sheer identities, that is, as iden- tical and essentially the same. This is a rhetoric of metaphor and irony that keeps boundaries appropriately fuzzy within a prevailing framework of inter- pretation and political motivation. Fuzzy boundaries are conducive to locat- ing points of identification between adversaries who position themselves on either side of a dividing line. They make it possible for rivals to become con- currently adverse and consubstantial, which is to say suitably conflicted and democratically inflected.

For Burke, this kind of rhetorical flexibility, with the healthy ambivalence that it promotes, functions positively as an exercise in democratic casuistry. By stealing symbols back and forth, he observes, political "Ins" can articulate a more balanced ecology of motives, and "Outs" can avoid "being driven into a corner" of black-and-white choices by a simplistic sense of absolute virtue. Casuistic stretching, symbolic convertibility, categorical liquidity, planned in- congruity, and strategic ambiguity are the bridging devices that make coop- eration between adversaries possible.[74]

Speaking in the democratic idiom is not a luxury reserved just for address- ing friends and allies or venting frustrations and opinions. Preventing rivals from becoming outright enemies requires a fluid discourse of identification to articulate some minimal basis of cooperation. As Burke observes, strife, en- mity, and faction are characteristics of rhetorical expression that can be per- verted into the tragedy of war unless redirected toward changing a boundary that separates adversaries too completely. This kind of change is a construc- tive form of symbolic killing that transforms perceived antinomies into "am- biguities of substance," ambiguities that enable rivals to be "both joined and separate, at once distinct substance and consubstantial with another." A rhetoric of identification "deals with the possibilities of classification" and re- classification in their "*partisan* aspects" and by "confront[ing] the implica- tions of *division*." Thus, "identification is compensatory to division" as a func- tion of the fractured human condition in which people and nations are not "wholly and truly of one substance," and rhetoric is required to proclaim a unity that bridges existing differences where otherwise strife might boil over into war.[75]

To abandon the rhetoric of identification for a rigid discourse of absolute evil at the very moment of crisis is to abandon the democratic idiom when it is most needed. In the words of United States senator Robert Byrd, uttered after first lamenting that the Senate chamber had fallen "ominously, dreadfully silent" and "passively mute" on the issue of preemptive war, "This Administration has turned the patient art of diplomacy into threats, labeling, and name calling of the sort that reflects quite poorly on the intelligence and sensitivity of our leaders, and which will have consequences for years to come. Calling heads of state pygmies, labeling whole countries as evil, denigrating powerful European allies as irrelevant—these types of crude insensitivities can do our great nation no good."[76]

Just as a robust rhetoric of identification is most needed in times of crisis, attempts to make ambiguous otherwise sharp divisions between rivals should not be confused with making friends out of enemies, attaining a state of harmonious accord, eliminating serious differences, or even just appealing to lofty ideals. Rhetoric operates, as Burke says, in the "Human Barnyard," taking us through the "Scramble," negotiating "the wavering line of pressure and counterpressure." It is concerned with "the state of Babel after the Fall."[77] Accordingly, rivals must be made consubstantial on earth, not in heaven.

One might have reasoned, for example, that the secular dictator Saddam Hussein would not have wanted to risk his own security by making common cause with the Islamic revolutionist Osama bin Laden to combat an impending American invasion of Iraq, just as the interests of the United States and the stability of the Middle East could not be well served in the long run by a war that might well goad more despairing Muslims into joining an Islamic revolution. Both the United States and Saddam Hussein could well have been made relatively more secure, that is, by a peaceful process of UN arms inspections to minimize Iraq's chemical, biological, and nuclear weapons. Similarly, the condition under which Saddam Hussein most likely would have used any chemical or biological weapons he may have possessed (which at this writing have yet to be found, months after the United States took control of Iraq), even at the risk of triggering a nuclear response from the United States or Israel, was precisely if Iraq were invaded for the purpose of overthrowing his regime, that is, when he no longer had anything to lose. No one's security, including that of the United States, would have been improved by establishing a legitimizing precedent for preemptive war or for using weapons of mass destruction, which was yet another substantive reason, based on what was known at the time, for both sides to make common cause with the UN weapons inspection program rather than resort precipitously to war.

This more complex way of thinking less sanctimoniously about remaining options beyond capitulating to evil and short of military invasion was no mere fantasy of uninitiated and naïve critics operating outside the constraints of informed judgment. As insider and seasoned analyst Kenneth Pollack underscored, "As best we can tell, Iraq was not involved in the terrorist attacks of September 11, 2001," just as Saddam Hussein's ties to Osama bin Ladin and Al Qaeda "were always fairly limited" because "Saddam generally saw bin Ladin as a wild card he could not control and so mostly shied away from al-Qa'eda for fear that a relationship could drag him into a war with the United States that was not of his making." Moreover, bin Ladin placed Iraq's dictator high on his list of enemies because Saddam was "an avowed secularist." Only if these two found themselves "desperate in the face of U.S. attacks" might they "put aside their differences to make common cause against their common American enemy." Although Saddam was not likely to provide terrorists with weapons of mass destruction, he might change his mind, Pollack noted, if he believed that his overthrow by U.S. forces was "imminent and unavoidable." Saddam, in Pollack's estimation, was also most likely, if at all, to use any arsenal of weapons of mass destruction at his disposal, including lashing out "in a final paroxysm toward Israel," to defend his regime from destruction or if he believed he was "doomed." He was a nasty tyrant and a risk taker, but he was not "irrational" beyond influence.[78]

I could continue in this vein, but my purpose here is more limited than to make a full case against the preemptive war on Iraq that began with U.S. missile strikes against Baghdad in the predawn of March 20, 2003, and developed from there into a full-fledged invasion and occupation.[79] Besides, the crux of the administration's case for war was spelled out explicitly by Lawrence Kaplan and William Kristol as a matter of confronting the "face of evil." In their lucid presentation of the administration's perspective on foreign policy in the post-9/11 world, Kaplan and Kristol endorsed the Bush doctrine of preemption, regime change, and U.S. military preeminence as perfectly suited in its "moral clarity" to the task of liberating a tortured Iraq from Saddam Hussein's sinister tyranny. They dedicated their opening chapter to describing in lurid detail Saddam's horrible crimes against his own people and his brutal record of aggression against neighboring countries. They chronicled the difficulties encountered by George W. Bush's "realist" and "liberal" predecessors in the White House in their attempts to manage, contain, and deter Saddam's menacing presence. And they applauded the present President Bush's policy of "marrying American power to American ideals," a "distinctly American internationalism" that followed properly from "American exceptionalism" and adopted as its mission the spread of liberal democracy by preemptive force. The "ultimate goal of regime change," they noted, "is liberal democracy," and "achieving liberal democracy in Iraq is a principal objective of the Bush administration's campaign against Saddam," a goal that, they argued optimistically, "should be a manageable task for the United States." Transforming the Middle East into a democratic oasis, even when imposed by military force, was the answer to the problem revealed on September 11. Indeed, the project of exporting democracy to replace evil tyrannies throughout the world promised lasting peace and security because "democracies rarely, if ever, wage war against one another." Thus, there was nothing wrong with world dominance "in the service of sound principles and high ideals," especially when the alternative to American leadership was Hobbesian chaos and sinister regimes. The urgency of the threat existed prior to the events of 9/11; "September 11 did not create the threat of Saddam Hussein." All that changed, according to Kaplan and Kristol, was the administration's ability to see evil where it lurked and willingness to do something definitive about it. The problem of terror would be solved by removing the face of evil.[80]

Given that the Bush administration's post-9/11 case for war was a function of suddenly perceiving the presence of evil instead of any significant change or upsurge in Iraq's status as a threat to world peace, my aim is limited to addressing the crux of that case by suggesting the kind of down-to-earth discourse that the rhetoric of identification can entail in the democratic idiom of constructing consubstantial rivals. Such a discourse of strategic identification adds rough texture and grimy complexity to any working definition of a problematic situation. Problems construed less simplistically than under the sign of evil cannot be solved simply by obliterating an enemy. Yet, a rhetoric that is flexible enough to identify nitty-gritty points of converging interest between potential enemies need not also abandon higher ideals. Just as George W. Bush justified the inevitable loss of life from a war in Iraq as a sacrifice to freedom, a leader wishing to avoid war could have legitimized arms inspections over regime change as the way to save precious lives and prevent a further deterioration of the quality of life in Iraq, improve U.S. and world security by not fostering more terrorism, and serve other similarly venerated principles. The stain of consubstantial rivalry can be cleansed by the ideals it serves, no less than the blood of war can be buried beneath a nation's conscience by bellicose appeals to righteous patriotism.

Just as articulating appropriately fuzzy boundaries opens the way for adversaries to share some substantive symbolic space, which is requisite to adopting a democratic perspective, it reinfuses the lexicon of democracy with a presumption of humility and the spirit of positive (that is, agonistic) peace. So animated, these are the very terms with which to enact the primacy of the democratic perspective and the stiff burden of proof it imposes on any call to arms. The tension embedded in the language of liberty and equality, for instance, builds on and keeps in play the agonistic ethic of holding diverging terms accountable to one another, not allowing the implication of individualism in terms such as liberty and freedom to cancel the implication of community in terms such as equality and unity, and vice versa. The democratic notions of dissent, protest, spirited debate, and contested elections privilege tension and keep categories malleable. The values of pluralism and diversity resist simplistic conceptions of patriotism. The rule of the people and their representatives is counterbalanced by the language of human rights, civil liberties, and constitutional constraints. Even the rule of law, which strives to ensure justice by treating people alike when they fall into the same category, must operate on the uncertain principle of similitude rather than perfect identity and through practical argument rather than universal reason.[81]

A critical distinction needs to be made here between a discourse of defending democracy and a discourse of practicing democracy. Mr. Bush speaks of the former, not in the latter. In his first State of the Union address, for example, he declared:

America will lead by defending liberty and justice because they are right and true and unchanging for all people everywhere. No nation owns these aspirations and no nation is exempt from them. We have no intention of imposing our culture, but America will always stand firm for the non-negotiable demands of human dignity, the rule of law, limits on the power of the state, respect for women, private property, free speech, equal justice and religious tolerance.[82]

In this discourse, the lexicon of democratic values serves as a source of hollowed-out symbols used to legitimize an open-ended and global war on terrorism. This is a war ostensibly to defend freedom, protect the principles of tolerance and equal justice, and so on. Yet it is a war of terror, more than a war on terror, which can be fought only by curtailing freedom, sacrificing civil liberties, encouraging citizens to spy on one another, denying suspects legal representation and their right to trial, and silencing political dissent to the point of "sacrificing the core democratic values that have guided [the U.S.] since its founding."[83] The notorious USA PATRIOT Act and the Terrorism Information and Prevention System, or TIPS snitch program, contradict any professed commitment to democratic practices and institutions.[84]

Contrary to Mr. Bush's example of hollowing and collapsing the rudiments of democratic rule, Senator Byrd spoke in the language of democracy to evaluate the president's call to arms. The terms of democracy set the senator's principal criteria and established his guiding perspective on the issue of war and peace. In opposing the passage of Senate Joint Resolution 46, for example, a resolution authorizing the president's resort to force as he saw fit, Senator Byrd warned that the resolution "reinterprets the Constitution to suit the will of the Executive Branch"; that it is an "unprecedented and unfounded interpretation of the President's authority under the Constitution"; that "nowhere in the Constitution is it written that the President has the authority to call forth the militia to preempt a perceived threat"; that giving the president "blanket authority" to launch a unilateral preemptive attack "concentrates too much power in one individual" and "brings oppression upon us," which is why "the Framers bestowed on Congress, not the President, the power to declare war"; that "the people, through their elected representatives," must make the decision to embark on war; that "the full spectrum of the public's desires, concerns, and misgivings must be heard" and considered in "informed debate"; and that "the principle of one government deciding to eliminate another government, using force to do so, and taking that action in spite of world disapproval, is a very disquieting thing."[85] Byrd's is not the definitive example of evoking democratic criteria, but it illustrates the difference between a discourse of coercion in the name of democracy and a discourse of persuasion guided by the terms of democracy.

Within a robustly democratic context, the arguments against preemptive war are not so easily trumped, for the game is no longer one of certain evil with its low threshold of violence but instead an ongoing contest of uncertain, necessarily mistaken, and even conflated interpretations. Such a contest minimizes the deadly consequences of hubris, or what Burke calls the "mistaken heroics of war," and maximizes opportunities for tolerance, contemplation, and security, in Burke's words, by acknowledging that "getting along with people is one devil of a difficult task" and by viewing "human antics" within the "comic frame," which is to recognize and underscore that political relations are "ever on the verge of the most disastrous tragedy."[86] In a condition of uncertainty and ambiguity, a decision to terminate the adversary must be based on a strong and thoroughly vetted case that establishes a clear and imminent threat that cannot be contained, deterred, or otherwise ameliorated by peaceful means (such as continued diplomacy and a strengthened regime of arms inspections that would have precluded the need for an invasion of Iraq) and that proves preempting such a threat by initiating armed conflict will not cause greater harm than it purports to prevent.

The Bush administration's preinvasion case fell far short of the democratic standard by failing to establish the substantial presence of weapons of mass destruction in Iraq; by exaggerating the ability and willingness of Saddam Hussein to use them under conditions of containment and deterrence; by understating the probability of immediate and long-term negative consequences of invading Iraq, including the certain cost in human lives and material resources as well as the likelihood of further escalating the problem of terrorism; and by refusing to engage the worldwide protests against preemptive warfare. A case for war articulated within the framework of democratic values must establish that there is no other way of correcting the errors of an adversary without suffering a devastating consequence. It is not enough to say the adversary is loathsome, to articulate a vaguely defined threat, and to suggest advantages that may be derived from a preemptive invasion, not from the perspective of enacting democratic attitudes instead of hollowing them out on the battlefield of good versus evil.

The strongest case for invading Iraq came not from the Bush administration's hyperbolic rhetoric of evil but instead from a former CIA analyst and National Security Council official, Kenneth Pollack. In his widely cited book, *The Threatening Storm*, Pollack systematically compared the relative advantages and disadvantages of five options for managing the menace of Saddam Hussein, concluding somewhat reluctantly that invasion was the "least bad" option, i.e., better than relying on containment (the only other reasonable choice), deterrence, covert operations to effect a coup d'état, or U.S. airpower in support of indigenous opposition forces to overthrow the Iraqi regime. The policy of containing Saddam Hussein worked well after the 1991 Gulf War, he argued, but had begun to erode and would have to be bolstered to avoid reaching a crisis point. It would require, for example, "finding a way to restore the inspectors to Iraq and allow them to do their job for as long as it takes." Given the "window of opportunity created by the tragedy of September 11," however, a full-scale invasion to remove Saddam Hussein, eliminate his weapons of mass destruction, and build a model democratic state in the troubled Persian Gulf had "unfortunately become our best option." Even this choice was not without serious drawbacks, Pollack underscored, and would have to be "done right" if the United States was to avoid trading "the threat of a nuclear-armed Saddam for the threat of an Iraq in chaos and civil war."[87]

Pollack reluctantly abandoned the option of containment largely because he was skeptical that the UN Security Council members could be motivated to support a strong and sustained new regime of weapons inspections in Iraq (even under the threat of a U.S. invasion) and beyond that to develop a new, more effective sanctions regime (one that eliminated the remaining economic sanctions that hurt Iraq's civilian population so badly but added secondary sanctions and incentives to prevent countries and companies from trading with Iraq in nefarious goods).[88] His analysis, however, preceded the debate in the Security Council after the United States actually threatened invasion, a debate that underscored the effectiveness of ongoing UN weapons inspections and generated a desire on the part of key UN and Security Council members to strengthen and maintain the inspections regime. Moreover, Pollack's argument for invasion as the "least bad option" included a number of strong provisos that the administration failed to meet. He warned that acting more or less unilaterally without a broad coalition could "alienate our allies and convince much of the rest of the world to band together against us to try to keep us under control," a development that would "drastically undermine" rather than increase U.S. "security and prosperity." He emphasized that the U.S. administration, in advance of any such invasion, would need "to do an honest job explaining to the American people" the substantial "costs of rebuilding Iraq and the commitment of time and resources necessary," allowing "the American people to participate in the debate." Moreover, the United States should avoid making "facile arguments" about Iraq's support of terrorism. Indeed, in Pollack's view, the United States should not even "indulge in a distraction as great as toppling Saddam" until after Al Qaeda was "defanged enough" to quell the threat of terrorism and until progress had been made to "cool the tensions of the region, especially the Israeli-Palestinian violence."[89]

At the root of even Pollack's more cerebral case for preemptive war and against containment and deterrence, however, was the premise that Saddam Hussein was too reckless and megalomaniacal to be restrained. Nothing in Saddam's "track record or personality," Pollack averred, suggested that he would behave in a "risk-averse" manner. Thus, he should be attacked by the

United States while he was still relatively weak and before he acquired nuclear weapons.[90] However, John Mearsheimer (codirector of the Program on International Security Policy at the University of Chicago) and Stephen Walt (academic dean of Harvard University's John F. Kennedy School of Government) took strong exception to this reasoning based on the war hawks' image of Saddam Hussein as "reckless, relentless, and aggressive." They argued instead that Saddam, "though cruel and calculating," was "eminently deterrable" and that "the historical record shows that the United States can contain Iraq effectively—even if Saddam has nuclear weapons." Neither the war he started with Iran in 1980 nor his invasion of Kuwait in 1990 was a reckless adventure. "Both times, he attacked because Iraq was vulnerable and because he believed his targets were weak and isolated." These were acts of aggression, Mearsheimer and Walt insist, but not evidence that he could not be deterred. Saddam was vulnerable to Khomeini's Islamic revolution in Iran and even received material support from the United States while he was using chemical weapons to thwart "Khomeini's attempt to topple him and dominate the region." His invasion of Kuwait was another attempt to "deal with Iraq's continued vulnerability," this time its economic vulnerability, and he received a green light to invade from U.S. ambassador April Glaspie. In neither instance was his decision to invade "irrational or reckless," nor were they cases of failed deterrence because deterrence was never tried. Moreover, Saddam's deplorable record of using chemical weapons was never against a formidable adversary such as the United States. He would not resort to using weapons of mass destruction, including nuclear weapons, against the United States or those it protected because that would mean the end of his own power.[91]

Pollack himself noted that "intelligent and patriotic men and women" could reasonably disagree with him on the invasion scenario as a matter of perspective, that is, from "a different point of view."[92] The administration, though, saw it in one way only and, then, not even consistent with Pollack's refinements. Terrorism was the point and perspective of the administration's call to arms against Iraq. As Norman Mailer put the matter so clearly, a war with Iraq from Bush's perspective would gratify America's "need to avenge September 11" even though, Mailer noted, "Saddam, for all his crimes, did not have a hand in September 11." According to the president's logic, as Mailer put it, "September 11 was evil, Saddam is evil, all evil is connected. Ergo, Iraq." Moreover, in Mailer's view, the "unstated, ever-denied subtext beneath the Iraqi project" for "flag conservatives" was that "America is not only fit to run the world" but it must remain committed to empire, or "the country will go down the drain." Yet, as Mailer also observed, to "assume blithely that we can export democracy into any country we choose can serve paradoxically to encourage more fascism at home and abroad."[93]

Finally, it is worth observing briefly that not only does the rhetoric of preempting evil trump and undermine democratic sensibilities to the point of making the U.S. complicit with terrorism but also that adopting the democratic idiom would better serve national and international interests. America's military might and economic strength can be squandered on belligerence or perceived as a secure platform on which to enhance the practice of democracy. Addressing rivals as agonistic Others rather than as evil enemies should be relatively unthreatening from a posture of strength and would appear to be obligatory for a nation that considers itself a model of democracy and an agent of democratization, especially if democratization is taken seriously as an ongoing struggle for increased equality and greater self-rule rather than reduced to a convenient, conscience-clearing rationalization of American exceptionalism and global hegemony that confounds free markets with democratic polities.[94] Moreover, exercising a modicum of rhetorical flexibility to make boundaries appropriately fuzzy and to achieve a degree of consubstantiality between rivals would open the United States and its controlling frame of reference to the constructive influence of continuing critique, keeping the nation's foreign policy flexible and adaptive to changing circumstances in a dynamic world and thus extending its viability.

Most immediately, the United States could opt out of reciprocating terror and could reduce the incentive for international terrorism by turning its attention directly to the sources of alienation and despair. So long as the rhetoric of evildoers preempts speaking in the democratic idiom of agonistic pluralism, however, the roots of terrorism will continue to be fertilized by the blood of a self-sustaining war. Terrorism haunts human history and cannot be eradicated by force. Counterterror breeds more terror. It can be reduced only by engaging conflicting worldviews—not by ignoring or suppressing them—only by identifying common ground and by addressing the sources of alienation and despair. A daily dose of democratic humility would go a long way toward preventing a tragic fall into the abyss of escalating death and destruction.

Adopting democracy as the perspective of perspectives and criterion of positive peace begins precisely when rhetoric is exercised with far more flexibility than has become customary in the White House. War is the bitter fruit of rhetorical rigidity, but peace gains the presumption and war becomes harder to rationalize when we choose to speak democratically to adversaries across rhetorically blurred boundaries. Taking democracy seriously does not mean relegating it to the status of an irrelevancy in the manner of an undeterred President Bush, who dismissed the mid-February, preinvasion protests of millions of people around the world by saying, "Democracy is a beautiful thing. . . . People are allowed to express their opinion."[95] Indeed, democracy must mean more than that, more than a pretty knickknack or just a way of venting steam, if it is worth killing and dying for. And if it is worth fighting for, it is worth practicing vigorously enough to prevent unnecessary wars or an overdependence on military force in a war of terror.

This commitment to the rhetorical idiom of democracy does not reduce to a simple matter of relativism versus truth, as many supporters of a war on terror would have it. It also is not a matter of a mere equivalency of evil between the acts of religious fanatics and the hubris of an American president, as many of the administration's critics maintain. It is not even a question of discarding America's faith in its ideals and abandoning its quest for a just peace. Those who argue otherwise deal in false dichotomies and rigid divisions that purport to place them on the side of angels in a war on evil.

The problem of evil is a rhetorical reality, a paradox of symbolic action that inclines human relations toward tragedy, but a tragic trajectory that remains subject in some degree to the influence of corrective measures. Under the most robust rhetorical circumstances, such correctives would sustain democratic visions of the good life by resisting shortsighted rituals of purification, self-indulgent rites of victimization, and escalating cycles of devastating warfare. A more fully articulated and deliberated understanding of terrorism from multiple perspectives would complicate the problem of evil beyond a simplistic and rigid choice between condemning foreign Others or taking the blame ourselves. It would widen the circumference of the prevailing perspective in order to develop more balanced and apt plans of action. It would speak to the problem of evil by seeking workable solutions and taking prudent actions in a thoroughly conflicted world rather than resorting frightfully and counterproductively to the conceit of righteous force. It would not confuse leadership with dominion or security with annihilation.

Yet evil remains something to be eradicated by means of a just war on terrorism, argues Jean Bethke Elshtain, the Laura Spelman Rockefeller Professor of Social and Political Ethics at the University of Chicago. Like President Bush, she grounds her case for the maximum use of military force by featuring a nearly unmitigated image of evil, thus reducing complex issues to relatively simple matters of right and wrong. Elshtain begins by extracting the lesson of blindness to evil from Albert Camus' novel *The Plague*. Humanists, she declares, are those misguided people who believe the world is amenable to rational discussion, negotiation, argument, and adjudication and who refuse to peer into the heart of darkness. They are the ones who "have banished the word *evil* from their vocabularies," thus denying "the enormity of what is going on" around them by substituting logical explanation for "harsh evidence" and thereby rationalizing "political pathology." By the humanists' way of thinking, the United States should appease terrorists by withdrawing from the world into a state of isolationism rather than standing its ground and fighting "to defend who we are and what we, at our best, represent." By Elshtain's way of thinking, "Only when we stop the spread of evil can good flourish and manifest itself."[96]

From the perspective of evil, Elshtain develops her case for a just war against terror, including a warning about the danger of appeasement, by drawing on a World War II analogy to Nazism and fascism. One cannot reason with such fanatics or, by extension, "sit down at a table and hammer out some sort of 'peace agreement' or 'nonaggression pact' with terrorists." Thus, the problem of terrorism is that the ideological fanatics who perpetrate this viciousness are beyond compromise, reason, and negotiation. Indeed, the problem of terrorism reduces to the fact of the radical Islamic fundamentalist terrorist. In Elshtain's words, "Terrorism is extremism. And Islamist fundamentalism is an extreme repudiation of modernity itself—another reason why it is impossible to negotiate and split the differences between its adherents and those immersed in the Western politics of negotiation and compromise." Terrorists hate Americans for "*what we are and what we represent and not for anything in particular that we have done*." No changes in U.S. foreign policy, therefore, can "disarm radical Islamism." There is no distinction to be made between church and state in the Islamic world of theocracies, nor any guarantee of human rights to women in particular. Nor is there any "prophylaxis" within Islam "to curb or limit the waging of war in the name of spreading the house of Islam," for "as radical fundamentalism has risen, tolerance of multiple tendencies within Islam has fallen." Thus, "authentic cultural dialogue can go forward only when the threat of terror is removed" by force of American arms. Religious motives are the root cause of terrorism, in her view, where a fanatic like Osama bin Laden can operate without the constraint of any legitimate or central line of Islamic authority and when most

Muslim leaders have not condemned terrorist violence against civilians, who are considered infidels in the eyes of Islamic "martyrs."[97]

Elshtain extends her argument to criticize not just "humanists" who deny the reality of evil and rationalize political pathology but also the "dominant intellectual class" of leftist "negators" who are against everything and have removed all affirmation from their collective vocabulary. These purveyors of "automatic oppositionism" have let their youthful resistance to the Vietnam War "harden into identity." From their "subjectivist perspective," facts themselves have taken a "beating." How can one "make a case that facts are being distorted," Elshtain asks, "if one's opponent believes there is no such thing"? Their complaint that dissent against the war on terrorism is being stifled would be laughable except that the "unstated purpose in such proclamations of quashed dissent is to discredit the policymakers under attack and to silence serious opponents by linking them to dissent stifling." Thus, quoting Salman Rushdie, Elshtain dismisses this "sanctimonious moral relativism" because a country that has "suffered the most devastating terrorist attack in history, a country in a state of deep mourning and horrible grief, is being told, heartlessly, that it is to blame for its own citizens' deaths." These heartless intellectual relativists—cynics who indulge themselves in a "blame-the-victim mentality" by arguing that 9/11 was blowback from American imperialism—would place the United States on the horns of an impossible dilemma between conquest and isolationism, for any involvement in world affairs is condemned by leftist negators as unwarranted imperialism and conquest.[98]

Rather than conquest, Elshtain insists, America's legitimate role as the world's only superpower and "longest lived constitutional republic" is to prevent and interdict violence in other countries. The Bush administration has correctly reconceptualized U.S. foreign policy to put into play the theme of a great power with a great responsibility, including the obligation to go beyond punishing the terrorists who assaulted American civilians so brutally on September 11—to go further, that is, by relying on itself "above all" and in "full awareness that states that are too weak to prevent the parasitical outcroppings of terrorists within their borders pose a threat to their own people as well as to their neighbors." The time has arrived "to put warmaking, peacekeeping, and justice together" and to spread "democratic ideals." Thus, the defense of democracy and human dignity requires "a return of imperialism," a term with which Elshtain says she is not completely comfortable but nevertheless endorses as a project of "the world's great superpower taking on an enormous burden and doing so with a relatively, though not entirely, selfless intent." This is a project of nation building for the purpose of deterring "failed states, within which hapless citizens are victimized by the ruthless and terrorists are given carte blanche to operate." The alternative is "something like the nightmare of Thomas Hobbes's war of all against all." America cannot have "empire 'on the cheap,' ruling the world without putting in place any new imperial structure," she avers, and in fighting terrorism the United States "may err on the side of protecting the populace and ensuring basic security" over rigorously respecting legal protections and civil liberties.[99]

This is the dichotomizing position of fighting a just war against evil terrorists in defense of democracy rather than practicing democracy robustly to engage divisive relations rhetorically. By this dichotomizing logic, a continuous, global, imperialistic war is given the strong presumption over other, more nuanced efforts. Those who object are rendered dangerous influences. Democracy must be protected from such irresponsible humanist negators, relativists, and appeasers who hold to no principles and who deny facts just as it must be protected from Islamic fanatics who kill civilians intentionally while the United States military tries to minimize collateral damage. Healthy democracy depends on right thinking that is based on "making the right distinctions," and right thinking requires the world's superpower to provide international stability, "whether much of the world wants it or not." Imperialism may be politically incorrect, but "endangered people around the globe will be able to count on us when American enlightened self-interest and the universal language of human rights and civil society come together in significant and robust warp."[100]

There are no fuzzy boundaries here between good and bad, just and evil. Evasive language, by Elshtain's account, amounts to a loss of meaning that separates words from reality. The choice is between isolation and appeasement on the one hand and a just war and beneficent imperialism on the other. The United States either must be involved in the world as an imperial force or must withdraw from the world as an appeaser. There is no room to debate seriously other ways of involvement. The problem of terrorism reduces basically to the matter of ridding the world of Islamic fanatics and their supporters.

Elshtain's rhetoric of evil, like the president's, is too rigid to cope aptly with the complexities of a divisive world. It substitutes a deadly ritual of vilification and victimization for a more comprehensive reflection on the characteristics and sources of terror. It undermines a thorough consideration of how

America's response might be calibrated along various dimensions to reduce the danger of terror rather than to exacerbate it by relying so exclusively on the coercive power of war. It erodes the nation's democratic culture instead of drawing on the more flexible rhetorical idiom of democracy to maximize the constructive management of adversarial relations.

Adopting a rhetorical perspective of the sort discussed here for the purpose of suggesting a more democratic and efficacious response to the problem of terror is not tantamount to nihilism or wallowing aimlessly in a sea of relativism. It amounts instead to a recognition that any prevailing perspective is necessarily delimited in its account or interpretation of reality and therefore is rendered more serviceable in a divided world by spirited critique from various points of view. This kind of rhetorical agonistics is the source of correctives that affirm and extend the life of a prevailing perspective, keeping it pliable and viable in the face of changing circumstances by resisting debilitating tendencies toward reification and calcification that the vilification of Others promotes. As a rhetoric of identification, it is a positive exercise in constructing bridges between adversaries where possible within and between polities rather than excusing violence deployed in the name of a righteous cause with the intent of obliterating sheer enemies. It is a robustly democratic idiom from which to confront terror as deadly wrong, horribly misguided, and terribly motivated and thus a matter that must be corrected in the most comprehensive way possible, not something that can be fixed simply by reducing the problem of terrorism to the demonic actions and aims of religious fanatics and the solution to a protracted and righteous exercise in overwhelming military force.

Addressing terror in the rhetorical idiom of democracy gives primacy to liberal democratic values and places a strong burden of proof where it should fall, on the shoulders of those who would routinely resort to arms instead of those who counsel less desperate and a more balanced set of measures, on those who would maximize the use of coercive power rather than those who would resort to it as little as possible and then only in combination with a full range of the other measures mentioned in chapter 4 minus the unrealistic expectation of eliminating the threat of terrorism completely and permanently. This is not a pacifist attitude that rejects any and all use of military force, nor is it an amoral position that tolerates the killing of civilians for political purposes intentionally or as the inevitable consequence of an unwarranted, prolonged, and ultimately counterproductive war of terror. It is instead a prudent attitude that would invest more confidence in a rhetorically robust democratic culture of agonistic pluralism, foment less fear of democratic distemper, and resist overstated, overextended, simplistic representations of menacing Others that privilege warfare and curtail the practice of democracy in the here and now. Although this attitude by itself falls short of a complete answer to the question of escalating violence and reciprocal terror, it does go to the heart of the matter by focusing critical attention on the construction of sheer enemies and affirming a strong predisposition toward the articulation of consubstantial rivals.

Conclusion

In his sweeping study of democracy and war, published at the end of the cold war and in the very year the Berlin Wall finally came down, Peter Manicas argues that the extended rivalry between the United States and the Soviet Union created conditions "which made democracy of any sort an increasingly precarious alternative in the contemporary world." Rather than taking a risk for democracy in the decades of the 1950s, 1960s, and 1970s, the CIA, as an instrument of the American security state, covertly undermined democracy in what were deemed risky places such as the Philippines, Guatemala, Ecuador, the Dominican Republic, Brazil, and Chile, all this without effective congressional oversight and in an era of an emerging imperial presidency. The context of the cold war consensus gave the CIA license and transformed the United States into a security-conscious warfare state, silencing and containing the demos by means of a series of international crises through which presidents "fashion[ed] the terms of elite debate and, accordingly, of media coverage." Just as war is a consequence of too little democracy and of the American republic overreaching itself, Manicas concludes, peace is the hope of preserving and enriching civilization by fostering more democracy.[1]

Yet, the prospects of augmenting democratic practice have become considerably less than optimal. The lingering cold war institutionalized a cultural pathology of perpetual peril under the guise of seeking peace and in the form of a national security state, transforming the nation's historic quest for absolute security into a continuing crusade for universal freedom. Dwight Eisenhower, as I have argued elsewhere, played the presidential role of cold warrior in exemplary fashion with a large and lasting influence and without diminishing his image as a man of peace despite his commitment to a New Look policy of containing communism by threatening nuclear extermination. As an agent of cold war acculturation, he augmented a rhetorical legacy of fear that survived even the demise of the Soviet Union, leaving the United States without a vision of national security in a post–cold war era of increasing diversity and deepening globalization other than the old one of enforcing what President George H. W. Bush soon declared to be the "New World Order," a so-called new order that amounted to little more than repackaging the old and bitter fruit of fearful exceptionalism and aggressive triumphalism.[2] These are not the conditions that promote confidence in democratic practices and institutions.

Moreover, the ruling conception of democracy in U.S. political culture, as Noam Chomsky has remarked, narrowly conceives the legitimate role of citizens as consumers and observers, not as active and informed participants who "take part in inquiry and discussion and policy formation . . . and advance their programs through political action." This is a doctrine of passive, compliant citizenship, he rightly notes, formulated by the nation's founders. It extends to restricting the purpose of the news media to the limited function of "vigilant guardians protecting privilege from the threat of public understanding and participation."[3] Chomsky's propaganda model postulates an ideologically driven, self-regulating, voluntary, and decentralized system of thought control in a democratic society where the news-media machine automatically censors itself and dutifully serves the interests of political elites consistent with an "internalized sense of political correctness."[4]

Rather than offering up a conspiracy theory, Chomsky conceptualizes the manufacturing of consent in the United States as a cultural phenomenon, the product of a number of converging economic and social forces, not the forced result of direct government orders, threats, or other forms of coercion characteristic of totalitarian regimes. Media corporations as corporations, for instance, naturally serve corporate interests. Maintaining the impression of an open society and freedom of expression requires more sophisticated measures of thought control than overt manipulation and violence provide. Continuing and ready access to government experts and other news sources is crucial, for example, to gathering the news that's fit and profitable to print. Straying from the straight and narrow risks such access for members of the press and their employers. Within the corporate news fraternity, journalists with the right attitude are hired, pressured to conform, and disciplined if they stray into dissent. Other factors undermining the intellectual independence of journalists include an elemental patriotism, the comparative ease of expressing conventional wisdom, and the tendency to internalize beliefs and attitudes that have infused their own reports.[5] As a result, the mainstream press is anything but a source of the fabled "excess of democracy" that so worries elites who remain convinced of the necessity of restraining the demos in defense of freedom.[6]

Indeed, the deep and abiding fear of an untethered demos so concerns political elites that they see a threatening surplus, instead of a troublesome deficit, of democracy. Fareed Zakaria, for example, warns of an outbreak of "illiberal democracy" over the last two decades especially, a widespread and escalating process of democratization into all aspects of life; "hierarchies are breaking down" under the "pressures from the masses," he complains, so that "everywhere we are witnessing the shift of power downward." Terrorism itself is perceived from this angle as the "democratization of violence," one of the "fundamental—and terrifying—features of the world today." The "dark side of democracy" in an "age of terror" is that it thwarts the proper "inequality of power between the state and the citizen [which] created order and was part of the glue that held modern civilization together." Democracy now flourishes at liberty's expense. Congress has become dysfunctional in a rush to democratize itself. Professional elites, from lawyers to medical doctors and bankers, have lost their prestige and authority. The voluntary but undemocratic service organizations that previously made civil society work have been weakened by pressures to democratize their operations. Government is now reduced to "perpetual campaigning and pandering," "genuflecting" before the public, reading polls as if they were "chicken entrails," a "lemminglike rush" to popular views, and a "roller-coaster ride" of "ritual homage to the American public." Liberty is threatened by the "chaos" of this outbreak of "unfettered, direct democracy" at the expense of "regulated, representative democracy" that otherwise characterizes a healthy republic. "There can be such a thing as too much democracy," Zakaria counsels in his "call for self-control, for a restoration of balance between democracy and liberty."[7]

Order and a strong bourgeoisie, from this perspective, precedes liberty, and liberty is prerequisite to a stable democracy where the government controls the governed and itself by means of strong constitutional liberalism. Otherwise, an illiberal democracy votes the likes of Hitler into power. Rule by violence and demagoguery, i.e., "totalitarian democracy," is the unhappy and certain alternative to "rule of law, equality before the law, private property, free enterprise, [and] civil liberties."[8] The key to liberal democracy's success is, by the measure of Occam's razor, economic success: once rich with "earned wealth," liberal democracies are "immortal." A modernized economy that embraces capitalism and creates a bourgeoisie establishes the base conditions for liberal democracy, a principle that applies even to Islam, Zakaria argues. Americans have lost faith in their government because the democratization of politics has gone too far: "The American people have watched their leaders bow and scrape before them for the last three decades—and they are repulsed by it." This decline of authority will amount to the country's undoing, smothered under a democratic wave that is ruining journalism and restricting the civilizing influence of elites. "The deregulation of democracy has . . . gone too far." Just as delegation is the right way to run a modern business, democracy delegated to experts who are experienced in public affairs will produce better government. Less democracy rather than more is the key to overcoming the current crisis of legitimacy, fighting terrorism successfully, managing globalization intelligently, improving decision making generally, and making the world safe for democracy but also, and more important, making "democracy safe for the world."[9]

This is the sort of demophobia that promotes belligerence and squanders the nation's soft power. As the dominant power in the Middle East, Zakaria suggests, the United States must press for political and economic reform, for capitalism and constitutional liberalism, not for elections and democracy. America must require Saudi Arabia to "rein in its religious and educational leaders and force them to stop flirting with fanaticism," demand that Egypt's "state-owned press drop its anti-American and anti-Semitic rants and begin opening itself up to other voices in the country," and "dislodge" Saddam Hussein in Iraq in order to "engage in a serious, long-term project of nation-building" that would establish a "genuinely entrepreneurial business class" and create an "infectious" example of the first Arab country that combines "Arab culture with economic dynamism, religious tolerance, liberal politics, and a modern outlook on the world."[10] Here we have the outline of yet another badly motivated project that amounts to constructing an impermeable container of liberalism around the stereotypical dangers of democracy—of running away from a frightening caricature, the specter of "total, unfettered democracy"—in a sustained exercise of hard power that would eradicate enemies rather than build minimal bridges between adversaries.[11]

Accenting liberalism so strongly over democracy (with the latter conceived in the extreme as an irrational, demagogic politics) leads all too easily to a militant articulation of the nation's peril. For Paul Berman, then, the

"Terror War" is nothing short of a "liberal war of liberation" from "Muslim totalitarianism." Noting that George W. Bush spoke of defending freedom and defeating totalitarianism and thus "held out the hope for liberal freedom in the Muslim world," Berman criticizes the president not for prosecuting an ill-motivated war but instead for deploying an underdeveloped rationale for such a war, relying on a rhetoric of freedom that sounded "tinny and false" and that held back from offering a "systematic explanation" of this opportunity to "undo the whole of Muslim totalitarianism." Thus, Bush squandered the post-9/11 waves of world sympathy for America and its cause by failing to "appeal to the higher motives of a liberal civilization," that is, by failing to launch a full-fledged "war of ideas" in support of his military strategies for defeating this newest outbreak of totalitarianism. In short, Americans must be made to understand that the terror war "between liberalism and Islamism" mirrors "earlier wars between liberalism and other forms of totalitarianism" and that the battle to preserve liberal civilization is never ending until freedom finally prevails over nihilism.[12]

What goes unnoticed by Berman in his analysis of this newest threat to freedom is that the rites and symbols deployed by murderous totalitarians to whip chanting masses into a mindless state of arousal and submission are not exclusive to the enemy. The "ur-myth" of aggressive totalitarian rhetoric, as he observes, has biblical origins, where Saint John tells of a people of God under attack from within by the abominations of the city dwellers of Babylon and from without by the forces of Satan. Contemporary, secularized versions remain true to the basic shape and texture of the biblical original, including the notion that the peaceful and moral life of a people of God is being destroyed by evil forces from within and without and that after a great battle the final victory achieved by unfaltering faith in a great leader will secure the safety and unity of humankind. This is a form indigenous to war rhetoric generally, at least in the Western tradition and for certain in the American experience. Yet Berman believes it applies today only to the crazed and antiliberal ideologies of modern-day totalitarians.[13]

Whereas Berman faults Bush for relying on a "grandiloquent" rhetoric and an underdeveloped rationale for a liberal war of ideas on Islamist totalitarianism —a counterproductive understatement, he believes, that resonates too strongly with the alienating overtones of preemption and unilateralism—others warn that unilateralism, even in the guise of good intentions, risks transforming the United States into a rogue nation that is at war with itself and the world.[14] The perception is growing around the world, as documented in

detail by the conservative (but not neoconservative) critic Clyde Prestowitz, that despite much talk about "democracy, human rights, and free trade
America's real aim is to control the destiny of other nations in pursuit of
its own short-term interests or ideological preoccupations." America's unacknowledged empire suffers from a bout of myopia and arrogance as the
United States pursues its own interests while telling itself that it is spreading
prosperity and liberal values that are universally respected and desired, except by the dark forces of evil. National invulnerability and absolute security
can be achieved, Americans want to believe, by an application of overwhelming military superiority that the rest of the world need not fear because of America's exceptional virtue and positive intentions. Yet, the reality
is that "there is no such thing as absolute military security," and many non-
Americans increasingly are unwilling to endorse the universality of American
values while the United States more and more is conducting a unilateralist
foreign policy in the name of hollowed-out symbols for which it evidences
too little actual regard. Indeed, unless the United States learns to cooperate
better with the international community, the likelihood of increasing resistance to American imperialism will continue to rise.[15] Already, on the eve of
America's invasion of Iraq, international public opinion registered George W.
Bush as more of a threat to world peace than Saddam Hussein. Even as the
world's so-called überpower, or grand overseer of the global system, Michael
Hirsh insists, America must manage its "twin burdens of power and vulnerability" carefully by giving due attention to the ambiguities and complexities
of an interdependent world beyond the sheer projection of military power.[16]

Yet, a manifest lack of prudence combined with an excess of indifference
to unfavorable world opinion by the nation's neoconservative leaders in their
unrelenting quest for global domination risks losing the war on terror at
home and abroad. Terrorism, Richard Falk notes, has been reduced mainly
to the function of "a surrogate enemy" that disguises the administration's
principal goal of "geopolitical intimidation." Portraying the nation's adversaries in absolutist terms as evil incarnate hyperinflates narrow-minded patriotism, dampens the democratic spirit and thus the marketplace of ideas, and
creates an oppressive environment of fear and intimidation. "We will surely
lose the war," Falk insists, "if we betray the values of democracy." Winning
the great terror war requires instead respect for the opinions of others; commitment to dialogue, debate, and dissent; the prudence of humility; and "a
capacity for acknowledging the non-contradiction of opposites" in a world
of necessarily fluid and fuzzy boundaries and competing perspectives. "Such

an acknowledgement," Falk recognizes, "does not come easily in the West, which since the Enlightenment has accepted a kind of either/or rationality that cannot accommodate contradiction."[17] But as Kenneth Burke underscores, the tragic inclinations of an either/or mentality necessitate an acquired taste for both/and thinking.

In this spirit, Falk outlines a number of constructive steps the United States might undertake to enhance its security if it could overcome the present "deformation of political language" that overgeneralizes and misdirects the nation's understanding of terrorism. Exempting its own state violence from "the stigma of terrorism" under the guise of "counterterrorism" miscues the nation to respond to nihilism with nihilism and thus perpetuates a righteous dance of destruction and death. Instead of relying so exclusively on military might and presuming unrealistically that terrorism will be eradicated, the United States can weaken the overall appeal of terrorism's message by addressing legitimate grievances and attending to root causes. In addition to a festering resentment over America's insensitivity to Palestinian aspirations and support of Israel's desperate countermeasures, Falk argues, the deeper roots of terrorism include an Arab sense of colonial and postcolonial disempowerment and a grassroots belief that Middle East oil reserves have benefited the West far more than the aggrieved people of the region. Accordingly, the constructive steps Falk contemplates include working to reduce poverty, to enhance human rights, to overcome the global democratic deficit, and to reinvigorate a "vibrant political democracy" at home.[18]

Falk's conclusion returns us directly to the challenge of invigorating democratic culture in order to achieve a stronger and more balanced expression of liberal democracy's commitment to freedom, equality, and self-rule and to articulate the primacy of those values in any assessment of a call to arms, especially a call to preemptive and prolonged war against a vaguely defined enemy in pursuit of a unilateral policy of global domination. Featuring the principles and discourse of a robust democracy is key to returning the presumption to peace, where the presumption should reside, and shifting a substantial burden of proof back onto those who advocate war. But overcoming a deeply ingrained fear of democracy, a demophobia inherited from the nation's founders, makes the task of responding constructively to the exigency of terror especially challenging. Filling the democratic deficit, in other words, requires more than just acknowledging this lingering deficiency of political agency, although that is an important first step. It also requires revising the very conception of democracy from one grounded in the frightful trope of disease to a healthier notion of democratic persuasion as an exercise in contested and contingent pluralism, an ongoing drama of adversaries who may bridge the divide sufficiently to achieve a relationship of consubstantial rivalry or fall short and into the abyss of sheer enemies. Where difference and diversity prevail, forcing a unity of prescribed truth and univocal values within and between polities through an empowered fiction of rational deliberation among political elites is a prescription for victimization and violence.

Short of rearticulating democracy's troubled representation as a distempered discourse, it will remain a dysfunctional source of republican terror and liberal desire for world dominion instead of becoming a principal resource for managing the tensions of the global information age. Reconfigured into a flexible discourse of identification, democracy becomes a medium of addressing antagonists as adversaries, enemies as consubstantial rivals. And it is a rich medium at that for adding texture and detail back into distorted abstractions of the Other's threatening visage so long as it is practiced widely and vigorously at least within and by the United States in order to hold its leaders and their power accountable to a public who can choose between contested accounts of reality.

Addressing the Other in the democratic idiom of partial identification is a powerful medium of international exchange, especially for a nation so strong as the United States, because it does not require adhering to a principle of reciprocity in order to achieve its end of articulating a minimal condition of consubstantial rivalry in any given case. Identification is achieved rhetorically, i.e., strategically, not by a mutually agreed upon process of dialogue and dialectic that purports to bracket power and to pursue universal truths and values that erase all differences in a wholly rational manner. A democratic rhetor courts the Other, even the nondemocratic Other, by articulating similarities between perceived differences and distinctions within supposedly pure categories, constructing a limited convergence of interests that is sufficient to warrant a degree of adherence and cooperation in a moment of otherwise disaffecting divisions. Keeping linguistic boundaries flexible, fuzzy, and fluid is the function of rhetoric in the democratic idiom of constructive agonistic relations as opposed to a rigid and antagonistic rhetoric of good versus evil, which exaggerates danger and promotes war.

Speaking in a balanced discourse of liberal democracy—one in which liberalism does not quarantine democracy—activates a full lexicon for promoting a positive peace and gives cause for participating in international forums with due regard for the viewpoints of others. Moreover, giving primacy to a lexicon of constitutional rights, equality, freedom, rule of law, self-rule, and so on does not easily abide contrary practices, loosely justified by an ill-defined and indefinitely prolonged state of war on terrorism—nefarious practices contrary to the liberal democratic ethos such as instituting a regime of domestic spying and government surveillance on a wide spectrum of society, increasing government secrecy and reducing judicial supervision, holding prisoners under conditions that violate the Geneva convention, denying American citizens due process of law, abdicating the responsibility to rigorously debate matters of war and peace in Congress, reporting the news from the singular perspective of the administration, treating political criticism and dissent as unpatriotic, and so on.

Democracy's rhetorical idiom is the nation's great untapped resource for constraining the hubris of pugnacious unilateralism and empire, for appreciating the limitations of human perspectives by holding them accountable to one another, and for addressing the nation's exaggerated fear of foreign influence constructively through strategies of identification instead of violently in escalating rituals of reciprocal victimization. It is a beneficial mode of agonistic politics that can be practiced in the here and now without first making the world safe for democracy, that is, without achieving the impossible dream of world domination. And it is an expression of liberal democracy that is not unsafe for the nation or the world. As Chantal Mouffe argues, an agonistic model of democracy respects constitutional liberalism and protects pluralism, negotiates the tensions between liberal regimes of individual rights and democratic values of equality and self-government, and preserves both liberty and equality as a project of converting enemies into legitimate adversaries. Moreover, she insists, "a well-functioning democracy calls for a vibrant clash of democratic political positions. . . . Too much emphasis on consensus and the refusal of confrontation lead to apathy and disaffection with political participation" and ultimately to alienation. Rhetorical deliberation, unlike models of deliberative democracy that operate under the guise of universal reason, acknowledges what Mouffe refers to as "the dimension of undecidability and the ineradicability of antagonism which are constitutive of the political." Such a rhetoric converts antagonism into the provisional, temporary, and partial condition of friendly enemies.[19] Enriching democratic culture and practice in this way does not threaten freedom, undermine individual rights, or tyrannize minorities, but it does promote a positive tension within a mixed constitution that holds elites more accountable to the people and treats the human divide as a condition for politics rather than as a basis of terror and cause for war.

Thus, America's soft power can be strengthened and extended into a national motive to participate confidently and cooperatively in world affairs where otherwise a singular and unilateral application of the nation's hard power to enforce its will globally will prove counterproductive and will intensify an already inflated sense of national insecurity. The United States not only can afford to embrace democracy at home as its modus operandi but also can deploy the rhetorical idiom of democracy to endorse and develop more participatory forums internationally. This is a commitment to practicing democracy more robustly now rather than seeking to impose it on others in a crusade for universal peace at the mythical end of history. It is an opportunity to explore what the likes of David Held and Richard Falk call, respectively, "cosmopolitan democracy" and "cosmopolitan patriotism" in order to supplement, not supplant, national forums of deliberation and governance.[20] Whether this leads toward establishing more regional parliaments or even a global people's parliament within the United Nations, making international trade and financial institutions more transparent and equitable, conducting international referendums, or experimenting with other specific ways of strengthening participatory politics, the basic commitment is to democratic persuasion as an alternative to militant arrogance. Popular rhetoric does not deteriorate into demagoguery and bellicose patriotism except in a politically impoverished culture absent the moderating influence of contested opinions. To speak in the rhetorical idiom of liberal democracy is to serve the most fundamental purpose of politics by enabling divided peoples to live more peacefully together in a shrinking world without sacrificing their cherished diversity.

The alternative is to succumb in this new century to the "terrible violence of the twentieth century." Such violence, Jonathan Schell eloquently insists, is "always a mark of human failure" and is now a "dysfunctional" political instrument that "destroys the ends for which it is employed." It "has become the path to hell on earth." The United States will condemn the world to repeating the cycle of terrible violence in the twenty-first century, he warns, by "responding disproportionately and unwisely" to the "unappeased demons of national, ethnic, religious, and class fury" and by pursuing "the Augustan path of force and empire." The idea of peace based on American global hegemony "carries the rule of force to an extreme," concealing "coarse self-interest behind a veil of noble ideals," tilting unrealistically against "the resolve of peoples to reject foreign rule and take charge of their own destinies," and completing "the transition from republic to empire." Even if such a project were feasible, it violates America's liberal-democratic principles. Rather than narrowing our vision to one of unmitigated force and violence, Schell turns our attention toward "structures of cooperative power" as a basis of peace premised on the necessity of coexistence. This approach privileges a robust democratic practice at home and chooses "a cooperative, multilateral international system over an imperial one."[21] It is a course correction toward a more balanced and prudent deployment of American power that, I believe, will be made all the more feasible by engaging a divisive world in the rhetorical idiom of democracy.

Notes

Introduction

1. Michael S. Sherry, *In the Shadow of War: The United States since the 1930s* (New Haven, Conn.: Yale University Press, 1995).

2. For a discussion of Roosevelt's call to arms in this context, see Robert L. Ivie, "Franklin Roosevelt's Crusade against Evil," in *Great Speeches for Criticism and Analysis*, ed. Lloyd Rohler and Roger Cook, 3rd ed. (Greenwood, Ind.: Alistair Press, 1998), 106–13.

3. Joseph S. Nye Jr., *The Paradox of American Power: Why the World's Only Superpower Can't Go It Alone* (New York: Oxford University Press, 2002), 12, 40. Nye develops these themes throughout the book but summarizes them in his chapter titled "The American Colossus," 1–40.

4. Ibid., 75–76, 99.

5. Kenneth Burke, "Terministic Screens," in *Language as Symbolic Action: Essays on Life, Literature, and Method* (Berkeley and Los Angeles: University of California Press, 1968), 46.

6. Kenneth Burke, "Definition of Man" and "Terministic Screens," in *Language as Symbolic Action*, 3–24, 44–62; Kenneth Burke, "Literature as Equipment for Living," in *The Philosophy of Literary Form: Studies in Symbolic Action*, 3rd ed. (Berkeley and Los Angeles: University of California Press, 1973), 293–304.

7. Friedrich Nietzsche, *The Will to Power*, ed. Walter Kaufmann (New York: Vintage Books, 1968), 193, 202.

8. Kenneth Burke, *A Rhetoric of Motives* (1950; repr., Berkeley and Los Angeles: University of California Press, 1969), 20.

1. Republic of Fear

1. James Chace and Caleb Carr, *America Invulnerable: The Quest for Absolute Security from 1812 to Star Wars* (New York: Summit Books, 1988), 318.

2. Ibid., 37.

3. David Campbell, *Writing Security: United States Foreign Policy and the Politics of Identity*, rev. ed. (Minneapolis: University of Minnesota Press, 1998), 1–4.

4. See the essay titled "Terministic Screens" in Burke, *Language as Symbolic Action*, 44–62.

5. Ernesto Laclau and Chantal Mouffe, *Hegemony and Socialist Strategy: Towards a Radical Democratic Politics* (London: Verso, 1985), 108.

6. Campbell, 13.

7. Russell L. Hanson, *The Democratic Imagination in America: Conversations with Our Past* (Princeton, N.J.: Princeton University Press, 1985), 16–19.

8. Kenneth Burke, *Attitudes toward History*, 3rd ed. (Berkeley and Los Angeles: University of California Press, 1984), 248.

9. Roger Burbach, "The Tragedy of American Democracy," in *Low Intensity Democracy: Political Power in the New World Order*, ed. Barry Gills, Joel Rocamora, and Richard Wilson (London: Pluto Press, 1993), 100, 106–7, 119–20.

10. On the matter of "thin democracy," see Benjamin Barber, *Strong Democracy: Participatory Politics for a New Age* (Berkeley and Los Angeles: University of California Press, 1984), especially 3–25, and Benjamin R. Barber, *A Passion for Democracy: American Essays* (Princeton, N.J.: Princeton University Press, 1998).

11. James Chace, "A Quest for Invulnerability," in *Estrangement: America and the World*, ed. Sanford J. Ungar (New York: Oxford University Press, 1985), 228–29.

12. Richard K. Matthews, *If Men Were Angels: James Madison and the Heartless Empire of Reason* (Lawrence: University of Kansas Press, 1995), 22, 24.

13. Hanson, 56, 60, 62, 75, 84, 87.

14. I am indebted to Stephen Olbrys, rhetorician, classicist, and folklorist, for introducing me to his term "demophobia" in "'Tis Folly to Be Wise: A Comic Corrective to the 'Problem of the Folk' in Science," a paper he wrote in May 1998 for a graduate class on rhetorical criticism I taught that spring semester.

15. Robert L. Ivie, "Eisenhower as Cold Warrior," in *Eisenhower's War of Words: Rhetoric and Leadership*, ed. Martin J. Medhurst, 7–25 (East Lansing: Michigan State University Press, 1994); Robert L. Ivie, "Dwight D. Eisenhower's 'Chance for Peace': Quest or Crusade?" *Rhetoric and Public Affairs* 1 (1998): 227–43.

16. Tony Smith, *The United States and the Worldwide Struggle for Democracy in the Twentieth Century* (Princeton, N.J.: Princeton University Press, 1995), 144.

17. Barry Gills, Joel Rocamora, and Richard Wilson, "Low Intensity Democracy," in Gills, Rocamora, and Wilson, *Low Intensity Democracy*, 9; Burbach, 100; Smith, *Worldwide Struggle*, 320.

18. Amos Perlmutter, *Making the World Safe for Democracy: A Century of Wilsonianism and Its Totalitarian Challengers* (Chapel Hill: University of North Carolina Press, 1997), 9, 162, 164–65.

19. John Lewis Gaddis, *The United States and the End of the Cold War: Implications, Reconsiderations, Provocations* (New York: Oxford University Press, 1992), 13–14, 196, 208–9, 212, 215–16.

20. Frederick M. Dolan and Thomas L. Dumm, "Introduction: Inventing America," in *Rhetorical Republic: Governing Representations in American Politics*, ed. Frederick M. Dolan and Thomas L. Dumm (Amherst: University of Massachusetts Press, 1993), 2, 6.

21. On the point about hubris and tragic fear in a rhetorical republic, see Robert L. Ivie, "Tragic Fear and the Rhetorical Presidency: Combating Evil in the Persian Gulf," in *Beyond the Rhetorical Presidency*, ed. Martin J. Medhurst (College Station: Texas A&M University Press, 1996), 166–68, 172–78.

22. Gaddis, 216.

23. Hanson, 22–23, 25, 53.

24. Thomas B. Farrell, *Norms of Rhetorical Culture* (New Haven, Conn.: Yale University Press, 1993), 277, 6–10, 1.

25. Hanson, 37–38.

26. Farrell, 188, 190, 194, 199, 211–12.

27. James W. Ceaser et al., "The Rise of the Rhetorical Presidency," *Presidential Studies Quarterly* 11 (1981): 158–71; Jeffrey K. Tulis, *The Rhetorical Presidency* (Princeton, N.J.: Princeton University Press, 1988); James S. Fishkin, *Democracy and Deliberation: New Directions in Democratic Reform* (New Haven, Conn.: Yale University Press, 1991), 1, 18, 21, 25, 40, 47–48.

28. Ceaser et al., 161.

29. Tulis, 112, 114, 128, 130–36.

30. Gary L. Gregg, *The Presidential Republic: Executive Representation and Deliberative Democracy* (Lanham, Md.: Rowman and Littlefield Publishers, 1997), 1.

31. Joseph M. Bessette, *The Mild Voice of Reason: Deliberative Democracy and American National Government* (Chicago: University of Chicago Press, 1994), 3, 5, 21, 34–35, 203, 217–18.

32. Bessette, 236–37, 241, 238, 240, 245.

33. Dolan and Dumm, 1–2, 6.

34. Farrell, 2, 8 10–13, 15.

35. Anne Norton, *Republic of Signs: Liberal Theory and American Popular Culture* (Chicago: University of Chicago Press, 1993), 1.

36. Dana R. Villa, "Postmodernism and the Public Sphere," in Dolan and Dumm, *Rhetorical Republic*, 227–48.

37. William E. Connolly, "Democracy and Territoriality," in Dolan and Dumm, *Rhetorical Republic*, 264–66. On the matter of transnational, border-crossing democracy, see Douglas Lummis, *Radical Democracy* (Ithaca, N.Y.: Cornell University Press, 1996) 138–41.

38. For a discussion of radical democracy, see Sue Golding, *Gramsci's Democratic Theory: Contributions to a Post-Liberal Democracy* (Toronto: University of Toronto Press, 1992); Laclau and Mouffe, *Hegemony and Socialist Strategy*; Lummis, *Radical Democracy*; Chantal Mouffe, ed., *Dimensions of Radical Democracy: Pluralism, Citizenship, Community* (London: Verso, 1992); and David Trend, ed., *Radical Democracy: Identity, Citizenship, and the State* (New York: Routledge, 1996).

39. Farrell, 1–3, 9–11, 29, 32, 39, 47–49, 75–76, 80.

40. Bessette, 223.

41. Simone Chambers, *Reasonable Democracy: Jürgen Habermas and the Politics of Discourse* (Ithaca, N.Y.: Cornell University Press, 1996), 8–9.

42. Amy Gutmann and Dennis Thompson, *Democracy and Disagreement* (Cambridge, Mass.: Belknap Press of Harvard University, 1996), 1. In addition to other works cited in my discussion of deliberative democracy and its intellectual cognates, see the following: James Bohman and William Rehg, eds., *Deliberative Democracy: Essays on Reason and Politics* (Cambridge, Mass.: MIT Press, 1997); John S. Dryzek, *Discursive Democracy: Politics, Policy, and Political Science* (New York: Cambridge University Press, 1990); Jon Elster, ed., *Deliberative Democracy* (New York: Cambridge University Press, 1998); Gerald M. Mara, *Socrates' Discursive Democracy: Logos and Ergon in Platonic Political Philosophy* (Albany, N.Y.: State University of New York Press, 1997); and Carlos Santiago Nino, *The Constitution of Deliberative Democracy* (New Haven, Conn.: Yale University Press, 1996).

43. Gutmann and Thompson, 2, 7, 12, 14–15, 17–18, 27, 41.

44. James Bohman, *Public Deliberation: Pluralism, Complexity, and Democracy* (Cambridge, Mass.: MIT Press, 1996), 5, 6, 15.

45. Ibid., 17–18, 20.

46. Ibid., 24–25, 58–59, 127, 33–34, 42.

47. Ibid., 57–58, 83–84, 89, 97, 103, 240.

48. Farrell, 199, 141–46, 149–50, 152, 154, 182, 199, 230–31, 273.

49. For a discussion of the comic corrective, see Burke, *Attitudes toward History*, and William H. Rueckert, *Encounters with Kenneth Burke* (Urbana: University of Illinois Press, 1994), 110–31.

50. Hanson, 13–14.

51. Lloyd C. Gardner, "Ideology and American Foreign Policy," in *Ideology and Foreign Policy: A Global Perspective*, ed. George Schwab (New York: Cyrco Press, 1978), 136.

52. Alan Nadel, *Containment Culture: American Narratives, Postmodernism, and the Atomic Age* (Durham, N.C.: Duke University Press, 1995), 7, 277, 293.

53. Tom Engelhardt, *The End of Victory Culture: Cold War America and the Disillusioning of a Generation* (New York: Basic Books, 1995), 303.

54. Smith, *Worldwide Struggle*, 7, 94. Clinton quoted in Smith, 320.

55. Bruce Russett, *Grasping the Democratic Peace: Principles for a Post-Cold War World* (Princeton, N.J.: Princeton University Press, 1993), 3–4, 16, 24, 29, 32, 38–39, 119, 123.

56. Ibid., 135–36.

57. Barber, *Strong Democracy*, xvii, xx, xxiii, 20–21.

58. Ibid., *Strong Democracy*, 36–37, 151, 160, 162, 167, 177, 189.

59. Ibid., *Strong Democracy*, 31–37, 178.

60. See Robert L. Ivie, "Presidential Motives for War," *Quarterly Journal of Speech* 60 (1974): 337–45; Robert L. Ivie, "Images of Savagery in American Justifications

for War," *Communication Monographs* 47 (1980): 279–94; Robert L. Ivie, "The Ideology of Freedom's 'Fragility' in American Foreign Policy Argument," *Journal of the American Forensic Association* 24 (1987): 27–36; and Peter T. Manicas, *War and Democracy* (Cambridge, Mass.: Basil Blackwell, 1989), 380.

61. Smith, *Worldwide Struggle*, 342, 332, 318; Ivie, "Tragic Fear and the Rhetorical Presidency."

62. Smith, *Worldwide Struggle*, 323–26.

63. "Remarks by the President at Commemorative Event for the 50th Anniversary of the Marshall Plan," May 28, 1997, White House Press Briefings and Releases, 3–4. See *Public Papers of the Presidents of the United States 1997: Book 1: William J. Clinton: January 1 to June 30, 1998* (Washington, D.C.: U.S. Government Printing Office, 1999). Hereafter cited as *Public Papers*.

64. "Remarks by the President at the United States Military Academy Commencement," May 31, 1997, White House Press Briefings and Releases, 4–5. See *Public Papers 1997: Book 1: William J. Clinton*.

65. "President Clinton's Speech to the Nation on Bosnia," November 27, 1995, Office of the Press Secretary. See *Public Papers 1995: Book 1: William J. Clinton* (Washington, D.C.: U.S. Government Printing Office, 1996).

66. Chace and Carr, 318–20.

67. G. Thomas Goodnight and David B. Hingstman, "Studies in the Public Sphere," *Quarterly Journal of Speech* 83 (1997): 351, 368–69.

68. Chantal Mouffe, *The Return of the Political* (London: Verso, 1993), 130.

69. Chaim Perelman and L. Olbrechts-Tyteca, *The New Rhetoric: A Treatise on Argumentation*, trans. John Wilkinson and Purcell Weaver (Notre Dame, Ind.: Notre Dame University Press, 1969), 31–32.

70. Chaim Perelman, "Philosophy, Rhetoric, Commonplaces," in *The New Rhetoric and the Humanities: Essays on Rhetoric and Its Application*, trans. William Kluback (Dordrecht, Holland: D. Reidel Publishing, 1979), 55.

71. Farrell, 203, 208–11.

72. Iris Marion Young, "Communication and the Other: Beyond Deliberative Democracy," in *Democracy and Difference: Contesting the Boundaries of the Political*, ed. Seyla Benhabib (Princeton, N.J.: Princeton University Press, 1996), 120, 122. Young also discusses her views on rhetoric and political communication in Iris Marion Young, *Inclusion and Democracy* (New York: Oxford University Press, 2000), 52–80.

73. Young, "Communication and the Other," 122–27.

74. Ibid., 128–32.

75. Scott Welsh, "Deliberative Democracy and the Rhetorical Production of Political Culture," *Rhetoric and Public Affairs* 5 (Winter 2002): 680, 688, 692, 698–99.

76. Rueckert, *Encounters with Kenneth Burke*, 44; for a relatively efficient insight into these Burkean themes, see Burke, *Attitudes toward History*; Burke, *Rhetoric of Motives*; and Kenneth Burke, "Dramatism," in *International Encyclopedia of the Social Sciences*, ed. David L. Sills (New York: Macmillan, 1968), 445–51.

204 / Notes to Pages 37–42

77. Rueckert, 7; Burke, *Rhetoric of Motives*, xv; Burke, *Attitudes toward History*, "Introduction," 4, 107, 171, 173.

78. Chantal Mouffe, "Decision, Deliberation, and Democratic Ethos," *Philosophy Today* (Spring 1997): 24–26.

79. Mouffe, *Return of the Political*, 4–7, 75–76, 57. As Mouffe writes, drawing on Hanna Pitkin, the construction of a collective "we" in political discourse concerns a public or community, "requires a plurality of viewpoints from which to begin," and reconciles varied perspectives "into a single public policy, though that reconciliation will always be temporary, partial and provisional" (50).

80. Ibid., 71, 82, 84–86.

81. Ibid., 6, 4.

82. Burke, *Rhetoric of Motives*, 19–26.

83. Burke, *Philosophy of Literary Form*, 76, 83, 107–8, 69–71.

84. Burke, *Rhetoric of Motives*, xiv, 34.

85. Burke, *Attitudes toward History*, 41, 102–3, 106–7, 344, 348, 396, 402, 411.

86. Rueckert, 112–14, 118–22, 124–26.

87. Barbara A. Biesecker, *Addressing Postmodernity: Kenneth Burke, Rhetoric, and a Theory of Social Change* (Tuscaloosa: University of Alabama Press, 1997), 38–43, 48–49, 54, 100.

88. I am grateful to Russell Hanson for suggesting to me in our conversations and e-mail exchanges during September 1996 the thoroughly rhetorical nature of the problem of revitalizing the nation's democratic imagination. In his view, as I understand it, writing a rhetorical prescription that would reduce the tendency of skeptics to exaggerate the risks of democracy requires an explicit diagnosis of the disease that has symbolically afflicted democracy. If the disease has something to do with the perception that reason is too easily displaced by will in politics, and if disease is a function of the body, then Hanson would suggest that we scrutinize the image of the "body politic" that has informed both deferential and democratic politics. The force of metaphors of disease and distemper in our rhetorical universe might be moderated, Hanson suggests, by deemphasizing the image of the body politic and cultivating a concept of politics as a discourse. Such a concept would reinforce the notion of democracy as an open, deliberative style of collective decision making by placing it in a rhetorical universe that treats politics itself as symbolic activity rather than essentially bodily function. Within this universe, the notion of having too much democracy would seem more odd than threatening. To become viable, of course, such a universe would require at minimum a notion of deliberation that is thoroughly rhetorical rather than strictly logical by some universal standard and a conception of symbolic action that privileges politics and political discourse in particular as the arbiter of egalitarianism.

89. Ivie, "Presidential Motives," 337–45.

90. Stephen E. Lucas, "Democracy and the Rhetorical Imagination in America, 1760–1800," paper presented to the Fifth Biennial Public Address Conference, University of Illinois, Urbana, September 27, 1996.

91. Quotations from Belknap and other early republic rhetors are taken from Lucas, "Rhetorical Imagination."

92. Hanson, 13.

93. Philip S. Foner, *The Democratic-Republican Societies, 1790–1800: A Documentary Sourcebook of Constitutions, Declarations, Addresses, Resolutions and Toasts* (Westport, Conn.: Greenwood Press, 1976), 17, quoted in Hanson, 84.

94. Hanson, 114, 116.

95. For a discussion of the image of savagery, see Ivie, "Images of Savagery," 279–94. For a brief synthesis of my work focused on metaphorical criticism, see Robert L. Ivie, "Cold War Motives and the Rhetorical Metaphor: A Framework of Criticism," in Martin J. Medhurst et al., *Cold War Rhetoric: Strategy, Metaphor, and Ideology*, rev. ed. (East Lansing: Michigan State University Press, 1997), 71–79.

96. In addition to my own work on these rhetorical images and vehicles, see Sam Keen, *Faces of the Enemy: Reflections of the Hostile Imagination* (San Francisco: Harper and Row, 1986).

97. Ivie, "Ideology," 27–36.

98. For a discussion of strategies of literalization, see especially Robert L. Ivie, "The Metaphor of Force in Prowar Discourse: The Case of 1812," *Quarterly Journal of Speech* 68 (1982): 240–53; Robert L. Ivie, "Speaking 'Common Sense' about the Soviet Threat: Reagan's Rhetorical Stance," *Western Journal of Speech Communication* 48 (1984): 39–50; and Robert L. Ivie, "Literalizing the Metaphor of Soviet Savagery: President Truman's Plain Style," *Southern Speech Communication Journal* 51 (1986): 91–105.

99. The design, drafting, presentation, and reactions to the Truman Doctrine, focusing on its conceptual metaphors, are discussed in Robert L. Ivie, "Fire, Flood, and Red Fever: Truman's Global Emergency," *Presidential Studies Quarterly* 29 (September 1999): 570–91. For a discussion of how this same rhetorical universe framed even the resistance to McCarthy and thus diminished confidence in democracy, see Robert L. Ivie, "Diffusing Cold War Demagoguery: Murrow versus McCarthy on 'See It Now,'" in Medhurst et al., *Cold War Rhetoric*, 81–101.

100. Robert L. Ivie, "George Kennan's Political Rhetoric: Realism Masking Fear," in *Post-Realism: The Rhetorical Turn in International Relations*, ed. Francis A. Beer and Robert Hariman (East Lansing: Michigan State University Press, 1996), 59.

2. Distempered Demos

1. Josiah Ober, *Mass and Elite in Democratic Athens: Rhetoric, Ideology, and the Power of the People* (Princeton, N.J.: Princeton University Press, 1989), 9, 8, 338, 35.

2. Harvey Yunis, *Taming Democracy: Models of Political Rhetoric in Classical Athens* (Ithaca, N.Y.: Cornell University Press, 1996), 7, 5, 2.

3. Ober, *Mass and Elite*, 128, estimates that the twenty thousand to thirty thousand Athenian citizens amounted to between 15 percent and 20 percent of the total population and about half of the adult male population.

4. Ibid., 82; Demosthenes, "First Olynthiac," in *Demosthenes I: Olynthiacs, Philippics, Minor Public Orations I–XVII and XX*, trans. J. H. Vince (Cambridge, Mass.: Harvard University Press, 1930), 13, 15. For a general characterization of democratic institutions and norms in Athens, also see Yunis, 2–7.

5. Ober, *Mass and Elite*, 7, 31–32, 45.

6. Demosthenes, "First Olynthiac," 5. Yunis, 9–12, observes that rhetors enabled Athenians to achieve effective leadership without sacrificing political equality and democratic decision making. As he explains, the term *rhetor* literally means "speaker." It referred to any citizen who addressed the assembly but especially those who frequently spoke to the masses and concerned themselves with politics fulltime. These politicians, who came predominantly from the social and economic elite class, had no professional standing or legal position but provided effective leadership through their ability to speak persuasively to the demos, who comprised a particularly demanding audience.

7. For a useful explanation of the range of meanings for the rhetorical concept of topoi, see James Jasinski, "Topics/Topoi," in *Sourcebook on Rhetoric: Key Concepts in Contemporary Rhetorical Studies* (Thousand Oaks, Calif.: Sage, 2001), 578–82.

8. Ober, *Mass and Elite*, 35, 40–45, 90, 124.

9. Ibid., 124, 178, 189–90, 314, 337.

10. On the linguistic assumption of citizens' competency for self-rule, see Russell L. Hanson and George E. Marcus, "Introduction: The Practice of Democratic Theory," in *Reconsidering the Democratic Public*, ed. George E. Marcus and Russell L. Hanson (University Park: Penn State University Press, 1993), 3, and Benjamin R. Barber, "Reductionist Political Science and Democracy," in Marcus and Hanson, 65–72. For further discussion of the role of the orator and citizenship in the Athenian democracy, see Takis Poulakos, *Speaking for the Polis: Isocrates' Rhetorical Education* (Columbia: University of South Carolina Press, 1997).

11. Ober, *Mass and Elite*, 308, 122–25.

12. Ibid., 121–25. For Ober's extension of his analysis of the strength of democratic government in Athens, despite the intellectual critiques advanced by its own elites, see Josiah Ober, *Political Dissent in Democratic Athens: Intellectual Critics of Popular Rule* (Princeton, N.J.: Princeton University Press, 1998).

13. Yunis, 24.

14. Ibid., 12, 28, 29, 280, 257.

15. Demosthenes, "First Philippic," in *Demosthenes I*, 69, 73, 75, 93, 97, 99. Demosthenes carried out the analogy to barbarian boxing as follows: "The barbarian, when struck, always clutches the place; hit him on the other side and there go his hands. He neither knows nor cares how to parry a blow or how to watch his adversary. So you, if you hear of Philip in the Chersonese, vote an expedition there; if at Thermopylae, you vote one there; if somewhere else, you still keep pace with him to and fro. You take your marching orders from him; you have never framed any plan of campaign for yourselves, never foreseen any event, until you learn that something has happened or is happening" (93).

16. Demosthenes, "Third Philippic," in *Demosthenes I*, 235–37, 225, 227, 233, 241–43.

17. Ibid., 241, 243, 239 (see also 255, 261).

18. Ibid., 231. (In this use of example, one of many throughout the speech, Demosthenes goes on to explain the deceit against the Olynthians, then against the Phocians, and then still other such instances, 233–35, 249–51.)

19. Yunis, 86, 196, 223.

20. Ibid., 2, 45, 280.

21. Ibid., 257, 85, 80, 78, 76, 148–49.

22. Ibid., 124–25, 168, 164, 181, 193–205, 314, 214, 216–30.

23. Ibid., 123, 149, 220, 124–26, 129–30.

24. Susan C. Jarratt, *Rereading the Sophists: Classical Rhetoric Refigured* (Carbondale: Southern Illinois University Press, 1991), 98, 104–5.

25. Ibid., 31. Also see Harold Barrett, *The Sophists* (Novato, Calif.: Chandler and Sharp Publishers, 1987), 39.

26. Eric A. Havelock, *The Liberal Temper in Greek Politics* (New Haven, Conn.: Yale University Press, 1957), 230.

27. See Jarratt, 47–61.

28. Poulakos, *Speaking for the Polis*, 5, 9–10.

29. Werner Jaeger, *Paideia: The Ideals of Greek Culture*, trans Gilbert Highet (New York: Oxford University Press, 1944), 3:90.

30. Isocrates, "Nicocles," in *Isocrates*, trans. George Norlin (Cambridge, Mass.: Harvard University Press, 1928), i, 5–7.

31. Poulakos, 88–89.

32. Aristotle, *Politics*, trans. Benjamin Jowett, in *The Basic Works of Aristotle*, ed. Richard McKeon (New York: Random House, 1941), 1287a28–32.

33. Aristotle, *Rhetoric*, 1404a1–8. Lane Cooper (*The Rhetoric of Aristotle* [New York: Appleton-Century-Crofts, 1932]) translates this passage as "the sorry nature of an audience," Rhys Roberts (*Rhetoric* [New York: Modern Library, 1954]) as "the defects of our hearers," and George A. Kennedy (*Aristotle on Rhetoric: A Theory of Civic Discourse* [New York: Oxford University Press, 1991]) as "the corruption of the audience."

34. Stephen Halliwell, "The Challenge of Rhetoric to Political and Ethical Theory in Aristotle," in *Essays on Aristotle's Rhetoric*, ed. Amélie Oksenberg Rorty (Berkeley and Los Angeles: University of California Press, 1996), 177. On this point, see also George A. Kennedy, *A New History of Classical Rhetoric* (Princeton, N.J.: Princeton University Press, 1994), 56, 58.

35. Halliwell, 185. See also C. D. C. Reeve, "Philosophy, Politics, and Rhetoric in Aristotle," in Rorty, *Essays on Aristotle's Rhetoric*, 202–3.

36. Eugene Garver, *Aristotle's Rhetoric: An Art of Character* (Chicago: University of Chicago Press, 1994), 6–7, 13.

37. Kennedy, 16.

38. Max Farrand, ed., *The Records of the Federal Convention of 1787*, rev. ed.

(New Haven, Conn.: Yale University Press, 1966), 1:299, 301. Hamilton was not alone in the expression of this antidemocratic sentiment. James Madison agreed that governance up to that point "had been too democratic" (1:49). Roger Sherman, a delegate from Connecticut, "opposed the election [of members of the House] by the people," adding that the people "want information and are constantly liable to be misled" and therefore "should have as little to do as may be about the Government" (1:48). Elbridge Gerry of Massachusetts concurred and, while warning against "the danger of the levilling [sic] spirit," asserted that "the evils we experience flow from the excess of democracy. The people do not want virtue; but are the dupes of demagogues." Thus, he wished to restrain "the fury of democracy" (1:48, 58).

39. James Madison, Alexander Hamilton, and John Jay, *The Federalist,* ed. Isaac Kramnick (New York: Penguin Books, 1987), 128, 122, 336. George Mason, delegate to the Constitutional Convention from Virginia, deployed Madison's disparaging trope with an added twist when he argued that the representatives of the new government should be drawn "immediately from the people" so "that even the Diseases of the people shd. be represented—if not, how are they to be cured—?" (Farrand, 1:142).

40. Matthews, *If Men Were Angels,* 48–49.

41. Madison, Hamilton, and Jay, 10:122, 126, 127.

42. Matthews, *If Men Were Angels,* 51, 55.

43. Madison, Hamilton, and Jay, 373; emphasis in original.

44. Farrand, 1:218, 261, 432, 473, 512, 514, 517, 430–31. Emphasis in original.

45. Ibid., 1:422–23, 381, 291; 2:647, 6. Gerry opposed popular election of the president because he believed "the people are uninformed, and would be misled by a few designing men" (2:57). Morris, too, reflected the distance existing between a democratic notion of self-rule and the preferred republican remedy by characterizing "the Executive Magistrate" as "the guardian of the people" (2:52).

46. Madison, Hamilton, and Jay, 55:336.

47. Matthews, *If Men Were Angels,* 23, 66, 240, 243.

48. Ibid., 4–5. See Robert A. Rutland, *The Presidency of James Madison* (Lawrence: University Press of Kansas, 1990), 20, 105–6; Irving Brant, *James Madison,* 6 vols. (Indianapolis: Bobbs-Merrill, 1941–1961), 1:106–7.

49. Madison, Hamilton, and Jay, 51:319.

50. Matthews, *If Men Were Angels,* 244.

51. Mary B. Black, "Belief Systems," in *Handbook of Social and Cultural Anthropology,* ed. John J. Honigmann (Chicago: Rand McNally College Publishing, 1973), 542.

52. Colin Murray Turbayne, *The Myth of Metaphor,* rev. ed. (Columbia: University of South Carolina Press, 1970), 19, 59.

53. Northrop Frye, "The Koine of Myth: Myth as a Universally Intelligible Language," in *Myth and Metaphor: Selected Essays, 1974–1988,* ed. Robert D. Denham (Charlottesville: University Press of Virginia, 1990), 7.

54. Ernst Cassier, *The Philosophy of Symbolic Forms* (New Haven, Conn.: Yale University Press, 1955), 2:67.

55. Stephen H. Daniel, *Myth and Modern Philosophy* (Philadelphia: Temple University Press, 1990), 10, 12, 4, 6.

56. Ibid., 10.

57. Ibid., 33.

58. William G. Doty, "Myth," in *Encyclopedia of Rhetoric and Composition: Communication from Ancient Times to the Information Age*, ed. Theresa Enos (New York: Garland Publishing, 1996), 449, 452, 451.

59. Bruce Lincoln, *Discourse and the Construction of Society: Comparative Studies of Myth, Ritual, and Classification* (New York: Oxford University Press, 1989), 24, 25.

60. Bernard Bailyn, ed., *The Debate on the Constitution: Federalist and Antifederalist Speeches, Articles, and Letters during the Struggle over Ratification* (New York: Library of America, 1993), 1:13, 15, 33, 132, 133.

61. Gordon S. Wood, *The Creation of the American Republic, 1776–1787* (New York: W. W. Norton, 1969), 595.

62. Madison, Hamilton, and Jay, 63:372.

63. Wood, 599, 606, 613, 614, 513, 517.

64. Edmund S. Morgan, *Inventing the People: The Rise of Popular Sovereignty in England and America* (New York: W. W. Norton, 1988), 267, 282, 286.

65. Wood, 562.

66. Madison, Hamilton, and Jay, 58:351; 63:371; 14:141; 63:371; 10:122; 51:319–20.

67. Cited in Richard K. Matthews, *The Radical Politics of Thomas Jefferson: A Revisionist View* (Lawrence: University Press of Kansas, 1984), 1.

68. On Leviathan, see Matthews, *Thomas Jefferson*, 18; on healing, see Matthews, *If Men Were Angels*, 241, 250; on moral sense, see Matthews, *Thomas Jefferson*, 20, and Matthews, *If Men Were Angels*, 239; on pastoral, see Matthews, *Thomas Jefferson*, 43.

69. On ward politics and revolution, see Matthews, *Thomas Jefferson*, 81; on anarchy, see Matthews, *If Men Were Angels*, 259 and 262, Matthews, *Thomas Jefferson*, 85, and Matthews, *If Men Were Angels*, 244.

70. Michael Kazin, *The Populist Persuasion: An American History*, rev. ed. (Ithaca, N.Y.: Cornell University Press, 1998), 17.

71. Isaac Kramnick, "Editor's Introduction," in Madison, Hamilton, and Jay, 41, 37.

72. Just as the Federalist notion of representation as a filter (especially as articulated by Alexander Hamilton in *Federalist* 35) resembled somewhat Edmund Burke's notion of "virtual representation," the Anti-Federalist counterimage drew from American revolutionary rhetoric that characterized representation as a mirror and, in John Adams's terms, as "an exact portrait, in miniature, of the people at large." James A. Morone, *The Democratic Wish: Popular Participation and the Limits of American Government*, rev. ed. (New Haven, Conn.: Yale University Press, 1998), 40.

73. Farrand, 1:50.

74. Madison, Hamilton, and Jay, 126–27.

75. "Letters from the 'Federal Farmer' to 'The Republican,'" in Bailyn, 1:282, 254, 257, 260, 261.

76. Madison, Hamilton, and Jay, 233–35.

77. "Melancton Smith and Alexander Hamilton Debate Representation, Aristocracy, and Interests," in Bailyn, 2:759.

78. Kramnick, "Editor's Introduction," in Madison, Hamilton, and Jay, 46; see also James Madison, in Madison, Hamilton, and Jay, 37:243.

79. "'Brutus' I," in Bailyn, 1:171–74.

80. Anti-Federalists maintained that circumstances under the Articles of Confederation were not as bad as Madison, Hamilton, and other Federalists suggested, that they were improving, and that they certainly were not sufficient to justify a hasty and ill-advised remedy that would sacrifice the long-term liberties of the people to the financial exigencies of the moment. The "Federal Farmer" (Bailyn, 1:246–47), for example, asked rhetorically whether the country's present situation warranted the precipitate adoption of the proposed constitution, answering: "If we remain cool and temperate, we are in no immediate danger of any commotions; we are in a state of perfect peace, and in no danger of invasions; the state governments are in the full exercise of their powers; and our governments answer all present exigencies, except the regulation of trade, securing credit, in some cases, and providing for the interest, in some instances, of the public debts. . . . We are hardly recovered from a long and distressing war: The farmers, fishmen, &c. have not yet fully repaired the waste made by it. Industry and frugality are again assuming their proper station. Private debts are lessened, and public debts incurred by the war, have been, by various ways, diminished; and the public lands have now become a productive source for diminishing them more. I know uneasy men, who wish very much to precipitate, do not admit all these facts; but they are facts well known to all men who are thoroughly informed in the affairs of this country." Similarly, on June 3, 1788, during the ratification debates in Virginia, Patrick Henry protested the specter of terrible "dangers" that could not be "demonstrated" and argued that the government that "carried us through a long and dangerous war," with "liberty . . . its direct end and foundation," had "secured us a territory greater than any European Monarch possesses" and thus deserved "the highest encomium" rather than the "ropes and chains of consolidation" (Ralph Ketcham, ed., *The Anti-Federalist Papers and the Constitutional Convention Debates* [New York: Penguin Books, 1986], 203, 208).

81. "'Brutus' III," in Bailyn, 1:322; "'Brutus' IV," 1:427.

82. "'John DeWitt,' Essay III (November 5, 1787)," in Ketcham, 315–16.

83. Ralph Ketcham, "Introduction," in Ketcham, 3–4, 17.

84. Marvin Meyers, *The Jacksonian Persuasion: Politics and Belief* (1957; repr., Stanford, Calif.: Stanford University Press, 1960), 7, 13–14. Bancroft quoted in Robert H. Wiebe, *Self-Rule: A Cultural History of American Democracy* (Chicago: University of Chicago Press, 1995), 38.

85. Robert V. Remini, *Andrew Jackson*, vol. 3, *The Course of American Democracy, 1833–1845* (Baltimore: Johns Hopkins University Press, 1984), 337.

86. Ibid., 3:338–42.

87. Editorial, *Richmond (Va.) Whig*, reprinted in *Washington (D.C.) Globe*, August 22, 1835, quoted in ibid., 3:270; emphasis in original. On the Jacksonian belief in the intelligence of the people, see also 3:269, 273.

88. Meyers, 10–11.

89. James L. Bugg Jr., "Introduction," in *Jacksonian Democracy: Myth or Reality?* ed. James L. Bugg Jr. (New York: Holt, Rinehart and Winston, 1962), 1.

90. Barnet Baskerville, *The People's Voice: The Orator in American Society* (Lexington: University Press of Kentucky, 1979), 72. See also Robert Gray Gunderson, *The Log-Cabin Campaign* (Lexington: University Press of Kentucky, 1957), 174–82.

91. Baskerville, 32–36, 59–64, 67, 74.

92. Kenneth Cmiel, *Democratic Eloquence: The Fight over Popular Speech in Nineteenth-Century America* (New York: William Morrow and Company, 1990), 14–17, 31, 39, 56–61, 64, 90. On the notion of impassioned reasoning, see Baskerville, 6.

93. On the rise of the party system as the mark of Jacksonian America, see Michael Schudson, *The Good Citizen: A History of American Civic Life* (Cambridge, Mass.: Harvard University Press, 1998), 110–113.

94. Morone, 75, 87.

95. Kazin, 19.

96. Cmiel, 66–67, 71–73.

97. Baskerville, 90–91, 93, 98. The best speaking in the years between 1865 and 1890, according to Baskerville (100–101), occurred outside the political arena on the lyceum and Chautauqua lecture circuits by such notables as Henry Ward Beecher, Wendell Phillips, Henry Grady, Robert Ingersoll, Ralph Waldo Emerson, Susan B. Anthony, Anna Dickinson, and others.

98. See Cmiel, 248–50, 259–62; Baskerville, 123–34.

99. J. Michael Sproule, *Propaganda and Democracy: The American Experience of Media and Mass Persuasion* (Cambridge: Cambridge University Press, 1997), 27, 38–39, 62, 76–78, 92, 93–94, 104, 207, 213, 222.

100. Bruce Ackerman, *We the People: Foundations* (Cambridge, Mass.: Belknap Press of Harvard University Press, 1991), 15–16, 19, 22–24, 27.

101. Robert G. Gunderson, "Introduction: A Setting for Protest and Reform," in *The Rhetoric of Protest and Reform: 1878–1898*, ed. Paul Boase (Athens: Ohio University Press, 1980), 7, 9.

102. Kazin, 1–6.

103. Gunderson, "Introduction," in Boase, 7–9.

104. Robert W. Smith, "The One-Gallus Uprising: Southern Discontent," in Boase, 155, 164, 173.

105. Robert G. Gunderson, "Calamity Howlers," *Quarterly Journal of Speech* 26 (October 1940): 402, 405–7, 409.

106. *Chicago Herald*, April 5, 1894, 107, quoted in Malcolm O. Sillars, "The Rhetoric of the Petition of Boots," in Boase, 29–30.

107. J. Harold Beaty, "Labor in the Age of Protest," in Boase, 64–66.

108. Frances McCurdy," Women Speak Out in Protest," in Boase, 202.

109. Ibid., 203–4.

110. Quoted in Justus Buck, *The Agrarian Crusade: A Chronicle of the Farmer in Politics* (New Haven, Conn.: Yale University Press, 1920), 33–34; see also Paul Crawford, "The Farmer Assesses His Role in Society," in Boase, 111.

111. Gunderson, "Introduction," in Boase, 9.

112. Charles W. Lomas, "Urban Mavericks and Radicals," in Boase, 39–49. As Lomas reports, "Only Dennis Kearney succeeded in developing a mass movement by means of this tool [of violent language], and with minor exceptions his threat never materialized into action" (43).

113. Kazin, 35, 54–57.

114. Kevin Mattson, *Creating a Democratic Public: The Struggle for Urban Participatory Democracy during the Progressive Era* (University Park: Penn State University Press, 1999), 37–39, 41–47.

115. Ibid., 48, 52, 56–57, 65–66, 81, 84.

116. See Schudson's aptly titled chapter, "Cures for Democracy? Civil Religion, Leadership, Expertise—and More Democracy," 188–232. And for his opinion that citizenship since then has not declined, see 294–314.

117. Mattson, 131.

118. Jeffrey C. Isaac, "The Poverty of Progressivism: Thoughts on American Democracy," *Dissent* 43 (Fall 1996): 47–48; Jeffrey C. Isaac, *Democracy in Dark Times* (Ithaca, N.Y.: Cornell University Press, 1998), 4, 120–21, 146–47, 202.

119. Isaac, *Democracy in Dark Times*, ix, 2–3, 11, 24–25, 38.

120. Mattson, 1–3.

121. Isaac, *Democracy in Dark Times*, 11, 57, 71, 104–5, 108–9, 136–37, 223n57.

122. Schudson, 304–5.

123. Chris Baldick, *The Concise Oxford Dictionary of Literary Terms* (New York: Oxford University Press, 1991), 143; Black, "Belief Systems," in Honigmann, 542.

124. Robert C. Rowland, "On Mythic Criticism," *Communication Studies* 41/42 (1990): 103–4.

125. Homer, *The Iliad*, trans. A. T. Murray (Cambridge, Mass.: Harvard University Press, 1924), 2:71, lines 280–85.

3. Democratic Peace

1. Nadel, *Containment Culture*, 2–3, 14. For an additional account of Cold War culture, see Stephen J. Whitfield, *The Culture of the Cold War* (Baltimore: Johns Hopkins University Press, 1991).

2. Russett, *Grasping the Democratic Peace*, 5, 10.

3. Ibid., 11, 14–15, 19.

4. Ibid., 30–31.

5. Russett, 123, 126, 135–36.

6. Immanuel Kant, "To Perpetual Peace: A Philosophical Sketch," in *Perpetual Peace and Other Essays*, trans. Ted Humphrey (Indianapolis, Indiana: Hackett Publishing, 1983), 111–15, 117.

7. Michael W. Doyle, "Kant, Liberal Legacies, and Foreign Affairs," in *Debating the Democratic Peace: An International Security Reader*, ed. Michael E. Brown, Sean M. Lynn-Jones, and Steven E. Miller (Cambridge, Mass.: MIT Press, 1996), 4–5, 10, 21. Doyle's two-part essay was originally published in *Philosophy and Public Affairs* 12 (1983): 205–35, 323–53.

8. R. J. Rummel, *Power Kills: Democracy as a Method of Nonviolence* (New Brunswick, N.J.: Transaction Publishers, 1997), 24.

9. Ibid., 105, 108.

10. Francis Fukuyama, *The End of History and the Last Man* (New York: Avon Books, 1992). Russett, 3–4, explicitly states that "the ideological conflict dissolved with the end of communism. . . .The end of ideological hostility matters doubly because it represents a surrender to the force of Western values of economic and especially political freedom."

11. Rummel, 23, 10, 25, 51, 63, 85, 91. "Democide" is a term Rummel has coined to refer to "genocide and mass murder by a regime" (91).

12. Ibid., 43. See David E. Spiro's response to Russett's critique of his statistical counterargument, a critique in which Rummel concurs: "The Liberal Peace—And Yet It Squirms," in Brown, Lynn-Jones, and Miller, 351–54.

13. Rummel, 80.

14. Ibid., 121, 143, 203, 160–61, 165, 143, 134, 52, 8–9. Emphasis in original.

15. Ibid., 9.

16. As Rummel makes clear, "By democracy is meant liberal democracy, where those who hold power are elected in competitive elections with a secret ballot and wide franchise (loosely understood as including at least two-thirds of adult males); where there is freedom of speech, religion, and organization; and a constitutional framework of law to which the government is subordinate and that guarantees equal rights" (11). He would avoid the mistake of putting "too much faith in the masses," for unchecked majorities, "superheated" with hate and revenge, can "drive democratic nations to war" under the "irresistible" influence of "ambitious politicians" (105).

17. Ibid., 16 (emphasis in original); Jack S. Levy, "Domestic Politics and War," in *The Origin and Prevention of Major Wars*, ed. Robert I. Rotberg and Theodore K. Rabb (Cambridge: Cambridge University Press, 1989), 88 (quoted by Sean M. Lynn-Jones, "Preface," in Brown, Lynn-Jones, and Miller, ix). James Lee Ray, *Democracy and International Conflict: An Evaluation of the Democratic Peace Proposition* (Columbia: University of South Carolina Press, 1995), captures the purity of the universal spirit in democratic peace theory as follows: "The main strength of the democratic peace proposition is its simplicity. It is a relatively straightforward proposition, and the most important supporting evidence (the absence of war between democratic states) requires no complex technique to unearth. Yet the proposition is also able to

withstand complex, powerful, and sophisticated theoretical as well as empirical scrutiny. The proposition is deserving of the attention it has received up to this point and promises to become a standard feature of the academic field of international politics, influential ultimately among policymakers as well as the general public" (210).

18. Spencer R. Weart, *Never at War: Why Democracies Will Not Fight One Another* (New Haven, Conn.: Yale University Press, 1998), 13, 2, 296, emphasis in original. Weart envisions the ideal as "a democratic international political culture, with democratically oriented international institutions to sustain it." To establish and maintain such a regime most likely would require "every important nation to adopt a democratic political culture domestically" (269).

19. Ibid., 3, 269, 276, 11–12, 20, 12, 14, 121–22, 123, 293–95, 291–92, 292 288, 100.

20. Christopher Layne, "Kant or Cant: The Myth of the Democratic Peace," in Brown, Lynn-Jones, and Miller, 159. For a useful overview of scholarship challenging particular aspects of democratic peace theory, see Miriam Fendius Elman, "The Need for a Qualitative Test of the Democratic Peace Theory," in *Paths to Peace: Is Democracy the Answer?* ed. Miriam Fendius Elman (Cambridge, Mass.: MIT Press, 1997), 20–33.

21. Joanne Gowa, *Ballots and Bullets: The Elusive Democratic Peace* (Princeton, N.J.: Princeton University Press, 1999); Alexander V. Kozhemiakin, *Expanding the Zone of Peace? Democratization and International Security* (New York: St. Martin's Press, Inc., 1998).

22. Gowa, 26, 68, 44, 113, 55, 113, 4.

23. Kozhemiakin, 2, 3, 11, 13, 17, 27, 130, emphasis in original; 127, 130, 69, 133, 146–47, 149.

24. Elman, vii, vii–viii, 505.

25. Ibid., 6, 36–37, 38, 479, 480.

26. Ibid., 40, 41, 42, 489. Stephen R. Rock, "Anglo-U.S. Relations, 1845–1930: Did Shared Liberal Values and Democratic Institutions Keep the Peace?" in Elman, 149.

27. Alan Gilbert, *Must Global Politics Constrain Democracy? Great-Power Realism, Democratic Peace, and Democratic Internationalism* (Princeton, N.J.: Princeton University Press, 1999).

28. Ibid., 28–29, 33, 47.

29. Elman, 35, 483, 485; Gilbert, 5.

30. Glbert, 66–118; 5–6, emphasis in original; 222, emphasis in original; 29–30, 47, 56–57, 216–19, my emphasis.

31. Ibid., 12, 13, 10, emphasis in original.

32. Ibid., 183, 184, emphasis in original; 185, 188, 194–95, 195, 184, 189, emphasis in original; 12.

33. Chantal Mouffe, "Deliberative Democracy or Agonistic Pluralism?" *Social Research* 66 (Fall 1999): 745–58.

34. Barber, *Strong Democracy*, 31–32.

35. Burke, *Attitudes toward History*; Burke, *Rhetoric of Motives*.

36. Smith, *Worldwide Struggle*, 10, 143–44, 181–84.

37. Ibid., 239–42.

38. Ivie, "Fire, Flood, and Red Fever," 570–91.

39. Ivie, "Eisenhower as Cold Warrior," 7–25; Ivie, "Dwight D. Eisenhower's 'Chance for Peace,'" 227–43.

40. Dan F. Hahn, "The Rhetoric of Jimmy Carter, 1976–1980," *Presidential Studies Quarterly* 14 (1984): 280.

41. Gaddis Smith, *Morality, Reason, and Power: American Diplomacy in the Carter Years* (New York: Hill and Wang, 1986), 47–48.

42. Quotations from Carter's speech at the University of Notre Dame, May 22, 1977, are taken from the text released by the White House following the commencement address, a copy of which is located in "SP 3–37 1/20/77–1/20/81," Box SP-21, WHCF, Subject File—Speeches, Jimmy Carter Library, Atlanta, Georgia (hereafter Carter Library).

43. Speaking draft, State of the Union address, January 23, 1980, "1/23/80 (Material for State of the Union Address) (1)," Box 166, Handwriting File, Carter Library.

44. Erwin C. Hargrove, *Jimmy Carter as President: Leadership and the Politics of the Public Good* (Baton Rouge: Louisiana State University Press, 1988), 112.

45. Jimmy Carter, *Keeping Faith: Memoirs of a President* (Toronto: Bantam, 1982), 142–46.

46. Gills, Rocamora, and Wilson, "Low Intensity Democracy," in Gills, Rocamora, and Wilson, 8.

47. Ibid., 9–10.

48. Burbach, 101–4.

49. Smith, *Worldwide Struggle*, 268–71.

50. *American Foreign Policy: Current Documents*, January 20, 1989, 4, quoted in Smith, *Worldwide Struggle*, 313.

51. Perlmutter, 9. Perlmutter observes specifically about President George H. W. Bush that he "coined the phrase 'new' world order to define the post–Cold War era. By this he meant the end of totalitarianism and the spread of democracy and free markets to the former Soviet Empire. It was actually a disguise for American hegemonial conduct in international politics" (161).

52. Baker's speech to World Affairs Council, Dallas, Texas, March 30, 1990, quoted in Burbach, 100.

53. *New York Times*, April 2, 1992, quoted in Smith, *Worldwide Struggle*, 320.

54. Perlmutter, 162, 164–65.

55. The set of Clinton addresses examined here was compiled by accessing the White House Virtual Library (http://www.whitehouse.gov/WH/html/library.html) and asking for all of Clinton's presidential texts (through December 31, 1997) including the term "democracy" in them. From that set, forty were selected for closer examination (distributed fairly equally over the five years from 1993 through 1997)

because of the extent to which they were devoted to foreign policy questions and democracy themes. Of those forty, thirteen proved most revealing and thus are cited in the analysis that follows. The themes and images of the other twenty-seven, it should be noted, were consistent throughout with the thirteen on which I have focused the analysis. All references are to the electronic versions of the president's messages and speeches.

56. William J. Clinton, "Inaugural Speech," January 20, 1993, White House Virtual Library (accessed December 24, 1997).

57. William J. Clinton, "Remarks by the President at American University Centennial Celebration," February 26, 1993, White House Virtual Library (accessed December 24, 1997).

58. William J. Clinton, "Prepared Remarks of President William J. Clinton to the American Society of Newspaper Editors, 'A Strategic Alliance with Russian Reform,'" April 1, 1993, White House Virtual Library (accessed December 24, 1997).

59. William J. Clinton, "Remarks by the President in Address to the National Assembly of the Republic of Korea," July 10, 1993, White House Virtual Library (accessed December 24, 1997).

60. William J. Clinton, "Address by the President to the 48th Session of the United Nations General Assembly," September 27, 1993, White House Virtual Library (accessed December 24, 1997).

61. William J. Clinton, "Remarks by the President in CNN Telecast of 'A Global Forum with President Clinton,'" May 3, 1994, White House Virtual Library (accessed December 31, 1997).

62. William J. Clinton, "Remarks by the President to the Sejm," July 7, 1994, White House Virtual Library (accessed December 31, 1997).

63. William J. Clinton, "Address by the President at the 49th Session of the U.N. General Assembly," September 26, 1994, White House Virtual Library (accessed December 31, 1997).

64. William J. Clinton, "Remarks by the President in Address to the Nation," October 10, 1994, White House Virtual Library (accessed December 31, 1997).

65. William J. Clinton, "President William Jefferson Clinton Address to the Nixon Center for Peace and Freedom Policy Conference," March 1, 1995, White House Virtual Library (accessed December 31, 1997).

66. William J. Clinton, "Remarks by the President to Students of Moscow State University," May 10, 1995, White House Virtual Library (accessed December 31, 1997).

67. William J. Clinton, "Remarks by the President in Freedom House Speech," October 6, 1995, White House Virtual Library (accessed December 31, 1995).

68. William J. Clinton, "Inaugural Address of President William J. Clinton," January 20, 1997, White House Virtual Library (accessed December 31, 1995).

69. See Gills, Rocamora, and Wilson, "Low Intensity Democracy," in Gills, Rocamora, and Wilson, 6–7, on this point as well as Noam Chomsky, "The Struggle for Democracy in the New World Order," in Gills, Rocamora, and Wilson, 80–99.

70. On this point, see Daniele Archibugi and David Held, "Editors' Introduc-

tion," in *Cosmopolitan Democracy: An Agenda for a New World Order*, ed. Daniele Archibugi and David Held (Cambridge: Polity Press, 1995), 3–4. See also Samuel P. Huntington, *The Third Wave: Democratization in the Late Twentieth Century* (Norman: University of Oklahoma Press, 1991).

71. Archibugi and Held, "Editors' Introduction," in Archibugi and Held, 11–12.

72. Clinton, "Address to the 49th U.N. General Assembly," and Clinton, "Remarks to Students of Moscow State University."

73. Barber, *Strong Democracy*, 3–25; David Held, *Models of Democracy*, 2nd ed. (Stanford, Calif.: Stanford University Press, 1996), xi, 254; Hanson, 5, 13–19. Lummis (111–42) discusses the larger context of the problem in Western culture as "democracy's flawed tradition."

74. David Held, "Democracy and the New International Order," in Archibugi and Held, 96–97.

75. Burbach, 120; see also Norberto Bobbio, *Liberalism and Democracy* (London: Verso Press, 1990).

76. Burbach, 101, 117–19.

77. For a discussion of America's war mentality, see Sherry.

78. Barber, *Strong Democracy*, 20.

79. Archibugi and Held, "Editors' Introduction," in Archibugi and Held, 10; Lawrence J. Hatab, *A Nietzschean Defense of Democracy: An Experiment in Postmodern Politics* (Chicago: Open Court, 1995), 78–93, 108, 158–73, 191, 199, 220.

80. Held, "Democracy and the New International Order," in Archibugi and Held, 110–12.

81. Ibid., 106–8, 112, 115–16.

82. David Held, "The Transformation of Political Community: Rethinking Democracy in the Context of Globalization," in *Democracy's Edges*, ed. Ian Shapiro and Casiano Hacker-Cordón (New York: Cambridge University Press, 1999), 103. For an elaboration of the cosmopolitan model, see David Held, *Democracy and the Global Order: From the Modern State to Cosmopolitan Governance* (Stanford, Calif.: Stanford University Press, 1995).

83. Held, "Transformation of Political Community," in Shapiro and Hacker-Cordón, 103–7.

84. Will Kymlicka, "Citizenship in an Era of Globalization: Commentary on Held," in Shapiro and Hacker-Cordón, 112, 118–19, 120, 125.

85. Ian Shapiro, *Democratic Justice* (New Haven, Conn.: Yale University Press, 1999), 5–6, 8–10.

86. Ibid., 12–15, 21–22, 39, 40–41, 47–49, 51, 58, 239.

87. Chantal Mouffe, *The Democratic Paradox* (London: Verso, 2000), specifically 102 but also 65–74, 94–105.

4. Fighting Terror

1. "Top Secret—Special Interest to General Groves," Manhatten Engineering District Papers, Modern Military Branch, National Archives, quoted in Robert Jay

Lifton and Greg Mitchell, *Hiroshima in America: A Half Century of Denial* (New York: Avon Books, 1996), 4, 6–7.

2. Phil Scraton, "Introduction: Witnessing 'Terror,' Anticipating 'War,'" in *Beyond September 11: An Anthology of Dissent,* ed. Phil Scraton (London: Pluto Press, 2002), 7, 9.

3. John Pilger, "An Unconscionable Threat to Humanity," in Scraton, 21.

4. Herman Schwendinger and Julia Schwendinger, "Terrorism, Neighbours, and Nuremberg," in Scraton, 171.

5. Pilger, in Scraton, 27.

6. Noam Chomsky, "September 11 Aftermath: Where Is the World Heading?" in Scraton, 71.

7. Chalmers Johnson, *Blowback: The Costs and Consequences of American Empire* (New York: Henry Holt and Company, 2000), 5, 7, 33, 216–17, 223. On the matter of George H. W. Bush's new-world-order rhetoric of war, see Ivie, "Tragic Fear." Robert S. Litwak provides a thorough assessment of U.S. policy on this matter in his *Rogue States and U.S. Foreign Policy: Containment after the Cold War* (Baltimore: Johns Hopkins University Press, 2000), and Noam Chomsky scrutinizes the United States and its allies in his *Rogue States: The Rule of Force in World Affairs* (Cambridge, Mass.: South End Press, 2000). For a discussion of the transnational system of empire and the role of crisis management (using just-war claims to put down outbreaks of terrorism) in maintaining the system, see Michael Hardt and Antonio Negri, *Empire* (Cambridge, Mass.: Harvard University Press, 2000).

8. Clyde Prestowitz, *Rogue Nation: American Unilateralism and the Failure of Good Intentions* (New York: Basic Books, 2003), 20–22, 30–36, 41 (emphasis in original); Bush, quoted by Prestowitz, speaking on June 1, 2002, at the U.S. Military Academy at West Point; found at www.whitehouse.gov/news/releases/2002/06/20020601-3.html. For a systematic analysis of the feasibility and costs of the present project in war and empire, including the myth of the reluctant superpower and the conceits of globalization, see Andrew J. Bacevich, *American Empire: The Realities and Consequences of U.S. Diplomacy* (Cambridge, Mass.: Harvard University Press, 2002). For a specific critique of the policy of empire as it distorted the administration's actions following 9/11, see John Newhouse, *Imperial America: The Bush Assault on the World Order* (New York: Alfred A. Knopf, 2003).

9. Seymour Martin Lipset, *American Exceptionalism: A Double-Edged Sword* (New York: W. W. Norton, 1996), 20.

10. To the extent that the culture of exceptionalism reinforces a narrow-minded attitude of American superiority, righteousness, and mission, it undermines national security and promotes policies of global domination. Yet, one might hope there is a potential of transforming this deeply rooted cultural formation into a more functional version for coping with the circumstances and demands of the twenty-first century. Given the United States' economic and military might, one might hope that Americans would perceive an exceptional and pressing responsibility for world leadership by enriching its own democratic culture and eschewing violence and domination as its default response to global threats and challenges.

11. Jeffrey D. Simon, *The Terrorist Trap: America's Experience with Terrorism*, 2nd ed. (Bloomington: Indiana University Press, 2001), 9, 11.

12. Benjamin R. Barber, *Jihad vs. McWorld: How Globalism and Tribalism Are Reshaping the World* (New York: Ballantine Books, 1995).

13. For an extended critique of the dangers of the Bush administration's post-9/11 strategy, including its negative impact on democracy, see Douglas Kellner, *From 9/11 to Terror War: The Dangers of the Bush Legacy* (Lanham, Md.: Rowman and Littlefield, 2003).

14. Nietzsche, 193, 202, 302, 400, 428.

15. For a useful discussion of the risks of profiling in the war on terror, see Christopher Edley Jr., "The American Dilemma: Racial Profiling Post-9/11," in *The War on Our Freedoms: Civil Liberties in an Age of Terrorism*, ed. Richard C. Leone and Greg Anrig Jr. (New York: Public Affairs, 2003), 170–92.

16. On these points, see Kenneth Burke, *Permanence and Change: An Anatomy of Purpose*, 2nd rev. ed. (1954; repr., Indianapolis: Bobbs-Merrill, 1965), and Burke, *Attitudes toward History*.

17. Sander L. Gilman, Carole Blair, and David J. Parent, ed. and trans., *Friedrich Nietzsche on Rhetoric and Language* (New York: Oxford University Press, 1989), 21.

18. Bruce Hoffman, *Inside Terrorism* (New York: Columbia University Press, 1998), 14–15, and Caleb Carr, *The Lessons of Terror—A History of Warfare against Civilians: Why It Has Always Failed and Will Fail Again* (New York: Random House, 2002), 6.

19. Philip B. Heymann, *Terrorism and America: A Commonsense Strategy for a Democratic Society* (Cambridge, Mass.: MIT Press, 1998), xxxi.

20. Simon, vi, xix–xx, 10.

21. Walter Laqueur, *No End to War: Terrorism in the Twenty-first Century* (New York: Continuum, 2003), 7.

22. All excerpts of the State of the Union address, January 29, 2002, are from the text provided by the White House online at http://www.whitehouse.gov/.

23. Kenneth Burke, *The Rhetoric of Religion: Studies in Logology* (Berkeley and Los Angeles: University of California Press, 1970), 274–76, 279, 280–82, 303.

24. Hoffman, 14–15.

25. Carr, 6.

26. Heymann, 6–7.

27. Simon, 348–65.

28. Ibid., 6.

29. Hoffman, 109, quoting David Harrison, "Jackboot Stamp of the New Right," *Observer* (London), April 23, 1995.

30. Hoffman, 110.

31. Mark Juergensmeyer, *Terror in the Mind of God: The Global Rise of Religious Violence* (Berkeley and Los Angeles: University of California Press, 2000), 133.

32. Ibid., 135.

33. Http://aryan-nations.org/posse/mainpagenews/WTC.htm, quoted in Daniel Levitas, *The Terrorist Next Door: The Militia Movement and the Radical Right* (New

York: Stomas Dunne Books, 2002), 335; see also "Reaping the Whirlwind," *Intelligence Report* (Winter 2001): 19.

34. Rex A. Hudson, *Who Becomes a Terrorist and Why: The 1999 Government Report on Profiling Terrorists* (Guilford, Conn.: Lyons Press, 2002), 8–10.

35. Scott Atran, "Who Wants to Be a Martyr?" *New York Times*, May 5, 2003, http://www.nytimes.com/.

36. Scraton, "Introduction," in Scraton, 2.

37. Paul L. Williams, *Al Qaeda: Brotherhood of Terror* (Parsippany, N.J.: Alpha Books, 2002), 71.

38. Carr, 13, 20, 22–23.

39. Walter Laqueur, "Left, Right, and Beyond: The Changing Face of Terror," in *How Did This Happen: Terrorism and the New War*, ed. James F. Hoge Jr. and Gideon Rose (New York: Public Affairs, 2001), 71; Heymann, 154.

40. Simon, 9–10. Also see pages 309–45 on Simon's overview of the various roots of terrorism.

41. Ibid., 339.

42. Juergensmeyer, 123–24, 145–49, 158–69, 182–83.

43. Williams, 128–38.

44. Michael Scott Doran, "Somebody Else's Civil War: Ideology, Rage, and the Assault on America," in Hoge and Rose, 31–32. See ibid., 31, for Doran's citation of David Fromkin, "The Strategy of Terrorism," *Foreign Affairs* 53 (July 1975): 683–89.

45. Simon, vii, 376.

46. Heymann, xvii.

47. Fareed Zakaria, "The Return of History: What September 11 Hath Wrought," in Hoge and Rose, 313–14; and for a more extended treatment of these concerns, see James Bovard, *Terrorism and Tyranny: Trampling Freedom, Justice, and Peace to Rid the World of Evil* (New York: Palgrave Macmillan, 2003).

48. Williams, 182–83; Simon, 375, 379–81, 390–93, 401; Juergensmeyer, 230–31.

49. Doran, in Hoge and Rose, 37.

50. Juergensmeyer, 238; Samuel R. Berger and Mona Sutphen, "Commandeering the Palestinian Cause: Bin Laden's Belated Concern," in Hoge and Rose, 128.

51. Anatol Lieven, "The Cold War Is Finally Over: The True Significance of the Attacks," in Hoge and Rose, 296–97, 305–6; Johnson, 229.

52. Berger and Sutphen, in Hoge and Rose, 125; Doran, in Hoge and Rose, 51.

53. These and related themes are developed in Henry A. Giroux, *Public Spaces, Private Lives: Democracy beyond 9/11* (Lanham, Md.: Rowman and Littlefield, 2003).

54. Paul R. Pillar, *Terrorism and U.S. Foreign Policy* (Washington, D.C.: Brookings Institution Press, 2001), 217–20. Although the comparison of the problem of terrorism to a public health campaign instead of to a war is in some important respects an improvement, the metaphor of disease remains a culturally tricky way of talking about managing threats to the body politic, for example, when the temptation arises to speak of fighting a war on disease. Fighting the cold war, for example, was easily conflated with a notion of medical progress and the eradication of polio as

well as with threatening images of fire, flood, and red fever. For one highly influential discussion of the dangers of thinking of illness metaphorically, see Susan Sontag, *Illness as Metaphor and AIDS and Its Metaphors* (New York: Anchor Books, 1990).

55. Laqueur, *No End to War*, 8.

56. Pillar, 221–29. Unfortunately, President George W. Bush "loves to deal in moral absolutes," as explained by nationally syndicated columnist David Broder in "'Good and Evil' Designations Can't Solve All the Problems Facing U.S.," *Herald-Times* (Bloomington, Ind.), April 10, 2002, A6.

57. Pillar, 5–6.

58. Ibid., 97–110.

59. Barry Schweid, "Powell Ready for 'Very Long Conversation' with Sharon," *Herald-Times* (Bloomington, Ind.), April 12, 2002, A1, A7.

60. Carr, 12, 224, 231, 236, 256.

61. Pillar, 73–129.

62. Laqueur, *No End to War*, 222, 231.

63. Mouffe, *Democratic Paradox*.

64. Jonathan Schell, "American Tragedy," *Nation*, April 7, 2003, http://www.thenation.com/.

5. Idiom of Democracy

1. Some of these restrictions are chronicled in Nancy Chang, *Silencing Political Dissent: How Post–September 11 Anti-Terrorism Measures Threaten Our Civil Liberties* (New York: Seven Stories Press, 2002).

2. On the subject of agonistic pluralism, see Mouffe, *Democratic Paradox*.

3. George Lakoff, "Metaphors of Terror: The Power of Images," *In These Times.com*, October 29, 2001, http://www.inthesetimes.com/issue/25/24/lakoff2524.html.

4. "Remarks by the President after Two Planes Crash into World Trade Center," White House, Office of the Press Secretary, September 11, 2001, http://www.whitehouse.gov/news/releases/2001/09/20010911.html; "Remarks by the President upon Arrival at Barksdale Air Force Base," White House, Office of the Press Secretary, September 11, 2001, http://www.whitehouse.gove/news/releases/2001/09/20010911-1.html; "Statement by the President in His Address to the Nation," White House, Office of the Press Secretary, September 11, 2001, http://www.whitehouse.gov/news/releases/2001/09/20010911-16.html.

5. "President Pledges Assistance for New York in Phone Call with Pataki, Giuliani," White House, Office of the Press Secretary, September 13, 2001, http://www.whitehouse.gov/news/releases/2001/09/20010913-4.html; "Text: Bush Delivers Weekly Radio Address," *Washington Post On Line*, September 15, 2001, wysiwyg://778/http://www.washingtonpost . . . transcripts/bushradioad dress_091501.html.

6. Ibid.

7. Lakoff.

8. "President Pledges Assistance."

9. "President Holds Prime Time News Conference," White House, Office of the Press Secretary, October 11, 2001, http://www.whitehouse.gov/news/releases/2001/10/20011011-7.html; "President Announces Crackdown on Terrorist Financial Network," White House, Office of the Press Secretary, November 7, 2001, http://www.whitehouse.gov/news/releases/2001/11/20011107-4.html; "President Discusses War on Terrorism," White House, Office of the Press Secretary, November 8, 2001, http://www.whitehouse.gov/news/releases/2001/11/20011108-13.html.

10. Bush quoted in a news report by David Stout, "Bush Says He Wants Capture of Bin Laden 'Dead or Alive,'" *New York Times on the Web*, September 17, 2001, http://www.nytimes.com/.

11. "President Outlines War Effort," White House, Office of the Press Secretary, April 17, 2002, http://www.whitehouse.gov/news/releases/2002/04/20020417-1.html; "President Bush Delivers Graduation Speech at West Point," White House, Office of the Press Secretary, June 1, 2002, http://www.whitehouse.gov/news/releases/2002/06/20020601-3.html; "Bush Consulting Congress about Iraq," *New York Times on the Web*, August 10, 2002, http://www.nytimes.com/.

12. "President Outlines War Effort" and "President Bush Thanks Germany for Support against Terror," White House, Office of the Press Secretary, May 23, 2002, http://www.whitehouse.gov/news/releases/2002/05/20020523-2.html.

13. "Presidential Address to the Nation," White House, Office of the Press Secretary, October 7, 2001, http://www.whitehouse.gov/news/releases/2001/10/20011007-8.html.

14. Lakoff. For a fresh and insightful discussion of how to begin thinking beyond the destructive dialectic of terrorism and counterterrorism and to engage Islamism democratically as a political discourse, see Susan Buck-Morss, *Thinking Past Terror: Islamism and Critical Theory on the Left* (London: Verso, 2003).

15. Jeffrey C. Goldfarb, "Losing Our Best Allies in the War on Terror," *New York Times on the Web*, August 20, 2002, http://www.nytimes.com/.

16. "President's Remarks at National Day of Prayer and Remembrance," White House, Office of the Press Secretary, September 14, 2001, http://www.whitehouse.gov/news/releases/2001/09/20010914-2.html.

17. "Statement by the President in His Address to the Nation."

18. "Address to a Joint Session of Congress and the American People," White House, Office of the Press Secretary, September 20, 2001, http://www.whitehouse.gov/news/releases/2001/09/print/20010920-8.html.

19. "President Bush: 'No Nation Can Be Neutral in This Conflict,'" White House, Office of the Press Secretary, November 6, 2001, http://www.whitehouse.gov/news/releases/2001/11/20011106-2.html.

20. "President Bush Speaks to United Nations," White House, Office of the Press Secretary, November 10, 2001, http://www.whitehouse.gov/news/releases/2001/11/20011110-3.html.

21. "President: We're Fighting to Win—And Win We Will," White House, Office of the Press Secretary, December 7, 2001, http://www.whitehouse.gov/news/releases/2001/12/20011207.html.

22. Benjamin R. Barber, *Fear's Empire: War, Terrorism, and Democracy* (New York: W. W. Norton, 2003), 32. Barber calls for a strategy of preventative democracy to replace the Bush administration's badly flawed doctrine of preventative war.

23. Among the post–9/11 books that have chronicled, analyzed, and critiqued the Bush administration's curtailment of civil rights are, besides Nancy Chang's *Silencing Political Dissent*, Nat Hentoff, *The War on the Bill of Rights and the Gathering Resistance* (New York: Seven Stories Press, 2003); Leone and Anrig, *War on Our Freedoms*; David Cole and James X. Dempsey, *Terrorism and the Constitution: Sacrificing Civil Liberties in the Name of National Security* (New York: New Press, 2002); and Bovard, *Terrorism and Tyranny*.

24. Chang, 13.

25. Ibid., 11.

26. Burke, *Rhetoric of Motives*, 11–17 (Burke's italics).

27. "President Thanks World Coalition for Anti-Terrorism Efforts," White House, Office of the Press Secretary, March 11, 2002, http://www.whitehouse.gov/news/releases/2002/03/20020311-1.html.

28. "President Bush Delivers Graduation Speech at West Point."

29. "President Bush Thanks Germany for Support against Terror."

30. "President Delivers State of the Union Address," White House, Office of the Press Secretary, January 29, 2002, http://www.whitehouse.gov/news/releases/2002/01/20020129-11.html.

31. Quoted in Neil A. Lewis, "Ashcroft Defends Antiterror Plan and Says Criticism May Aid Foes," *New York Times on the Web*, December 7, 2001, http://www.newyorktimes.com/.

32. "Address to a Joint Session of Congress and the American People."

33. "Presidential Address to the Nation," October 7, 2001.

34. "Address to a Joint Session of Congress and the American People"; "President Announces Crackdown on Terrorist Financial Network."

35. "President: We're Fighting to Win—And Win We Will"; "President Speaks on War Effort to Citadel Cadets," White House, Office of the Press Secretary, December 11, 2001, http://www.whitehouse.gov/news/releases/2001/12/20011211-6.html.

36. "Address to a Joint Session of Congress and the American People."

37. "President Delivers State of the Union Address."

38. Ibid.

39. Katharine Q. Seelye, "Judge Questions Detention of American in War Case," *New York Times on the Web*, August 14, 2002, http://www.newyorktimes.com/.

40. Neil A. Lewis, "Ashcroft's Terrorism Policies Dismay Some Conservatives," *New York Times on the Web*, July 24, 2002, http://www.newyorktimes.com/.

41. "Informant Fever," *New York Times on the Web*, July 22, 2002, http://www.newyorktimes.com/.

42. Adam Clymer, "Ashcroft Defends Plan for National Hotline on Terrorism," *New York Times on the Web*, July 25, 2002, http://www.newyorktimes.com/.

43. I refer here to George W. Bush's State of the Union address on January 28, 2003, in which he anticipated war being "forced upon us" by Saddam Hussein's evil

recalcitrance. "Some have said we must not act until the threat is imminent," Bush observed. "Since when have terrorists and tyrants announced their intentions, politely putting us on notice before they strike? If this threat is permitted to fully and suddenly emerge, all actions, all words, and all recriminations would come too late. Trusting in the sanity and restraint of Saddam Hussein is not a strategy, and it is not an option." *New York Times*, January 28, 2003, http://www.nytimes.com/.

44. Chantal Mouffe, *Democratic Paradox*, 80–107. Also see Young, *Inclusion and Democracy*, 49–51.

45. On the matter of danger as an effect of interpretation, see Campbell, *Writing Security*.

46. Robin Wright, *Sacred Rage: The Wrath of Militant Islam*, rev. ed. (New York: Simon and Schuster, 2001); Juergensmeyer, *Terror in the Mind of God*; Rahul Mahajan, *The New Crusade: America's War on Terrorism* (New York: Monthly Review Press, 2002); George W. Bush, "State of the Union Address, January 28, 2003," *New York Times*, January 28, 2003, http://www.nytimes.com/.

47. Laurie Goodstein, "A President Puts His Faith in Providence," *New York Times*, February 9, 2003, http://wwww.nytimes.com/.

48. Ibid.

49. Ibid.

50. This is not the same as saying that all religious traditions or appropriations of religion default to a rhetoric of war and evil. Indeed, much of the history of peace activism and nonviolent social action in the United States, as well as other parts of the world, is religiously based.

51. On the definition of terrorism as politically motivated assaults on civilians, see Heymann, *Terrorism and America*, 6–7, and Carr, *Lessons of Terror*, 6.

52. "Full Text: Bush's National Security Strategy," *New York Times*, September 20, 2002, http://www.nytimes.com/.

53. Ibid.

54. David E. Sanger, "Bush Sees 'Urgent Duty' to Pre-empt Attack by Iraq," *New York Times*, October 8, 2002, http://www.nytimes.com/.

55. "Powell's Remarks to U.N.," *New York Times*, February 5, 2003, http://www.nytimes.com/.

56. "China's Remarks to the U.N.," *New York Times*, February 5, 2003, http://www.nytimes.com/.

57. "Russia's Remarks to the U.N.," *New York Times*, February 5, 2003, http://www.nytimes.com/.

58. "France's Remarks to the U.N.," *New York Times*, February 5, http://www.nytimes.com/.

59. "3 Nations Call for Alternative to Iraq War," *New York Times*, February 10, 2003, http://www.nytimes.com/.

60. Alan Cowell, "British Troops Deploy at London Airport over Fear of Attack," *New York Times*, February 11, 2003, http://www.nytimes.com/.

61. See, for instance, Giambattista Vico, *New Science*, trans. David Marsh

(1744; repr., New York: Penguin Books, 1999); John D. Schaffer, *Sensus Communis: Vico, Rhetoric, and the Limits of Relativism* (Durham, N.C.: Duke University Press, 1990); Ernesto Grassi, *Rhetoric as Philosophy: The Humanist Tradition* (University Park: Penn State University Press, 1980).

62. For a discussion of Burke's tropology along these lines, see Robert L. Ivie, "Metaphor and Motive in the Johnson Administration's Vietnam War Rhetoric," in *Texts in Context: Critical Dialogues on Significant Episodes in American Political Rhetoric*, ed. Michael C. Leff and Fred J. Kauffeld (Davis, Calif.: Hermagoras Press, 1989), 122–26.

63. "President Bush Thanks Germany for Support against Terror."

64. "President Bush Speaks to United Nations."

65. Burke, *Attitudes toward History*, rev. 2nd ed. (1937; repr., Boston: Beacon Press, 1959), 92–107.

66. Barber, *Fear's Empire*, 141.

67. Michael Walzer, *The Company of Critics: Social Criticism and Political Commitment in the Twentieth Century*, 2nd ed. (New York: Basic Books, 2002), xii–xviii.

68. Mouffe, *Democratic Paradox*, 13.

69. This point is adapted from Kenneth Burke's dramatism, discussed, for example, in his *Attitudes toward History*, 3rd ed.

70. Laclau and Mouffe, *Hegemony and Socialist Strategy*, x–xviii.

71. Paul Rabinow, "Polemics, Politics, and Problematizations: An Interview with Michel Foucault," in *Michel Foucault: Ethics, Subjectivity, and Truth*, ed. Paul Rabinow (New York: New Press, 1997), 112–13.

72. Burke, *Attitudes toward History*, 39–43, 166–75, 179 (emphasis in original).

73. Lewis Hyde, *Trickster Makes This World: Mischief, Myth, and Art* (New York: North Point Press, 1998), 9.

74. See Burke's discussion of these themes in his "Dictionary of Pivotal Terms," *Attitudes toward History*, 216–338.

75. Burke, *Rhetoric of Motives*, 19–23 (emphasis in original).

76. "Senate Remarks: Reckless Administration May Reap Disastrous Consequences," February 12, 2003, http://www.senate.gov/~byrd/.

77. Burke, *Rhetoric of Motives*, 23.

78. Kenneth M. Pollack, *The Threatening Storm: The Case for Invading Iraq* (New York: Random House, 2002), xxi–xxii, 149, 158, 178, 180, 347, 416, 422.

79. For more of the argument against the preemptive war on Iraq, see Michael Ratner, Jennie Green, and Barbara Olshansky, *Against War in Iraq: An Anti-War Primer* (New York: Seven Stories Press, 2003), and Milan Rai, *War Plan Iraq: Ten Reasons against War on Iraq* (London: Verso, 2002).

80. Lawrence F. Kaplan and William Kristol, *The War over Iraq: Saddam's Tyranny and America's Mission* (San Francisco, Calif.: Encounter Books, 2003), 63–64, 72–74, 91, 95, 98, 101, 104, 112, 121, 124.

81. Chaim Perelman, *The Idea of Justice and the Problem of Argument*, trans. John Petrie (London: Routledge and Kegan Paul, 1963). See also Perelman and Olbrechts-Tyteca, *New Rhetoric*.

82. Quoted in Todd S. Purdum, "Bush's Moral Rectitude Is a Tough Sell in Old Europe," *New York Times*, January 30, 2003, http://www.nytimes.com/.

83. Chang, *Silencing Political Dissent*, 13. For a chilling view of the future under a regime of counterterror national security measures, see Matthew Brzezinski, "Fortress America," *New York Times*, February 23, 2003, http://www.nytimes.com/.

84. See, for instance, "Informant Fever," *New York Times*, July 22, 2002, http://www.nytimes.com/.

85. Robert C. Byrd, "Senate Remarks: Rush to War Ignores U.S. Constitution," October 3, 2002, http://byrd.senate.gov/.

86. Burke, "Introduction," in *Attitudes toward History*. See also Burke, *Rhetoric of Motives*, xiv–xv.

87. Pollack, xxiv, xxiii–xxx.

88. Ibid., 222–26, 235–37.

89. Ibid., 353, 365–66, 370, 419–21.

90. Ibid., 416, 418–19.

91. John J. Mearsheimer and Stephen M. Walt, "An Unnecessary War," in *The Iraq War Reader: History, Documents, Opinions*, ed. Micah L. Sifry and Christopher Cerf (New York: Simon and Schuster, 2003), 414–19, 422–23.

92. Pollack, xv–xvi.

93. Norman Mailer, *Why Are We at War?* (New York: Random House, 2003), 53, 55, 70–71.

94. On this point of democratization versus rationalizing the conflation of economic and political domains, see Samir Amin, "Imperialism and Globalization," *Monthly Review* 53 (June 2001): 6–24, especially 10–13.

95. David Stout, "Bush Says Worldwide Protests Won't Change Approach to Iraq," *New York Times*, February 18, 2003, http://www.nytimes.com/.

96. Jean Bethke Elshtain, *Just War against Terror: The Burden of American Power in a Violent World* (New York: Basic Books, 2003), 1–2, 6, 143, 151.

97. Ibid., 10, 12, 22–23, 36, 45, 64, 132, 134, 137, 154; italics in the original. Elshtain approvingly quotes Michael Walzer to reinforce her view from the Right that Islamic fundamentalism is the root cause of terrorism when Walzer writes that "whenever writers on the left say that the 'root cause' of terror is global inequality or human poverty, the assertion is in fact a denial that religious motives really count" (84).

98. Elshtain, 71–74, 76, 83, 95–96.

99. Ibid., 151, 158, 160–62, 166–67, 170, 172–73, 177–78.

100. Ibid., 17, 20, 169, 178.

Conclusion

1. Manicas, *War and Democracy*, 380–90.

2. Ivie, "Eisenhower as Cold Warrior," 21–22.

3. Noam Chomsky, *Necessary Illusions: Thought Control in Democratic Societies* (Cambridge, Mass.: South End Press, 1989), 14.

4. Milan Rai, *Chomsky's Politics* (London: Verso, 1995), 46.

5. For a useful and concise summary of this model, see ibid., 33–47.

6. Chomsky, *Necessary Illusions*, 2, 5.

7. Fareed Zakaria, *The Future of Freedom: Illiberal Democracy at Home and Abroad* (New York: W. W. Norton, 2003), 13–17, 23–26. Zakaria, as is the case with other contemporary critics of democracy, rehearses approvingly Madison's critique of unchecked democratic passions, e.g., 246–47.

8. Zakaria, 65, quoting Jacob L. Talmon, *The Origins of Totalitarian Democracy* (London: Secker and Warburg, 1955), and E. E. Rich et al., eds., *The Economic Organization of Early Modern Europe*, vol. 5 of *Cambridge Economic History of Europe* (Cambridge: Cambridge University Press, 1977), 583.

9. Zakaria, 69, 70, 73, 87, 152, 162, 167, 231, 238, 240, 247, 248, 255, 256.

10. Ibid., 151–54.

11. Ibid., 245.

12. Paul Berman, *Terror and Liberalism* (New York: W. W. Norton, 2003), 23, 178, 183, 191, 194, 199, 200–2, 210.

13. Ibid., 46–51.

14. Ibid., 178, 196, 199, 200–202; Prestowitz, *Rogue Nation*; Michael Hirsh, *At War with Ourselves: Why America Is Squandering Its Chance to Build a Better World* (New York: Oxford University Press, 2003).

15. Prestowitz, 8, 36, 41–42, 44, 47, 49, 273–76, 283.

16. Hirsh, xi, 6–7, 19–20.

17. Richard Falk, *The Great Terror War* (New York: Olive Branch Press, 2003), 5, 29–31, 33–36, 146, 179, 189.

18. Ibid., xix, xxii–xxiii, xxv, xxviii, 22–29, 72, 77, 186.

19. Mouffe, *Democratic Paradox*, 80–105.

20. Falk, 27–29, 145–46; David Held, *Democracy and the Global Order*.

21. Jonathan Schell, *The Unconquerable World: Power, Nonviolence, and the Will of the People* (New York: Metropolitan Books, 2003), 6–8, 340–43, 345–47, 351.

Selected Bibliography

Ackerman, Bruce. *We the People: Foundations.* Cambridge, Mass.: Belknap Press of Harvard University Press, 1991.

Archibugi, Daniele, and David Held, eds. *Cosmopolitan Democracy: An Agenda for a New World Order.* Cambridge: Polity Press, 1995.

Bacevich, Andrew J. *American Empire: The Realities and Consequences of U.S. Diplomacy.* Cambridge, Mass.: Harvard University Press, 2002.

Bailyn, Bernard, ed. *The Debate on the Constitution: Federalist and Antifederalist Speeches, Articles, and Letters during the Struggle over Ratification.* 2 vols. New York: Library of America, 1993.

Barber, Benjamin R. *Fear's Empire: War, Terrorism, and Democracy.* New York: W. W. Norton, 2003.

———. *Jihad vs. McWorld: How Globalism and Tribalism Are Reshaping the World.* New York: Ballantine Books, 1995.

———. *A Passion for Democracy: American Essays.* Princeton, N.J.: Princeton University Press, 1998.

———. *Strong Democracy: Participatory Politics for a New Age.* Berkeley and Los Angeles: University of California Press, 1984.

Barrett, Harold. *The Sophists.* Novato, Calif.: Chandler and Sharp Publishers, 1987.

Baskerville, Barnet. *The People's Voice: The Orator in American Society.* Lexington: University Press of Kentucky, 1979.

Benhabib, Seyla, ed. *Democracy and Difference: Contesting the Boundaries of the Political.* Princeton, N.J.: Princeton University Press, 1996.

Berman, Paul. *Terror and Liberalism.* New York: W. W. Norton, 2003.

Bessette, Joseph M. *The Mild Voice of Reason: Deliberative Democracy and American National Government.* Chicago: University of Chicago Press, 1994.

Biesecker, Barbara A. *Addressing Postmodernity: Kenneth Burke, Rhetoric, and a Theory of Social Change.* Tuscaloosa: University of Alabama Press, 1997.

Boase, Paul, ed. *The Rhetoric of Protest and Reform: 1878–1898*. Athens: Ohio University Press, 1980.

Bohman, John. *Public Deliberation: Pluralism, Complexity, and Democracy*. Cambridge, Mass.: MIT Press, 1996.

Bohman, John, and William Rehg, eds. *Deliberative Democracy: Essays on Reason and Politics*. Cambridge, Mass.: MIT Press, 1997.

Bovard, James. *Terrorism and Tyranny: Trampling Freedom, Justice, and Peace to Rid the World of Evil*. New York: Palgrave Macmillan, 2003.

Brown, Michael E., Sean M. Lynn-Jones, and Steven E. Miller, eds. *Debating the Democratic Peace: An International Security Reader*. Cambridge, Mass.: MIT Press, 1996.

Buck-Morss, Susan. *Thinking Past Terror: Islamism and Critical Theory on the Left*. London: Verso, 2003.

Burbach, Roger. "The Tragedy of American Democracy." In *Low Intensity Democracy: Political Power in the New World Order*. Edited by Barry Gills, Joel Rocamora, and Richard Wilson. London: Pluto Press, 1993.

Burke, Kenneth. *Attitudes toward History*. 3rd ed. Berkeley and Los Angeles: University of California Press, 1984.

———. "Dramatism." In *International Encyclopedia of the Social Sciences*, edited by David L. Sills, 445–51. New York: Macmillan, 1968.

———. *Language as Symbolic Action: Essays on Life, Literature, and Method*. Berkeley and Los Angeles: University of California Press, 1968.

———. *Permanence and Change: An Anatomy of Purpose*. 2nd rev. ed. 1954. Reprint, Indianapolis: Bobbs-Merrill Company, 1965.

———. *The Philosophy of Literary Form: Studies in Symbolic Action*. 3rd ed. Berkeley and Los Angeles: University of California Press, 1973.

———. *A Rhetoric of Motives*. Berkeley and Los Angeles: University of California Press, 1969.

———. *The Rhetoric of Religion: Studies in Logology*. Berkeley and Los Angeles: University of California Press, 1970.

Campbell, David. *Writing Security: United States Foreign Policy and the Politics of Identity*. Rev. ed. Minneapolis: University of Minnesota Press, 1998.

Carr, Caleb. *The Lessons of Terror—A History of Warfare against Civilians: Why It Has Always Failed and Will Fail Again*. New York: Random House, 2002.

Cassier, Ernst. *The Philosophy of Symbolic Forms*. New Haven, Conn.: Yale University Press, 1955.

Ceaser, James W., Glen E. Thurow, Jeffrey Tulis, and Joseph M. Bessette. "The Rise of the Rhetorical Presidency." *Presidential Studies Quarterly* 11 (1981): 158–71.

Chace, James, and Caleb Carr. *America Invulnerable: The Quest for Absolute Security from 1812 to Star Wars*. New York: Summit Books, 1988.

Chambers, Simone. *Reasonable Democracy: Jürgen Habermas and the Politics of Discourse*. Ithaca, N.Y.: Cornell University Press, 1996.

Chang, Nancy. *Silencing Political Dissent: How Post–September 11 Anti-Terrorism Measures Threaten Our Civil Liberties*. New York: Seven Stories Press, 2002.

Chomsky, Noam. *Necessary Illusions: Thought Control in Democratic Societies.* Cambridge, Mass.: South End Press, 1989.

———. *Rogue States: The Rule of Force in World Affairs.* Cambridge, Mass.: South End Press, 2000.

Cmiel, Kenneth. *Democratic Eloquence: The Fight over Popular Speech in Nineteenth-Century America.* New York: William Morrow and Company, 1990.

Cole, David, and James X. Dempsey. *Terrorism and the Constitution: Sacrificing Civil Liberties in the Name of Security.* New York: New Press, 2002.

Daniel, Stephen H. *Myth and Modern Philosophy.* Philadelphia: Temple University Press, 1990.

Denham, Robert D., ed. *Myth and Metaphor: Selected Essays, 1974–1988.* Charlottesville: University Press of Virginia, 1990.

Dolan, Frederick M., and Thomas L. Dumm, eds. *Rhetorical Republic: Governing Representations in American Politics.* Amherst, Mass.: University of Massachusetts Press, 1993.

Doty, William G. "Myth." In *Encyclopedia of Rhetoric and Composition: Communication from Ancient Times to the Information Age,* edited by Theresa Enos, 449–52. New York: Garland Publishing, 1996.

Dryzek, John S. *Discursive Democracy: Politics, Policy, and Political Science.* New York: Cambridge University Press, 1990.

Elman, Miriam Fendius, ed. *Paths to Peace: Is Democracy the Answer?* Cambridge, Mass.: MIT Press, 1997.

Elshtain, Jean Bethke. *Just War against Terror: The Burden of American Power in a Violent World.* New York: Basic Books, 2003.

Elster, Jon, ed. *Deliberative Democracy.* New York: Cambridge University Press, 1998.

Engelhardt, Tom. *The End of Victory Culture: Cold War America and the Disillusioning of a Generation.* New York: Basic Books, 1995.

Falk, Richard. *The Great Terror War.* New York: Olive Branch Press, 2003.

Farrand, Max, ed. *The Records of the Federal Convention of 1787.* Rev. ed. New Haven, Conn.: Yale University Press, 1966.

Farrell, Thomas B. *Norms of Rhetorical Culture.* New Haven, Conn.: Yale University Press, 1993.

Fishkin, James S. *Democracy and Deliberation: New Directions in Democratic Reform.* New Haven, Conn.: Yale University Press, 1991.

Fukuyama, Francis. *The End of History and the Last Man.* New York: Avon Books, 1992.

Gaddis, John Lewis. *The United States and the End of the Cold War: Implications, Reconsiderations, Provocations.* New York: Oxford University Press, 1992.

Gilbert, Alan. *Must Global Politics Constrain Democracy? Great-Power Realism, Democratic Peace, and Democratic Internationalism.* Princeton, N.J.: Princeton University Press, 1999.

Gills, Barry, Joel Rocamora, and Richard Wilson, eds. *Low Intensity Democracy: Political Power in the New World Order.* London: Pluto Press, 1993.

Gilman, Sander L., Carole Blair, and David J. Parent, eds. and trans. *Friedrich Nietzsche on Rhetoric and Language*. New York: Oxford University Press, 1989.

Giroux, Henry A. *Public Spaces, Private Lives: Democracy beyond 9/11*. Lanham, Md.: Rowman and Littlefield, 2003.

Gowa, Joanne. *Ballots and Bullets: The Elusive Democratic Peace*. Princeton, N.J.: Princeton University Press, 1999.

Grassi, Ernesto. *Rhetoric as Philosophy: The Humanist Tradition*. University Park: Penn State University Press, 1980.

Gregg, Gary L. *The Presidential Republic: Executive Representation and Deliberative Democracy*. Lanham, Md.: Rowman and Littlefield Publishers, 1997.

Gunderson, Robert Gray. *The Log-Cabin Campaign*. Lexington: University Press of Kentucky, 1957.

Gutmann, Amy, and Dennis Thompson. *Democracy and Disagreement*. Cambridge, Mass.: Belknap Press of Harvard University, 1996.

Hanson, Russell L. *The Democratic Imagination in America: Conversations with Our Past*. Princeton, N.J.: Princeton University Press, 1985.

Hargrove, Erwin C. *Jimmy Carter as President: Leadership and the Politics of the Public Good*. Baton Rouge: Louisiana State University Press, 1988.

Hatab, Lawrence J. *A Nietzschean Defense of Democracy: An Experiment in Postmodern Politics*. Chicago: Open Court, 1995.

Havelock, Eric A. *The Liberal Temper in Greek Politics*. New Haven, Conn.: Yale University Press, 1957.

Held, David. *Democracy and the Global Order: From the Modern State to Cosmopolitan Governance*. Stanford, Calif.: Stanford University Press, 1995.

———. *Models of Democracy*. 2nd ed. Stanford, Calif.: Stanford University Press, 1996.

Hentoff, Nat. *The War on the Bill of Rights and the Gathering Resistance*. New York: Seven Stories Press, 2003.

Heymann, Philip B. *Terrorism and America: A Commonsense Strategy for a Democratic Society*. Cambridge, Mass.: MIT Press, 1998.

Hirsh, Michael. *At War with Ourselves: Why America Is Squandering Its Chance to Build a Better World*. New York: Oxford University Press, 2003.

Hoffman, Bruce. *Inside Terrorism*. New York: Columbia University Press, 1998.

Hoge, James F., Jr., and Gideon Rose, eds. *How Did This Happen: Terrorism and the New War*. New York: Public Affairs, 2001.

Honigmann, John J., ed. *Handbook of Social and Cultural Anthropology*. Chicago: Rand McNally College Publishing, 1973.

Hudson, Rex A. *Who Becomes a Terrorist and Why: The 1999 Government Report on Profiling Terrorists*. Guilford, Conn.: Lyons Press, 2002.

Huntington, Samuel P. *The Third Wave: Democratization in the Late Twentieth Century*. Norman: University of Oklahoma Press, 1991.

Hyde, Lewis. *Trickster Makes This World: Mischief, Myth, and Art*. New York: North Point Press, 1998.

Isaac, Jeffrey C. *Democracy in Dark Times*. Ithaca, N.Y.: Cornell University Press, 1998.

Ivie, Robert L. "Dwight D. Eisenhower's 'Chance for Peace': Quest or Crusade?" *Rhetoric and Public Affairs* 1 (1998): 227–43.

———. "Eisenhower as Cold Warrior." In *Eisenhower's War of Words: Rhetoric and Leadership*, edited by Martin J. Medhurst, 7–25. East Lansing: Michigan State University Press, 1994.

———. "Fire, Flood, and Red Fever: Truman's Global Emergency." *Presidential Studies Quarterly* 29 (September 1999): 570–91.

———. "George Kennan's Political Rhetoric: Realism Masking Fear." In *Post-Realism: The Rhetorical Turn in International Relations*, edited by Francis A. Beer and Robert Hariman, 55–74. East Lansing: Michigan State University Press, 1996.

———. "The Ideology of Freedom's 'Fragility' in American Foreign Policy Argument." *Journal of the American Forensic Association* 24 (1987): 27–36.

———. "Images of Savagery in American Justifications for War." *Communication Monographs* 47 (1980): 279–94.

———. "Presidential Motives for War." *Quarterly Journal of Speech* 60 (1974): 337–45.

———. "Tragic Fear and the Rhetorical Presidency: Combating Evil in the Persian Gulf." In *Beyond the Rhetorical Presidency*, edited by Martin J. Medhurst, 153–78. College Station: Texas A&M University Press, 1996.

Jarratt, Susan C. *Rereading the Sophists: Classical Rhetoric Refigured*. Carbondale: Southern Illinois University Press, 1991.

Johnson, Chalmers. *Blowback: The Costs and Consequences of American Empire*. New York: Henry Holt, 2000.

Juergensmeyer, Mark. *Terror in the Mind of God: The Global Rise of Religious Violence*. Berkeley and Los Angeles: University of California Press, 2000.

Kant, Immanuel. "To Perpetual Peace: A Philosophical Sketch." In *Perpetual Peace and Other Essays*, translated by Ted Humphrey, 107–43. Indianapolis: Hackett Publishing Company, 1983.

Kaplan, Lawrence F., and William Kristol. *The War over Iraq: Saddam's Tyranny and America's Mission*. San Francisco: Encounter Books, 2003.

Kazin, Michael. *The Populist Persuasion: An American History*. Rev. ed. Ithaca, N.Y.: Cornell University Press, 1998.

Keen, Sam. *Faces of the Enemy: Reflections of the Hostile Imagination*. San Francisco: Harper and Row, 1986.

Kellner, Douglas. *From 9/11 to Terror War: The Dangers of the Bush Legacy*. Lanham, Md.: Rowman and Littlefield, 2003.

Kennedy, George A. *A New History of Classical Rhetoric*. Princeton, N.J.: Princeton University Press, 1994.

Kozhemiakin, Alexander V. *Expanding the Zone of Peace? Democratization and International Security*. New York: St. Martin's Press, 1998.

Laclau, Ernesto, and Chantal Mouffe. *Hegemony and Socialist Strategy: Towards a Radical Democratic Politics*. London: Verso, 1985.

Lakoff, George. "Metaphors of Terror: The Power of Images." In *These Times.com*, October 29, 2001. http://www.inthesetimes.com/web2524/lakoff2524.html.

Laqueur, Walter. *No End to War: Terrorism in the Twenty-first Century*. New York: Continuum, 2003.

Leone, Richard C., and Greg Anrig Jr., eds. *The War on Our Freedoms: Civil Liberties in an Age of Terrorism*. New York: Public Affairs, 2003.

Levitas, Daniel. *The Terrorist Next Door: The Militia Movement and the Radical Right*. New York: Stomas Dunne Books, 2002.

Lifton, Robert Jay, and Greg Mitchell. *Hiroshima in America: A Half Century of Denial*. New York: Avon Books, 1996.

Lincoln, Bruce. *Discourse and the Construction of Society: Comparative Studies of Myth, Ritual, and Classification*. New York: Oxford University Press, 1989.

Lipset, Seymour Martin. *American Exceptionalism: A Double-Edged Sword*. New York: W. W. Norton, 1996.

Litwak, Robert S. *Rogue States and U.S. Foreign Policy: Containment after the Cold War*. Baltimore: Johns Hopkins University Press, 2000.

Lummis, Douglas. *Radical Democracy*. Ithaca, N.Y.: Cornell University Press, 1996.

Madison, James, Alexander Hamilton, and John Jay. *The Federalist*. Edited by Isaac Kramnick. New York: Penguin Books, 1987.

Mahajan, Rahul. *The New Crusade: America's War on Terrorism*. New York: Monthly Review Press, 2002.

Manicas, Peter T. *War and Democracy*. Cambridge, Mass.: Basil Blackwell, 1989.

Mara, Gerald M. *Socrates' Discursive Democracy: Logos and Ergon in Platonic Political Philosophy*. Albany: State University of New York Press, 1997.

Matthews, Richard K. *If Men Were Angels: James Madison and the Heartless Empire of Reason*. Lawrence: University Press of Kansas, 1995.

———. *The Radical Politics of Thomas Jefferson: A Revisionist View*. Lawrence: University Press of Kansas, 1984.

Mattson, Kevin. *Creating a Democratic Public: The Struggle for Urban Participatory Democracy during the Progressive Era*. University Park: Penn State University Press, 1999.

Medhurst, Martin J., Robert L. Ivie, Philip Wander, and Robert L. Scott. *Cold War Rhetoric: Strategy, Metaphor, and Ideology*. Rev. ed. East Lansing: Michigan State University Press, 1997.

Meyers, Marvin. *The Jacksonian Persuasion: Politics and Belief*. 1957. Reprint, Stanford, Calif.: Stanford University Press, 1960.

Morgan, Edmund S. *Inventing the People: The Rise of Popular Sovereignty in England and America*. New York: W. W. Norton, 1988.

Morone, James A. *The Democratic Wish: Popular Participation and the Limits of American Government*. Rev. ed. New Haven, Conn.: Yale University Press, 1998.

Mouffe, Chantal. "Deliberative Democracy or Agonistic Pluralism?" *Social Research* 66 (Fall 1999): 745–58.

———. *The Democratic Paradox*. London: Verso, 2000.

———. *The Return of the Political*. London: Verso, 1993.

———, ed. *Dimensions of Radical Democracy: Pluralism, Citizenship, Community.* London: Verso, 1992.

Nadel, Alan. *Containment Culture: American Narratives, Postmodernism, and the Atomic Age.* Durham, N.C.: Duke University Press, 1995.

Newhouse, John. *Imperial America: The Bush Assault on the World Order.* New York: Alfred A. Knopf, 2003.

Nietzsche, Friedrich. *The Will to Power.* Edited by Walter Kaufmann. New York: Vintage Books, 1968.

Norton, Anne. *Republic of Signs: Liberal Theory and American Popular Culture.* Chicago: University of Chicago Press, 1993.

Nye, Joseph S., Jr. *The Paradox of American Power: Why the World's Only Superpower Can't Go It Alone.* New York: Oxford University Press, 2002.

Ober, Josiah. *Mass and Elite in Democratic Athens: Rhetoric, Ideology, and the Power of the People.* Princeton, N.J.: Princeton University Press, 1989.

———. *Political Dissent in Democratic Athens: Intellectual Critics of Popular Rule.* Princeton, N.J.: Princeton University Press, 1998.

Perelman, Chaim. *The Idea of Justice and the Problem of Argument.* Translated by John Petrie. London: Routledge and Kegan Paul, 1963.

———. *The New Rhetoric and the Humanities: Essays on Rhetoric and Its Application.* Translated by William Kluback. Dordrecht, Holland: D. Reidel Publishing Company, 1979.

Perelman, Chaim, and L. Olbrechts-Tyteca. *The New Rhetoric: A Treatise on Argumentation.* Translated by John Wilkinson and Purcell Weaver. Notre Dame, Ind.: Notre Dame University Press, 1969.

Perlmutter, Amos. *Making the World Safe for Democracy: A Century of Wilsonianism and Its Totalitarian Challengers.* Chapel Hill: University of North Carolina Press, 1997.

Pillar, Paul R. *Terrorism and U.S. Foreign Policy.* Washington, D.C.: Brookings Institution Press, 2001.

Pollack, Kenneth M. *The Threatening Storm: The Case for Invading Iraq.* New York: Random House, 2002.

Poulakos, Takis. *Speaking for the Polis: Isocrates' Rhetorical Education.* Columbia: University of South Carolina Press, 1997.

Prestowitz, Clyde. *Rogue Nation: American Unilateralism and the Failure of Good Intentions.* New York: Basic Books, 2003.

Rabinow, Paul, ed. *Michel Foucault: Ethics, Subjectivity, and Truth.* New York: New Press, 1997.

Rai, Milan. *Chomsky's Politics.* London: Verso, 1995.

———. *War Plan Iraq: Ten Reasons against War on Iraq.* London: Verso, 2002.

Ratner, Michael, Jennie Green, and Barbara Olshansky. *Against War in Iraq: An Anti-War Primer.* New York: Seven Stories Press, 2003.

Ray, James Lee. *Democracy and International Conflict: An Evaluation of the Democratic Peace Proposition.* Columbia: University of South Carolina Press, 1995.

Remini, Robert V. *Andrew Jackson.* Vol. 3, *The Course of American Democracy, 1833–1845.* Baltimore: Johns Hopkins University Press, 1984.

Rueckert, William H. *Encounters with Kenneth Burke.* Urbana: University of Illinois Press, 1994.

Rummel, R. J. *Power Kills: Democracy as a Method of Nonviolence.* New Brunswick, N.J.: Transaction Publishers, 1997.

Russett, Bruce. *Grasping the Democratic Peace: Principles for a Post-Cold War World.* Princeton, N.J.: Princeton University Press, 1993.

Rutland, Robert A. *The Presidency of James Madison.* Lawrence: University Press of Kansas, 1990.

Schaffer, John D. *Sensus Communis: Vico, Rhetoric, and the Limits of Relativism.* Durham, N.C.: Duke University Press, 1990.

Schell, Jonathan. *The Unconquerable World: Power, Nonviolence, and the Will of the People.* New York: Metropolitan Books, 2003.

Schudson, Michael. *The Good Citizen: A History of American Civic Life.* Cambridge, Mass.: Harvard University Press, 1998.

Scraton, Phil, ed. *Beyond September 11: An Anthology of Dissent.* London: Pluto Press, 2002.

Shapiro, Ian. *Democratic Justice.* New Haven, Conn.: Yale University Press, 1999.

Shapiro, Ian, and Casiano Hacker-Cordón. *Democracy's Edges.* New York: Cambridge University Press, 1999.

Sherry, Michael S. *In the Shadow of War: The United States since the 1930s.* New Haven, Conn.: Yale University Press, 1995.

Sifry, Micah L., and Christopher Cerf, eds. *The Iraq War Reader: History, Documents, Opinions.* New York, Simon and Schuster, 2003.

Simon, Jeffrey D. *The Terrorist Trap: America's Experience with Terrorism.* 2nd ed. Bloomington: Indiana University Press, 2001.

Smith, Gaddis. *Morality, Reason, and Power: American Diplomacy in the Carter Years.* New York: Hill and Wang, 1986.

Smith, Tony. *The United States and the Worldwide Struggle for Democracy in the Twentieth Century.* Princeton, N.J.: Princeton University Press, 1995.

Sontag, Susan. *Illness as Metaphor and AIDS and Its Metaphors.* New York: Anchor Books, 1990.

Sproule, J. Michael. *Propaganda and Democracy: The American Experience of Media and Mass Persuasion.* Cambridge: Cambridge University Press, 1997.

Tulis, Jeffrey K. *The Rhetorical Presidency.* Princeton, N.J.: Princeton University Press, 1988.

Turbayne, Colin Murray. *The Myth of Metaphor.* Rev. ed. Columbia: University of South Carolina Press, 1970.

Vico, Giambattista. *New Science.* Translated by David Marsh. 1744. Reprint, New York: Penguin Books, 1999.

Walzer, Michael. *The Company of Critics: Social Criticism and Political Commitment in the Twentieth Century.* 2nd ed. New York: Basic Books, 2002.

Weart, Spencer R. *Never at War: Why Democracies Will Not Fight One Another.* New Haven, Conn.: Yale University Press, 1998.

Welsh, Scott. "Deliberative Democracy and the Rhetorical Production of Political Culture." *Rhetoric and Public Affairs* 5 (2002): 679–707.

Whitfield, Stephen J. *The Culture of the Cold War*. Baltimore: Johns Hopkins University Press, 1991.

Wiebe, Robert H. *Self-Rule: A Cultural History of American Democracy*. Chicago: University of Chicago Press, 1995.

Williams, Paul L. *Al Qaeda: Brotherhood of Terror*. Parsippany, N.J.: Alpha Books, 2002.

Wood, Gordon S. *The Creation of the American Republic, 1776–1787*. New York: W. W. Norton, 1969.

Wright, Robin. *Sacred Rage: The Wrath of Militant Islam*. Rev. ed. New York: Simon and Schuster, 2001.

Young, Iris Marion. "Communication and the Other: Beyond Deliberative Democracy." In *Democracy and Difference: Contesting the Boundaries of the Political*, edited by Seyla Benhabib. Princeton, N.J.: Princeton University Press, 1996.

———. *Inclusion and Democracy*. New York: Oxford University Press, 2000.

Yunis, Harvey. *Taming Democracy: Models of Political Rhetoric in Classical Athens*. Ithaca, N.Y.: Cornell University Press, 1996.

Zakaria, Fareed. *The Future of Freedom: Illiberal Democracy at Home and Abroad*. New York: W. W. Norton, 2003.

Index